WITHDRAWN

SOUTH AFRICA

SOUTH AFRICA

BACKGROUND TO THE CRISIS

Michael Attwell

SIDGWICK & JACKSON
LONDON

PICTURE ACKNOWLEDGEMENTS

Associated Press: 29; BBC Hulton Picture Library: 3, 6, 10, 11; Camera Press: 12, 15, 22, 23, 26; International Defence and Aid Fund: 19, 17, 24, 25; Sonia Halliday Photographs: 4; Mansell Collection: 1, 2, 7; National Army Museum: 14; Popperfoto: 5, 8, 9, 16, 18, 20, 21, 28; Royal Photographic Society: 13.

First published in Great Britain in 1986
by Sidgwick & Jackson Limited

Copyright © 1986 by London Weekend Television

Picture research by Juliet Brightmore

Maps drawn by Chris Etheridge

ISBN 0-283-99370-7 hardcover
ISBN 0-283-99371-5 softcover

Typeset by Rapidset and Design Limited
Printed and bound in Great Britain by
The Garden City Press Limited,
Letchworth, Hertfordshire SG6 1JS
for Sidgwick & Jackson Limited
1 Tavistock Chambers, Bloomsbury Way
London WC1A 2SG

CONTENTS

ACKNOWLEDGMENTS

I should like to express my sincere thanks to Professor Ray Inskeep, of the Pitt Rivers Museum, Oxford; to Professor Shula Marks, of the Institute of Commonwealth Studies, London; to Professor David Phillipson, Curator of the Museum of Archaeology and Anthropology, University of Cambridge; and to Dr Stanley Trapido, of the Institute of Commonwealth Studies, Oxford. Despite being extremely busy, they were all kind enough to devote much time and energy to helping me in my research for this book. I gained much important information and many ideas from them, and I am most grateful.

I should also like to take this opportunity of saying how much I appreciate the many long hours of patient discussion, sometimes going back many years, with friends and acquaintances in South Africa. I should like to thank particularly Dr Willie Breytenbach, formerly of the Department of Constitutional Development and Planning, and now at the University of Stellenbosch; John Kane-Berman, Director of the South African Institute of Race Relations; Patrick 'Terror' Lekota, of the United Democratic Front; Patrick Van Niekerk, formerly of the *Rand Daily Mail*; and Helen Zille, also formerly of the *Rand Daily Mail*. From them especially, but from many others too, I have learnt a great deal, and profited greatly in my understanding of our native country.

A special word of thanks must go, too, to Casper Venter, of the Department of Foreign Affairs, who, over many years, has been a source of unfailing kindness and assistance.

To my sometime colleagues on *Weekend World*, I must also express my gratitude. Over the last decade their constant intellectual challenging has helped clarify my ideas on and analysis of South Africa. In particular I should mention Bruce Anderson and Sarah Powell, with whom I have spent many happy hours in South Africa, and Paul Neuberg and Hugh Pile, the Deputy Editor and Editor respectively of the programme. Their guidance and support has been invaluable. Of all those at London Weekend Television, however, I owe most to David Cox, Head of Current Affairs. Not only has he been enormously kind and helpful to me, and a great source of wisdom and inspiration, but, as it happens, this book would not have been possible without him.

I am most grateful as well to Sarah Mahaffy, of Baker Mahaffy Publishers; to Juliet Brightmore, who researched the pictures; to Chris Etheridge, who drew the maps; to Carey Smith, of Sidgwick & Jackson; and especially to Elizabeth Blair. All contributed enormously to the production of this book.

South Africa being South Africa, I should make it absolutely clear that all errors, omissions, ideas and opinions in this book are my responsibility, and mine alone. Nor should any of the people I have thanked necessarily be identified with my conclusions: indeed I can guarantee that many of them will be horrified or offended by them. I can only apologize for that, and hope that they will be magnanimous.

LIST OF TERMS

AAC

All-African (National) Convention. An umbrella group formed in 1935 of blacks, Coloureds, and Indians to campaign against the removal of Cape blacks from the common voters' roll in 1936.

African Democratic Party

Founded in 1943, it was a radical black party, which nonetheless worked with liberal whites.

Afrikaans, Afrikaner, Boer

A descendant of Dutch settlers in South Africa was known during the nineteenth century as a *Boer*, which means farmer. By the early twentieth century such people were calling themselves Afrikaners, which means people of Africa. Their language is *Afrikaans*, a locally-evolved form of Dutch.

Afrikaner Volkswag

Afrikaner People's Sentinel – an umbrella organization for far-right political movements in the 1980s.

Akademie vir Wetenskap en Kuns

'Academy of Arts and Sciences' – an *Afrikaner* body designed to ensure *Afrikaner* control in these areas of policy.

ANC

African National Congress. This was the new name given to the *SANNC* in 1923.

assegai

A short, stabbing spear which the Zulu under Shaka made a potent weapon of war.

AWB

Afrikaner Weerstandsbeweging, or Afrikaner Resistance Movement. An extreme-right militaristic movement of the 1980s, designed to oppose compromises of apartheid.

AZAPO	Azanian People's Organization, a black exclusivist body formed in the 1980s, mainly of young intellectuals, with the *NF*.
Bantustan	See *homeland*
bitter-einder	'Bitter-ender' – *Boer* who fought until the very end of the Boer War. It has come to mean one who pursues their cause unfailingly.
Boer	See *Afrikaans*
BPA	Black Parents Association, formed during the 1976-7 Soweto protests by parents to represent the children's cause to white authorities.
BPC	Black People's Convention, a black consciousness umbrella body in the 1970s.
Broederbond	'Fraternal League' – secret organization formed in 1918 to promote *Afrikaans* and *Afrikaners* in public life.
burgher	A Dutch term meaning citizen, and conveying full civic rights.
bywoner	A tenant farmer – the term was applied in the late nineteenth and early twentieth centuries to a poor white sharecropper employed by another white farmer.
commando	The system of conscripting Dutch settlers into ad hoc military posses. Used from the *VOC* days till the Boer War. It was British familiarity with *Boer* commandos in that war that brought the term into general currency in English. Also used for an irregular soldier, as in a *commando*.
Congress of Democrats	A party of white radicals in the 1950s.
Conservative Party	A right-wing breakaway from the National Party, formed under Dr Andries Treurnicht in 1982 to reimplement traditional apartheid.

COSAS	Congress of South African Students. Black organization with the *UDF*
COSATU	Congress of South African Trade Unions. A powerful confederation of black unions, the largest such grouping, formed in 1985.
CUSA	Council of Unions of South Africa. A federation of black unions in the 1980s.
Die Sestigers	'People of the Sixties' – dissident cultural movement among young *Afrikaners* in the 1960s.
Die Spoorbond	'The Railway League' – an *Afrikaner* rail union formed in 1933 to promote *Afrikaner* interests in the industry.
Difaqane	A Sotho word meaning literally forced migration. It refers to the upheaval precipitated throughout South Africa's interior as a result of the Zulu wars of conquest in the early nineteenth century. The Zulu or Xhosa word is *mfecane*, or crushing.
drostdy	Magistrate's residence during Dutch government.
Ekonomiese Volkskongres	'People's Economic Congress' convened in 1939 to promote *Afrikaner* economic interests.
Federasie van Afrikaanse Kultuurverenigings	'Federation of Afrikaner Cultural Unions' – created in 1929 to promote *Afrikaner* culture.
FOSATU	Federation of South African Trade Unions. A co-ordinating body for black trade unions in the 1980s, loosely allied with the *UDF*.
FRELIMO	Mozambique Liberation Front. Political and guerrilla force which opposed Portuguese rule, and became the government of the territory in 1975.
'Gesuiwerde' National Party	See *NP*

hensopper	'Hands-upper' *Boer* who surrendered before the end of the Boer War. It has become synonymous with a traitor or a person of less than full commitment.
Heren XVII	The governing board of the VOC – literally, the Seventeen Gentlemen.
HNP	Herstigte (Re-established) National Party. A right-wing breakaway from the *NP*, formed in 1969 by Dr Albert Hertzog
homeland	From the early 1950s onwards, under 'separate development', the reserves set aside for black South Africans were divided into different *homelands*. Each black person was allocated to one depending on their presumed 'tribal' origin. A *homeland* was also known as a *Bantustan*.
ICU	Industrial and Commercial Workers' Union led by Clement Kadalie and active in the 1920s.
impi	The powerful regimental system introduced among the Zulu in the early nineteenth century. The regiment was a standing one, based on age rather than kinship.
Inkatha	A primarily Zulu organization under Chief Gatsha Buthelezi; politically 'moderate' and opposed to the *UDF*.
ISCOR	Iron and Steel Corporation. State body created in 1927. An important source of employment for *Afrikaners*. A new works at Vanderbijlpark in the Southern Transvaal shortly after the Second World War was known as VECOR.
Kaapse Patriotte	Literally, Cape Patriots – a movement of Dutch settlers in the Eastern Cape in the late eighteenth century, who demanded more say in the running of their own affairs.

Kappiekommando Literally, bonnet brigade – an *Afrikaner* women's protest movement in the early 1980s, whose members protested against the erosion of apartheid by dressing up in *Voortrekker* clothes and bonnets.

Khoikhoi The yellowy-brown-skinned descendants of prehistoric South Africans. They were *San* people, who took up sheep and cattle herding. Known by white settlers as Hottentots.

Khoisan A term embracing the *Khoikhoi* and the *San*.

kombuistaal Literally, a kitchen-language – the nineteenth-century status of *Afrikaans* which was the medium of communication between *Boers* and their servants and the native tongue of Coloured (mixed-race) people.

Kontak groups 'Contact' groups set up in the mid-1980s by women of the Dutch Reformed Church to get to know black women.

kragdadigheid Literally, efficiency or vigour – used generally to describe the quality of unhesitating willingness to employ force.

laager A defensive drawing into a circle of ox-wagons which the *Boers* used as a barricade from within which to ward off attackers.

MNR Mozambique National Resistance Movement. A post-independence guerrilla movement opposing the *FRELIMO* government, backed and trained by South Africa.

MPLA Popular Movement for the Liberation of Angola. A marxist guerrilla movement, one of three which opposed Portuguese rule, and which became the government in 1975.

NF	National Forum. A rival umbrella grouping to the *UDF*, formed in 1983 and comprising black exclusivist organizations.
NP	National Party. Formed by Barry Hertzog in 1914. When his party fused with the *SAP* in 1934 to form the *UP*, some NP supporters led by Dr D.F. Malan broke away to form the *Gesuiwerde* (Purified) NP, which became the modern NP and continued the tradition of the earlier party.
NUSAS	National Union of South African Students, predominantly white.
Oranjewerkers-vereniging	Orange Workers' Union right-wing Afrikaans movement of the 1980s which aimed to establish a white *homeland* without black workers.
Ossewabrandwag	'Ox-wagon Sentinel' – a terrorist, pro-Nazi organization during the Second World War.
PAC	Pan-Africanist Congress. Founded by Robert Sobukwe as a breakaway from the *ANC* in 1958, a black exclusivist party.
PFP	The Progressive Party was a liberal breakaway from the *UP* formed in 1959. In 1975 it became the Progressive Reform Party; in 1977 the Progressive Federal Party (PFP), its current name.
Poqo	An armed underground movement of the *PAC*.
predikant	preacher, minister
Progressives	See PFP
SACP	South African Communist Party
SAIC	South African Indian Congress. Founded in 1920 to campaign against all discriminatory legislation. Worked closely with the *ANC*.

San	The yellowy-brown-skinned descendants of pre-historic South Africans. They were hunters and gatherers of fruit and vegetation. Known by white settlers as *Bushmen*.
SANNC	South African Native National Congress. Formed 1912, and the forerunner of the *ANC*
Sanlam and Santam	*Afrikaner* financial institutions, set up in 1918 for investment and insurance respectively, to promote *Afrikaner* financial independence.
SAP	South African Party. Originally a Cape party, it received the support of Transvaal and Free State *Afrikaners* in 1910, and formally merged with them as a national party in 1911.
SASM	South African Students' Movement, a black consciousness body in the 1970s.
SASO	South African Students' Organization, a black consciousness body in the 1970s.
SASOL	South African Coal, Oil and Gas Corporation. A state enterprise set up in 1950, it created a huge oil-from-coal plant at Sasolburg in the Orange Free State. There are now two other such plants.
SACPO	South African Coloured People's Organization. Formed in the 1950s to oppose the removal of Coloureds from the common voters' roll.
stoep	The verandah of Dutch homes.
SWAPO	South West African People's Organization. Political and guerrilla movement opposing South African occupation of Namibia (South West Africa).
swartgevaar	'Black peril'

trekboer	A Dutch farmer in the late seventeenth and the eighteenth centuries who moved into the interior of the Cape and pursued pastoral farming. The word means migrating, or frontier, farmer.
tsotsi	A Bantu word meaning bandit or gangster.
Tuinhuis	Literally, the Garden House – the governor's residence in Cape Town.
UDF	United Democratic Front. A non-racial umbrella body formed in 1983, broadly sympathetic to the ANC.
uitlander	A Dutch word meaning foreigner. It referred to the immigrants who flocked to the Transvaal in the late nineteenth-century gold-rush, and who were a precipitating cause of the Boer War.
Umkhonto we Sizwe	The armed underground movement of the *ANC*.
UP	United Party. Formed in 1934 as a result of the fusion between the *SAP* and Hertzog's *NP*.
VECOR	See ISCOR
verkrampte	Literally, a person of cramped mind – used from the late 1960s onwards for an *Afrikaner* political reactionary; cf. *verligte*.
verligte	An enlightened person – used from the late 1960s onwards for politically progressive *Afrikaners*; cf. *verkrampte*.
VOC	Dutch East India Company (*Vereenigde Nederlandsche Ge-Octroyeerde Oost-Indische Compagnie*, or United Netherlands Chartered East India Company).
volk	The people – quasi-mystical concept of the *Boers* or *Afrikaners* as a separate nation.

xvi

Volkskas	Literally 'The People's Treasury' – an *Afrikaner* bank set up in 1934 to promote *Afrikaner* financial independence.
Volksraad	A Dutch word meaning people's council. It was used by all *Boer* republics for their highest policy-making body, and it is the name given to the Lower House of the modern all-white South African Parliament.
volksverraad	Betrayal of the people.
Voortrekker	The word means pioneer. A Dutch descendant who trekked away into the interior to escape British rule.
witdoeke	'White handkerchiefs' – the name given to black conservative vigilantes in the Crossroads squatter camp in 1986, who were distinguished by tying pieces of white cloth around their arms or necks.
Wit Kommando	'White Commando' – a shadowy *Afrikaans* terrorist movement in the early 1980s which attacked *verligte* targets.
ZANU	Zimbabwe African National Union. Political and guerrilla movement which opposed white rule in Rhodesia; it became the government of independent Zimbabwe in 1980.

LIST OF ILLUSTRATIONS

LIST OF MAPS

INTRODUCTION

South Africa is a land of extraordinary beauty and grandeur. Its peoples are warm, kind, and generous. It has a formidable economy, and is without doubt the most advanced and sophisticated country on the African continent. Yet is also a society of great violence and brutality. Its history is steeped in blood. For centuries, it has been a country at war with itself. And even now, as all the world knows, that war is not yet resolved.

The essentials of the South African conflict are familiar to everyone: it is a fundamental struggle for power between the country's white minority and its black majority. This stark contest, however, has only recently come so sharply into focus, and South Africa has been the scene of other wars for much longer. Before the Europeans arrived in 1652, it is probable that black fought black in a series of limited skirmishes to establish local and regional control. Once the whites had arrived, the great modern struggle between them and the blacks was always implicit in the country's affairs – but it took its time to reach this pure state of confrontation. The first Dutch settlers spent most of their early years fighting other native people in more localized wars. Then, at the end of the eighteenth century, the British arrived and added their weight to the white–black killing which was just getting under way in a limited area.

By the late nineteenth century, however, these local conflicts were being subsumed into a greater national contest. British imperialism and its desire to bring all of Southern Africa under its influence, explosively matched by the growth of a distinctly South African Dutch – or Boer – identity, ensured that smaller disputes were being resolved into a single all-out struggle for the entire territory we know today as South Africa. That battle was clearly going to be fought out by the two white powers – for the British had helped the Boers crush and break any potential the blacks may have had to play a part in it.

Thus was the stage set for a final showdown between Boer and Briton: the great Boer War of 1899 to 1902. And the irony is that although the British were the victors, they decided the game was not worth the candle. In 1910 they quit South Africa for good, leaving the Boers in sole control of the newly unified country. Even then, however, South Africa's protracted agony was not over. Indeed, in a very real sense, it was only just beginning.

The country's black majority, voiceless and powerless, had none the less ensured themselves a future by the ferocity of their struggle to avoid extinction and marginalization. The mere fact of their continued existence posed a fundamental threat to white supremacy.

The Boers – now calling themselves Afrikaners – groped towards the view that the practice of racial discrimination, which had long been characteristic of their social functioning, would have to be elevated into a more thoroughgoing political system. They began to embark on an elaborate exercise which history will judge as a stupefying monument to human greed and as evidence that human beings will embark on anything, no matter how apparently futile, in the pursuit of their own self-interest. It was not quite that simple, however: the Afrikaners' actions sprang from a long history of fear, from poverty and their own sense of injustice – and however deranged it may have seemed to outsiders, it worked. They ensured themselves a better future in the long term. The exercise they set in train was aimed at nothing less than the rebuilding of Europe in Africa, and in such a way as to exclude the Dark Continent itself. They created a system of enforced racial segregation surpassed only by Nazi Germany – a system which had as its corollary the bizarre notion that black South Africans should not be South Africans at all. In putting this system into effect, the Afrikaners bequeathed the world a term from their own indigenous language, a term which has become synonymous with evil: 'apartheid'.

It was the racial dimension of South Africa's peculiar government that brought it to the attention of the world. In earlier times it might not have attracted so much notice. But the world had moved on. Decolonization was nearing its apogee, founded on the newly triumphant ideals of racial equality. And in the broader world, the juxtaposition of people of different races, speeded up and given immediate importance by the acceleration of travel and communication, made it a matter of great significance to decent people everywhere to find a salve for the tensions of racial co-existence.

In that climate apartheid represented not just an immoral practice but a very special kind of affront to the whole direction of modern sensibilities. It was not that racism did not exist elsewhere, but a state which took that as its central organizing principle, enshrined it in its laws and institutions, and systematically used force and brutality to underpin its power, constituted a peculiarly regressive kind of country, deeply offensive to values which had become increasingly important to the rest of the world.

And so, if apartheid contained the key to continued white domination, it also contained the seeds of ultimate white disaster. For the appalling indignities it visited on black South Africans fuelled their determination to overthrow it. And the affront it gave the world ensured that when the crunch came, white South Africa would find itself alone and without allies. All this was predictable – and predicted. All this is coming to pass. In that way, the blood-letting now unleashed in South Africa conforms perfectly to the requirements of classical tragedy.

Today we stand on the threshold of the second great resolution in the country's history. For if the Boer War settled the question of which white group would win dominance in South Africa, current events are determining who, as between white and black, will ultimately triumph.

Everyone knows the answer, including South Africa's whites. But the incubus of history, pride, hope of some miraculous intervention, and fear of retribution help render whites incapable of averting the Nemesis they know awaits them. However, as we shall see, none of this is the real reason for their paralysis. That is to be found in the self-interest, for which one can hardly castigate them, of a section of the Afrikaner people who will lose out in the great reversal of power. They are desperate to stave off their fate, and the rest of Afrikanerdom, having climbed on their backs to achieve their own positions, is riddled by guilt and hesitation. Their own self-interest requires that they abandon their kith and kin, but their long attachment to them and the unedifying prospect of their own desertion is consuming them with weakness.

In the end, of course, they will do it. Self-interest always wins out, especially in South Africa. But it will take time to happen, and it will be a very bloody business altogether.

There are many illusions still, certainly about South Africa's past, and more particularly about its future. We hear many 'if only's; we shall hear a good deal more from those who have an interest in avoiding the hard choices, who will talk about 'dialogue' and promoting 'peaceful' change – this in relation to a country where the death toll has been rising unceasingly for two years, to say nothing of the more distant past.

A word from A. J. P. Taylor writing in 1947 about the fall of the Habsburg Monarchy is instructive:

> [An] earlier book [of mine] was still dominated by the 'liberal illusion'; many passages talked of 'lost opportunities' and suggested that the Habsburg Monarchy might have survived if only this or that statesman or people had been more sensible. It was difficult to escape from this approach after reading the in-numerable contemporary writers of goodwill, who either wrote before the fall of the Monarchy or still could not believe that it had vanished. These regrets are no part of the duty of a histo-rian, especially when the story he tells makes it clear, time after time, that there were no opportunities to be lost. The conflict between a super-national dynastic state and the national principle had to be fought to the finish; and so, too, had the conflict between the master and subject nations. Inevitably, any concession came too late and was too little; and equally inevitably every concession produced more violent discontent. The national principle, once launched, had to work itself out to its conclusion.

He might just as well have been writing about the conflict between white and black nationalism in South Africa forty years later.

Once white South Africa had set in train the process of domina-tion rather than of power-sharing, it had ensured the full maturation of black nationalism. All opportunities to negotiate some com-promise disappeared. No strong enough incentive could be thrown up by the system to force either side to compromise: for the privi-leged whites the immediate danger to their self-interest would al-ways outweigh longer-term considerations; the miserable crumbs immediately available to blacks would never be attractive enough to outweigh the utility of holding to a longer-term, but more radical, alternative.

And by the time black resistance had reached such a level of inten-sity that whites realized they would have to make more fundamental concessions, the blacks' success was already showing that they could achieve much more themselves than anything the whites could offer them. The only 'reform' which could now stave off a violent denouement is the one reform white South Africa cannot, and will not, countenance: the transfer of power.

So the mechanisms allow no opportunity to avert disaster in South Africa. There is no possibility of real compromise – nor has there been for forty years. There is only the interplay of two fundamentally irreconcilable nationalisms. We will thus witness a bloody struggle to the very end.

The only questions now are how long will the process take, what level of violence will accompany it, and what will South Africa look like when it is over?

This book will try to provide answers.

*   *   *   *

Telling the story of how South Africa came to this pass is, however, the main business of the book. It is based on the wealth of first-hand research acquired by London Weekend Television journalists in the course of making regular visits to South Africa and producing a stream of programmes on the subject for the company's distinguished current affairs series, *Weekend World*. Drawing on this research, then, we hope to provide a new historical overview for those interested in South Africa, a contemporary history, which has hardly been written so far at all, except in news reports, and also a proper framework for understanding events as they unfold in that unhappy country in the future.

The book begins with a brief background on who the pre-European South Africans were and where they came from. As South Africa's crisis attracts growing interest at home and abroad, there is especial curiosity to know more about the people white South Africans encountered when they set out to dominate the country. Those interested in this theme will rightly find themselves frustrated. It is a subject which has been obscured by scholarly disagreement and government propaganda, and in fact remains extraordinarily under-written. So attempts are made to bring together what can reasonably be said about it, and in so doing to dispel white-created myths which have been used to justify pernicious arguments.

But there are other reasons for starting so far back. It becomes apparent in considering all human interaction in South Africa that there have always been processes at work – which have nothing to do with race – which have played a critical role in shaping human relationships there. And it is easier, against such a background, to see that the modern conflict itself owes a good deal to those processes. The world has become obsessed with the racial dimension of South Africa's crisis, but we will argue that to see it in those terms alone, is to misunderstand it. It is hoped, in doing so, to provide new insights into the country's long-drawn-out agony, and to expose many of the over-simplifications which currently obscure discussion of it.

For example, very few writers have looked at the central question of exactly how racism came to take the form it did in South Africa. For although vast differences did exist between the races there, it was never self-evident that they would lead to the systematic segregation involved in apartheid. Many other countries have been composed of strongly differing races, and though they may have manifested some segregationist tendencies, the outcome of their racial contact has been very different from that in South Africa.

And as far as South Africa is concerned, a stranger who knew nothing of apartheid might be forgiven, if he found himself in a 'Coloured' area, for thinking South Africa little different from other multiracial societies. The Coloureds – a group nearly 3 million strong and about 10 per cent of the modern population – are people whose blood is mixed between white, black, and brown South Africans, and their presence in the country is living testimony to generation after generation of intermingling between all South Africa's people at the most fundamental level.

Further close examination of South African history shows quite startling evidence that racial segregation of the kind the contemporary South African government practices was historically absent, and that, until quite recently, there was a significant, if unsuccessful, impulse towards integration. It is thus a surprise to many, both within South Africa and without, to discover that apartheid as such has existed in South Africa for less than forty years, and that its full, unadulterated hold over the country has been of an extraordinarily short duration.

In discovering that the reality of South African history is much at odds with many beliefs about it, we discover, too, that many of the popular and traditional explanations about apartheid have been conflated with mystical concepts about the nature of Afrikanerdom.

These will not do. There is something more that needs explaining here and in providing a more subtle level of understanding of South Africa's complex difficulties, it is hoped to remove other over-simplifications, and in particular to throw light on the true nature of the South African conflict. For though it is clearly right to see it as a racial war, it is also misleading.

There are further oddities that counsel caution in describing the struggle as a purely racial one. It is not the case, for instance, that whites alone have acted to perpetuate apartheid, nor that it has served only their interests. Black South Africans are not at one in wishing to see an end to white rule, and significant elements are deeply opposed to majority rule. Even among those who agree on it, there are deep divisions about how the alternative South Africa should be governed.

In addition there is a long and honourable tradition of white resistance to apartheid. Indeed, it would not be an exaggeration to say that the foundations for the present resistance to apartheid were laid by generations of white South Africans, whose role, though often derided or dismissed, was crucial in keeping alive the possibility of dissent at a time when it might plausibly have been extinguished, if not forever, for many decades. And even today, an increasing number of whites are allying themselves with the cause of non-racialism in South Africa, a fact which may prove decisive in the end.

What all this suggests is that there is more to South Africa's war than meets the eye. And here again history holds vital clues. Like many human entanglements, the struggle for South Africa began as a contest between disparate groups of people, many of whom were very poor, for access to, and control of, limited economic resources. Even today, this is what the struggle ultimately remains: a battle for resources. And though with the passage of time those on the hitherto successful side, the whites, have grown rich beyond their forefathers' imaginings, the intensity of their fight as they see power slipping from their grasp is fuelled at the most profound level by a horror among many that they may slip back into an abyss from which their parents only escaped within living memory.

It is the astigmatism of seeing race as the only issue in South Africa that has led many critics of apartheid into the unhappy contradiction of making judgments which are ultimately racist themselves. For many people have come to believe that South Africa's whites are somehow set apart from other human beings, that there is something which makes them intrinsically wicked and morally inferior. In making this judgment, such observers fail to understand how racism really comes about, how it operates and is kept alive – and without such knowledge we cannot hope to escape from it in the future. In learning about South Africa, we shall also be learning about ourselves.

None of this is to excuse apartheid, but merely to understand it. It is not to deny the validity of the struggle for black liberation, but to understand the real obstacles in the path to its attainment.

It may be, too, that learning about South Africa will better inform opinion abroad, which has a role, if limited, to play in the unfolding drama. When one sees, for example, the crucial part played by the British in helping to lay the foundations for apartheid, it may perhaps also seem to them a more morally urgent imperative to play their modern role honourably – and more honourably than their forefathers did.

Finally, in outlining the possible future of South Africa, some of the immense problems which will face its rulers will be examined. They are caught up at present in current events. They have not found time to think about the country's future – and it seems unlikely under present circumstances that they can do so. But unless they do, they may find South Africa's future as agonizing as its past. The unbroken chain of war has the potential to endure unless a great effort is made to snap it once and for all.

So the need to enumerate South Africa's future difficulties is great: not only for South Africa itself, but for all the many people in the world whose interests, both material and psychological, are tied up in that remote country on the southernmost tip of the African continent.

It would be the cruellest blow of all if the predictions of South Africa's most convinced racists were to come true. South Africa's future rulers owe it to themselves, and to all of us, to make sure that they do not.

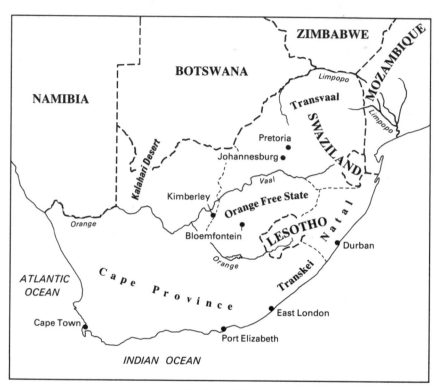

Southern Africa

1
BEFORE THE EUROPEANS

The foundations of South Africa's modern conflict were laid long before either black or white set foot in the country. Both these peoples are, in fact, comparatively recent arrivals when viewed against the background of all human history there. And it was the descendants of earlier inhabitants who were to play the crucial role in the opening stages of our contemporary drama.

These were the Khoisan or, as the Europeans called them, the Hottentots and the Bushmen. They were the first people the Dutch settlers encountered, and in that meeting the dynamic which informed all subsequent South African history first took shape. They were entirely innocent parties in the confrontation which arose and which, indeed, is only now reaching its gruesome climax. But the nature of their economy made them the object of white acquisitiveness, the structure of their society made them vulnerable, and their technology did not provide them with adequate protection. These factors encouraged the Europeans to opt for conflict rather than co-operation in South Africa, and once the habit was formed, they could not find it in themselves to give it up. An explanation of who and what the Khoisan were is thus a necessary starting-point in understanding the full nature of the modern drama we are witnessing.

The Khoisan were in a direct line of descent from the very first South Africans. The archaeological record suggests those earliest people made their appearance in the country at a time which is so distant we cannot really grasp what it means: some 1¾ million years ago, and it is generally thought they had wandered down from Eastern Africa, where the evolution from ape to human being is believed to have begun. Those first immigrants – if immigrants they were – were early stone-age people. They were not identical to modern humans. They had smaller brains and their general ana-

1

tomy was still evolving towards ours. As they meandered through South Africa, though, living off corpses of wild animals and the fruits of the veld, new closely related and bigger-brained human types – species – kept gradually emerging so that the earlier forms disappeared and the physical features of the stock were slowly transformed.

It is particularly fascinating to discover that certain patterns are suggested in this process, which if true, would be highly relevant to what has occurred in the last three centuries in South Africa. Each new species was a relative of its predecessor, and either came to South Africa by migration or evolved spontaneously within the country. It seems only logical to assume that their ability to displace or absorb each earlier species stemmed directly from the control of common sources of food which their greater brain capacity and thus technological inventiveness secured for them, and which made further independent existence impossible for their earlier relatives. In other words, where there was implied economic competition between peoples, technological advantages may have been literally vital in determining group dominance.

Implications for the modern South African conflict may already be seen peeping out, even to readers unfamiliar with details of the country's history. There are great dangers and pitfalls in extrapolating too directly from pre-history to modern history, where we are dealing not with very early and anatomically different species but with groups of exactly the same human beings with the same intellectual capabilities, and where misconceived notions of 'iron laws of nature' both distort the truth of human interaction and may be falsely taken as justification for inhuman behaviour. Nonetheless there do seem to be imperatives and dynamics here which are remarkable in the light of much later events.

The chain of evolution, succession, and absorption continued unbroken for hundreds of thousands of years, with the early humans' stone tools being constantly improved upon. Then, just over 100,000 years ago – fairly recently in the light of the periods we have been considering – South Africa's people reached a point where they had become the species known to science as *Homo sapiens sapiens*. This name may stir a faint resonance among the lay public, and for good reason. This was fully formed modern man. And it is a fact surprisingly well-hidden that South Africa's people have a unique and special claim on our esteem, for, as far as we know, they were the very

2

first people anywhere to attain this state of evolution. South Africa was, in short, the earliest home of modern human beings.

The Khoisan were their offspring. The Khoisan were not what is commonly called Negroid people. Their skin was yellowy-brown, they had tight peppercorn hair which could not really be 'frizzed', and they were generally smaller and scrawnier. The Khoisan actually pursued two divergent lifestyles, such that they were later seen as two different peoples. These were the Hottentots and the Bushmen of European description; the Khoikhoi and the San as they are now more generally referred to. They were, however, basically the same stock, and the term 'Khoisan' has been invented to embrace both. Chronologically, the San way of life developed first, and it was about 10,000 ago that their economy, their culture, and their languages had coalesced into the form in which they were to survive, modified but still recognizable, right into modern times. It is around this period then that we start thinking of the San as a people with a distinct and clearly delineated group identity.

The San were what anthropologists describe as hunter-gatherers: they lived by hunting game and by gathering fruit and vegetation from the veld. They combed South Africa's vast wildnesses, moving about in small wandering bands and usually sheltered in caves. They had bows and poisoned arrows; their implements included stone axes, cleavers, knives, and spears. Their languages were unique for they contained peculiar 'clicking' sounds. Indeed the European word for their later relatives – Hottentot – was a rather lame attempt at onomatopoeia.* They had no writing, but they developed rock-painting into a fine art which recorded their experience for all posterity, and they used reed pipes to make music which, to our ears, is strange, but beautiful and haunting. It is almost impossible to establish with any certainty the precise nature of their society, but many believe that crimes like theft and murder were virtually unknown, and many modern Europeans, Laurens van der Post being perhaps the most notable, see it in romantic terms as an almost ideal kind of existence. One archaeologist† describes it as 'a way of life perfected'.

---

* No one really knows why the Europeans called the San Bushmen. One theory is that it was because they lived in the bush, another that that was where they retreated whenever they saw white people.
† Professor Ray Inskeep of the Pitt Rivers Museum, Oxford.

Today their presence in South Africa over many millennia is recalled mainly in vestigial physical features in the modern population, in elements of their languages which have passed into the currency of other local languages, and in their magnificent rock paintings which they left in many parts of the country. As a separate and distinctly identifiable people, however, they continue to live only in small bands in the wastes of the Kalahari Desert. Even there the modern world has sought them out and is destroying what remains of their ancestral lives, though long interaction with other people has changed even that. Within a generation or two they will no longer exist as a separate people. They will have become totally absorbed by the modern world. When one considers, without being too starry-eyed about it, that their extended stewardship of Southern Africa was more benign than later peoples', and that their culture was rich and fertile, it is difficult to resist the feeling that something of value to South Africa is lost forever and not to regret the passing of their way of life. The story of how this came about will be seen to form an integral part of the long protracted struggle which is the main subject of this book.

The first Europeans, as they explored South Africa's interior, did come into contact with the San, but their main encounters were really with the Khoikhoi. As with so much else in South Africa's pre-European history, we are not clear how their distinctive way of life originated, but it was probably connected with the arrival in South Africa of metal-using farmers from north of the country's borders about 2,000 years ago, in the first century AD. These farmers are generally accepted as the ancestors of today's black South Africans. So not only were they to have a profound effect on the people already there, they were also destined to play an even more significant role in the conflict with white arrivals many centuries later.

The farmers brought sheep with them, and the more northerly San whom they met probably began to acquire flocks from them. Herding spread down through the country, and as more and more San turned to this form of economy, the Khoikhoi way of life began to develop. There was no neat division between Khoikhoi and San; many overlapped. But herding required different social organization from hunting. Though they moved about with their flocks, they had to spend longer in any one place; there also had to be a greater division of labour. Over time these less mobile people began to form clans with recognized chiefs. The evident difference between them

4

and the hunters led them to call themselves 'Khoikhoi': men of men. And these were the people the first whites would encounter.

Meanwhile the newly arrived farmers spread through the modern Transvaal and Orange Free State, down towards the east coast and into Natal. Herding tended to be an adjunct to their main activity which was planting crops, mainly cereals. Indeed, cereals, and especially maize, remain the staple diet of many black South Africans even today. It was this agriculture which determined the pattern of settlement: these areas were particularly suitable for it, but the Cape interior which was hot and parched and often desert, far less so. In the areas they settled the Khoisan lived among them, being slowly absorbed over the centuries. But in the Cape the Khoisan continued to maintain their distinct identity. The San ranged wherever there was game. The Khoikhoi clustered along the Orange River and the Cape's western and southern coasts, for these well-watered areas were most favourable for their sheep. The south-western corner of the modern province was especially lush and fertile. This was where the first white city, Cape Town, would be established, and why the Khoikhoi would be the first to feel the impact of European settlement.

The building-blocks on which a conflict-riddled society would later rise were thus unconsciously being laid in place. But there was one further development of very great significance. There seem to have been some cattle present in South Africa in the first centuries after the arrival of the farmers, but over time there were quantum increases until, between AD 1000 and 1500 cattle came to play a crucial role in both Khoikhoi and black South African societies. The reason is straightforward. Cattle were not only hardy and providers of meat, they also made a healthy addition to diet through milk and dairy products. Among both peoples they became the major store of wealth and the basis of exchange. Their importance can be gauged from the fact that among many black people there might be thirty or forty different words for our one word 'cattle', describing variations of breed, size, colour, and so on.

This significance of cattle, coupled with certain structural characteristics of the two societies, were to have implications in the future confrontation with the whites which fundamentally determined the shape and outcome of that struggle. Black South Africans greatly valued cattle, but they were not dependent on them because agriculture provided another source of sustenance. Farming also

5

tied them more solidly to one place, and that and the variety of their economic enterprises, allowed more complex and robust social and political structures to develop. They too lived in clans, but, unlike the Khoikhoi, the clans became mobilized in broader groupings called chieftaincies or kingdoms in which a hereditary paramount chief was acknowledged by the clans under him. Among virtually all black groups, descent passed through the male line only. However, queens-regent sometimes ruled if their sons were too young. Some queens-regent, indeed, played a most significant part in their people's history. One such was the fabled MaNthatisi of the Tlokwa people in the early nineteenth century, who enjoyed an especially lurid, though considerably exaggerated, reputation. A British missionary, Robert Moffat, wrote:

> It was said that a mighty woman was at the head of an invincible army, numerous as the locusts, marching onward among the interior nations, carrying devastation and ruin wherever she went; that she nourished the army with her own milk, sent out the hornets before it, and, in one word, was laying the world desolate.

Her people were known as 'the Mantatee [sic] hordes' and were dreaded wherever they passed. Even in modern times, queens-regent can still be important figures. In Swaziland, whose people are near-relatives of black South Africans, Queen Dziliwe enjoyed a short but politically explosive reign when the venerable King Sobhuza II died in 1982. She too suffered a bad press, though it had rather more to do with her style as 'the great white she-elephant' than her politics.

By comparison with black South African society, the Khoikhoi's way of life was much more fragile, though they did not yet realize it. Their political structures were weaker because their more nomadic existence inhibited the formation of stronger ones. And cattle were a somewhat vulnerable basis on which to build an entire society, for they could be stolen, or wiped out by drought and disease. Traditionally, if any of these events occurred, the Khoikhoi simply reverted to their ancestral San way of life to keep themselves going, and when once they had re-established themselves they could begin to build up their herds again. No one ever supposed – nor was there any reason to – that a situation might one day arise in which an ex-

6

ternal onslaught might deprive them of their cattle, and also prevent them returning to the San life. In that situation they would have nothing left. But that inherent weakness was not yet noticed because it had never been fundamentally tested. In due course, however, it would be.

Black South Africans, as they had established themselves, had evolved societies which were complex and sophisticated not just socially and politically, but technologically too. Many of their skills they brought with them, and it was probably related to, and reinforced by, spending time in one place and in a diverse social environment. They were great builders. Some constructed pole and thatch houses, with plastered floors and walls; some beehive-shaped huts. The Southern Transvaal saw substantial stone buildings clustered in what were effectively small towns. The sharing of this culture with other Southern African black people can be seen, for example, in the wonderful stone buildings of Great Zimbabwe in the modern country of the same name. It also provides an interesting instance of white racists' refusal to believe that black people could have been capable of such architecture. For many decades, white Southern African scholars busied themselves feverishly trying to solve the 'riddle' of who built Great Zimbabwe. After looking for lost white explorers and Arab traders and other similarly exotic explanations, they were finally compelled by the weight of evidence to settle for the obvious.

Black South Africans brought knowledge of metal-smelting with them too, and so their villages contained furnaces in which iron or copper tools and weapons were forged. From about the twelfth century, when they had discovered gold, extensive gold industries were set up, and early Portuguese explorers along South Africa's eastern coast remarked enviously on the impressive sight of women arriving to greet them decked out from head to foot in magnificent gold ornaments. They had elaborate pottery, and fired clay into objects for ritual and domestic use. A find of ornamental heads at Lydenburg in the Eastern Transvaal dates back to AD 500 and contains wonderful examples of their art. They carved soapstone, bone, and ivory, and these traditions still linger on, as the myriad curio shops in South Africa's tourist centres testify. It seems highly likely too that they traded with coastal areas, for Indian Ocean shells have been discovered far into the interior.

All in all, then, this was a rich and complex society, established

7

over many centuries. The precise number of those centuries is actually a matter of a considerable and important controversy. Although the overwhelming majority of scholars agree that black South Africans arrived in the first century AD, some argue on the basis of changes in pottery and stock-keeping that that event may not have happened until AD 1000. This is very much a minority view and, as more evidence is found, seems increasingly improbable, though it remains conceivable. Either way, it is beyond dispute that AD 1000 was the very latest date at which black South Africans could have arrived.

This is not simply an academic matter, but one which has important political implications. The South African Government, in their latest official accounts of black history, argue that the first blacks began to reach South Africa in the eleventh and twelfth centuries. As we have seen, the eleventh century is, in fact, the very last possible date, and one which most scholars regard as a thousand years too late. This latest government version of events is actually an improvement over earlier ones since they claimed for decades that it was not until sometime around the sixteenth and seventeenth centuries that blacks began making their way down through South Africa. The reason for this distortion of history is that the government wanted to claim that the white settlers had not displaced native peoples. They argued that the country had been more or less empty. It will be readily apparent that whatever else the land was, it was not empty, nor had it been for many hundreds of thousands of years.

By the seventeenth century, indeed, the pattern of Khoisan and black settlement had been established long enough to produce not only developed clan and chieftaincy systems, but a broad and mutually accepted division of the country into what might be called local spheres of influence. The mapping out of that pattern was later undertaken by white settlers, who imposed a more rigid framework on it than was true in reality, and who brought their own prejudices and interests to bear on their work. In particular they invented the concept of the 'tribe' and delineated the pre-European situation in tribal terms. 'Tribe' has come to be another highly charged political issue and it is certainly the case that black South Africans did not see themselves in quite this way and that the concept was only a crude approximation to what actually existed. They saw their political allegiance to their chief or king; the European 'tribe' was a much broader category which lumped together a number of separate and

8

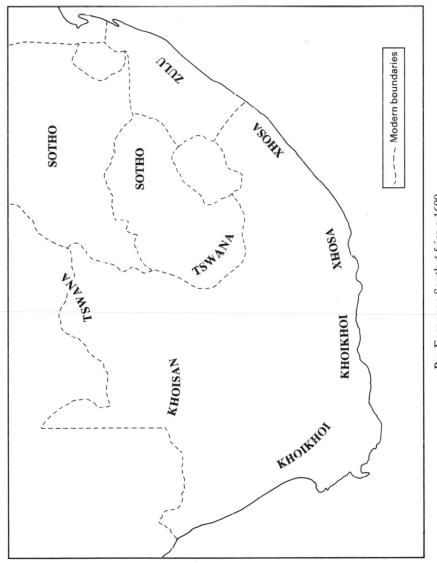

SOTHO

SOTHO

ZULU

XHOSA

TSWANA

TSWANA

XHOSA

KHOISAN

KHOIKHOI

KHOIKHOI

Modern boundaries

Pre-European South Africa c.1600

diverse kingdoms. The real basis of this European-imposed division was language, for they identified broad language groups which might comprise a number of different authorities and presumed that that cultural link was also a political link.

With that caveat in mind, we can say that by the mid-seventeenth century a number of black chieftaincies lay in a line down the Transvaal to the modern Lesotho, and that they spoke a roughly similar language which the Europeans called Sotho. Some of those people did call themselves Sotho, and the name of the modern kingdom of Lesotho actually means 'the land of the Sotho'. To the south-east, in the modern province of Natal, a number of other kingdoms were situated where a common language was also spoken. This was the language whites called Zulu. The Zulu were actually only one kingdom within Natal, but in the nineteenth century they did weld the others into a larger grouping under their own banner, so that today a larger Zulu identity does exist, with its members constituting the largest single language grouping in the country.

By this time blacks had settled in the eastern Cape too, and there the main language was Xhosa, which was quite closely related to Zulu. In the western Transvaal, the north-eastern Cape, and parts of the modern Orange Free State, Tswana was the name whites gave the common language spoken by the different chieftaincies. Readers may guess that the modern Botswana, into which the Tswana speakers extended, also derives its name from its people and means 'the land of the Tswanas'.

All these languages had begun life as South African dialects within the pan-African family of Bantu, but they were unique within it by having acquired 'click' sounds – most probably under the influence of Khoisan tongues, and are evidence that the interaction between the two peoples was by no means a one-way process.

By the seventeenth century, then, this was the pattern of co-existence in South Africa, and it was a fairly stable one. There was sporadic conflict at the margins between groups as conflicts over land and cattle periodically arose, but a carefully evolved balance had been long established.

In that fateful century, however, this was to be shattered forever, and the forces unleashed which would reverberate right up until today, when they would finally reach their long drawn-out climax. The upheaval was to be fundamental, and unparalleled in its violence and destructive power. For the Khoisan in particular, though they did not immediately realize it, the titanic struggle which was about to come upon them would mark the beginning of the end of their many thousands of years of existence as a people.

In discovering how this arose, we will find the key to understanding why South Africa has become what it has, and why the bloodletting is not yet over.

2
WHITE AND KHOIKHOI

The mortal threat to the Khoikhoi came in innocent guise, and on a day we can trace with deadly certainty. On 6 April 1652, a small group of sailing ships put in at the Cape of Good Hope. The leader of the party aboard was the Dutchman Jan van Riebeeck, and he came to establish the European presence in South Africa. Ironically enough, it was not his intention to colonize, or even to create any major form of settlement. He came with explicit instructions from his employers, the Dutch East India Company,* to do nothing more than establish a small revictualling station for Dutch ships *en route* to and from the Dutch East Indies. He had ninety men with him.

For Van Riebeeck and his men, the Cape assignment must have been one of mixed blessings. Cape Town, where they built their incongruous small Dutch houses, whitewashed and replete with gables, occupied a location which, in summer, was of breathtaking beauty. It sat beneath the majestic flat-topped outcrop of rock called Table Mountain, with twelve mountains crashing down into the sea behind it, and beaches of white sand marking the points of contact. It was an almost excessively lush, fertile location, with exotic flora and fauna. Sir Francis Drake, passing there on his journey around the globe, had called it 'the fairest cape in all the world'.

But there were pitiably few of them, gripping onto this toe-hold at the bottom of Africa and the known world. Beyond the blue mountains in the distance, which came to be called Hottentots-Holland, stretched a vast land, occupied by people of whom they had only the scantest impression. Their acute vulnerability and isolation in this

---

* Its full name was the *Vereenigde Nederlandsche Ge-Octroyeerde Oost-Indische Compagnie*, or the United Netherlands Chartered East India Company, and will hereafter be abbreviated in the normal form of VOC.

paradise, where the sun blazed down and sparkled on the mountains in summer, would have been starkly brought home to them in winter. Clouds would set in for months on end, and it would rain continuously. The winds would howl in from the South Atlantic, and suddenly huge storms would erupt around the coast, known, fittingly, to earlier European sailors as the Cape of Storms. Then, as they huddled in their tiny houses, as the elements hurtled in all around them, they must have felt an extraordinary sense of desolation.

They did not have much time to brood, however. They were there to work at getting the revictualling station set up, and it was sorely needed. The voyage from the Netherlands to the East Indies took many months. The provisions ships could hold were not large. Many coastlines were hostile, and even if they were not, supplies could not be guaranteed. Scurvy, disease, and malnutrition made it extremely attractive to have a halfway refuelling point.

So Van Riebeeck and his party set to work building a fort at the foot of Table Mountain, on the shores of Cape Town's Table Bay. It no longer stands but the Castle of Good Hope, a pentagonal building which replaced it a few years later, is still there, with its cobbled courtyard and the messages of doomed slaves scribbled on the walls of its dungeons. They established a small hospital for sick sailors, which has long since disappeared, and planted a vegetable garden on the slopes of Table Mountain. The vegetable garden is no longer a vegetable, but a flower, garden and still sits right in the middle of the city, alongside the modern Parliament building.

Almost at once these Dutch settlers came into contact with the Khoikhoi, since this was a highly fertile area of their grazing lands. The Khoikhoi were not unfamiliar with white people. Since the fifteenth century, explorers of various nationalities had passed along their shores, especially Portuguese, and ships of many European powers had taken to stopping and trading with them. It is unlikely that they were immediately alarmed by this European presence.

But a conflict of interest soon arose. The VOC was concerned to make the Cape station self-supporting and wanted to minimize their own input as much as possible. The Cape had to supply fresh fruit and vegetables, meat and dairy produce, and cereals to passing ships. Van Riebeeck soon found that the Company gardens could provide fruit and vegetables. But for meat and dairy produce, cattle were needed. At first, a certain amount of cattle could be bartered

13

from the Khoikhoi, but they very quickly began to resist the Company's blandishments. The Khoikhoi's wealth, after all, was measured in terms of cattle ownership, and by selling off his herd, a Khoikhoi man was destroying the very basis of his economy. The only solution was for the Company to acquire more breeding cattle and raise its own herds. So they continued to put pressure on the Khoikhoi's stock. Because of the Company's dependence on Khoikhoi goodwill, its board – the Heren XVII* – had at first insisted that the Khoikhoi be regarded as free people who could not be enslaved, and that they be treated with all due respect and courtesy. But very soon Van Riebeeck began to hold individual Khoikhoi hostage as a way of forcing the delivery of cattle. Within the very first years, then, tension between white and non-white† was already growing. But in addition, the Company needed pasturage if it was to raise cattle. They began to use land lying immediately beyond the encampment – Khoikhoi land. Furthermore, the Company gardens were quite unsuitable for wheat-growing since they were exposed to the destructive south-easterly winds. But just beyond the settlement lay sheltered land with good soil. Company employees were released from tutelage to the Company and allowed to acquire land there for their own use as free farmers, provided they sold their produce to the Company. This land was also regarded by the Khoikhoi as theirs.

The Khoikhoi must quite quickly have realized what a grave threat these people posed to them. With their sailing ships and guns, they obviously had technological superiority, and now they were beginning to behave in a most aggressive way, snatching people and cattle, and installing themselves on Khoikhoi land. How to counteract this threat posed an appalling dilemma. So the economic forces for colonization and conflict were in place from the moment Van Riebeeck's men set foot on South African soil. In 1659, barely seven years after the Dutch settlers had arrived at the Cape, the Khoikhoi tried to expel the free farmers from the land they had occupied, and the first Khoikhoi-Dutch War had broken out.

* Literally, the Seventeen Gentlemen.
† 'Non-white' is a loaded term, being extensively used by the South African Government, and regarded by many as inherently racist. It seems to me a useful shorthand, frequently obviating the need to specify which of the many different peoples are being distinguished from whites.

It lasted about a year. The Khoikhoi outnumbered the settlers many times over, but the settlers had guns and resourcefulness. The confrontation ended in a military stalemate. The Company made airy promises to respect the Khoikhoi's rights in future, and the Khoikhoi, unable to do anything else, in turn agreed to allow the farmers to stay.

Though it would be an exaggeration to say that this encounter was absolutely decisive in the relations between white and non-white in South Africa, it was to prove typical. In that sense, then, the summary given above could serve as a model for many future encounters, and tells, as simply as can be told, the broad story of the next 300 years in South Africa. The pattern was established, and it is only now, many centuries later, that it is finally to be broken.

For once Dutch settlers were ensconced beyond the confines of the Company stockade, European expansion was inevitable. Cape Town started to develop. It was the only port of any significance for literally thousands of miles in any direction, and this was a time when European ships were plying the world in search of trade. Many of them began to call regularly. Inns and taverns started up – brothels too. Slaves were brought from Madagascar and the East Indies, because the Khoikhoi were proving reluctant to provide labour in the quantities needed. Quite a little town started to grow up. More men came out from the VOC to work there. Immigrants of various types started arriving. Adventurers and blackguards of many kinds came out to seek their fortunes. Company employees got bored and their local bosses, being so far removed from any control, became corrupt. As the population reproduced, more and more men wanted their own bit of land as a way of amusing themselves and making a profit on the side. Expansion, and the usurpation of Khoikhoi land, followed inexorably.

By 1679 European South Africa's second town, Stellenbosch, had been established forty miles from modern-day Cape Town, and its Cape Dutch homesteads have been preserved on a large scale to remind visitors of what a beautiful and charming place it must have been for those early residents. Alongside the church – a central feature of any town created by these intensely God-fearing Calvinists – the slave-bell still stands, though the message of the darker side of that society tends to be forgotten among the touristic prettiness.

A third town, Paarl, followed soon after. In 1688 200 French Hug-

15

uenot refugees provided a new and significant infusion into the settler population – of whom, incidentally, a substantial proportion were actually German. The Huguenots were installed further afield, at Drakenstein and Franschhoek. There, in beautiful and lush sun-strewn valleys, they used the knowledge they had brought from France to plant vineyards and establish South Africa's fledgling wine industry. They quickly lost their Frenchness and became absorbed into the Dutch culture, but names like Malan, Le Grange, and De Villiers live on in the modern white population.

This expansion was facilitated by changing attitudes to the Khoikhoi. The first Khoikhoi-Dutch war had demonstrated that the Dutch could hold the Khoikhoi at bay. It soon became clear to them that the gun was a potent weapon in defending even isolated outposts. A new sense of security prevailed, and by the early 1670s the Heren XVII had lost interest in the treatment of the Khoikhoi and were prepared to turn a blind eye to what the settlers might do.

In 1673 this new attitude was underscored when the Dutch themselves launched a war on the Khoikhoi. It took the form of four major punitive expeditions, and ranged far into the interior of the modern Cape Province. The growing confidence of the Dutch was heightened when they achieved an important symbolic victory by breaking the resistance of Gonnema, one of the most powerful and most anti-Dutch Khoikhoi leaders. Gonnema was forced to submit to providing an annual tribute of cattle. With even his resistance broken, other Khoikhoi leaders were less inclined to withstand future settler depredations.

It was the start of a process of systematic subjugation and control of South Africa's native peoples. The law mirrored this developing pattern. At first, the Company had regarded the Khoikhoi as lying beyond their jurisdiction. Increasingly, now, the Company arrogated to itself the right to intervene in Khoikhoi disputes. More and more, it imposed decisions concerning Khoikhoi-settler disputes by force. In 1679, the new Governor at the Cape, Simon van der Stel, even went so far as to insist that he be allowed to approve the installation of new Khoikhoi chiefs, supplying them with official Company canes as a seal of approval, and which quickly became objects of popular resentment among the Khoikhoi. It is testimony to the longevity of political traditions that the current South African Government still operates a similar system of selective recognition of non-white chiefs – whose seals of office continue to excite resentment.

16

By now the decimation of Khoikhoi herds, especially in the South Western Cape, was proceeding apace. At the same time the demand for labour on settler farms was accelerating, a demand not satisfied even by the accelerating importation of slaves, many of whom were Malay – thus adding to the growing cosmopolitan character of the Cape their own distinctive Islamic culture. In these circumstances, the increasingly cattle-less Khoikhoi sought employment on settler farms, where their own independent identity gradually eroded as they tended to merge with the slave population, thus laying the basis for the modern Coloured people.

By the beginning of the eighteenth century, the breakdown of traditional Khoikhoi life in the South Western Cape was far advanced. In 1713 it was dramatically accelerated by an outbreak of smallpox – hitherto unknown among the Khoikhoi, who consequently had no immunity against it. As much as 90 per cent of the Khoikhoi in the South Western Cape may have perished, and this disaster greatly hastened their disintegration as a people in that particular corner of South Africa.

By this time, the settlers were steadily expanding further and further into the interior of the Cape Province, mainly northwards towards the Orange River. The agents of this penetration were a new breed of European: *trekboers*, or frontier farmers. Much of the terrain beyond the South Western Cape was relatively arid: intensive agricultural farming was much more difficult and expensive. Many of the men who sought to make a new life in the hinterland were impoverished and lacked agricultural experience, so, like the Khoikhoi, they took up pastoral farming, grazing cattle and sheep. The Company allowed them to acquire substantial tracts of land, which had to be large enough to make such enterprises viable.

It was a curious life. Living on isolated, far-flung farms, with Cape Town, itself rather provincial, several days' travel away, and with a distinct shortage of white women, it became a dispersed world of frontier living: hard, tough, entirely lacking in higher pursuits, and of easy morals. They brought their Bibles with them, but in the silence of pitch-black nights, they sought the solace of the gun, the brandy bottle, and non-white women. Their sole occupation was pastoral farming. Their hunger for land was the only way to enrichment. The niceties of negotiation and parleying were quickly dispensed with. The Khoikhoi, who had, of course, learnt immediately how to use guns, had considerable difficulty acquiring them from

17

the whites, who were not anxious to see them armed. The Khoikhoi, then, became comparatively easy prey. If they did not deliver what the *trekboers* wanted – cattle, land, and labour – they got a bullet through the head. It was a simple, brutal life. And as the *trekboers* expanded further and further afield, more and more Khoikhoi got sucked into the vicious cycle of conflict and dispossession. The same struggles over livestock and land were played out repeatedly, with the same results. The economy of the Khoikhoi remaining to the north of the Cape settlement slowly disintegrated. Those rendered landless flocked to white farms to eke out a living by the only alternative open to them: labouring.

This process was neither quick nor easy. It took nearly half a century – until about 1750. The Khoikhoi resisted as best they could. Sometimes they attacked the *trekboers* physically; a number of small wars occurred. More often, though, they resorted to stealing the Europeans' stock and trying to disrupt their farming. The Dutch authorities found an effective counter-weapon: the 'commando' system, by which they periodically conscripted *trekboers* into small posses for punitive raids against the Khoikhoi. The Khoikhoi had no answer to the gun. The disintegration of their way of life took time – but was inevitable.

It was a painful period for everyone, a time of great turbulence and insecurity. For the *trekboers* there was loneliness, vulnerability, fear, and resentment. It is no accident that today, when so many of their descendants suffer similar feelings, the idea of the commando remains a potent symbol of reassurance to whites. For the Khoikhoi, there was only despair. Their many centuries of independent existence in South Africa was drawing to an humiliating end. Only in the Eastern Cape did their presence remain strong. It would take another century for the same processes to destroy their identity and distinct existence there. But the same outcome awaited them.

So the Khoikhoi dwindled in number, decimated by alien diseases and routine slaughter. As a people they did not die out: those who went to the towns became labourers and artisans. Those who stayed on the farms not only worked on the land, but proved adept at horse-riding and served their new masters by hunting or even by providing troops for their expeditions against other Khoikhoi. But their culture, their distinct identity, and their independence disappeared. As they merged with the slaves, they became little better than slaves themselves. Interbreeding with their co-workers, and indeed with the whites, ensured that a new population would emerge – the modern Coloureds – which, with its rich mixture of different backgrounds and cultures, would provide an important new element in South Africa's long catalogue of human existence. But it was the end of the Khoikhoi as a distinct group.

In the latter half of the eighteenth century, the mantle of resistance in the Northern Cape passed to their San hunting brothers, who now also came under threat. They too put up a fierce struggle, but could not check the white advance. Their more flexible and self-sufficient lifestyle ensured their longer survival as a distinct people. But they too were gunned down, driven into servitude for the whites, and absorbed, to fuse into the Coloured population. Small bands maintained their independence by retreating gradually to the deserts, where not even the Europeans, for all their sophistication, could survive. There they preserved something of their traditional way of life, though that too had long been mediated by interaction with the Khoikhoi and Bantu. Theirs was a long twilight, their numbers dwindling steadily as modernity tempted people away, or ate into their refuge. Today what remains of San life is to be found only in the Kalahari, and as the twentieth century draws to a close, its end has surely come. The broader world, and the South African Army in what has become a sensitive border zone, has finally penetrated even its last retreat. It has taken less than four centuries finally to destroy a way of life which was evolved over millions of years.

Of course we should not be sentimental about this. Human evolution is an endless process of people meeting, interacting, changing each other, and evolving into something new and different. This is inevitable, perhaps even desirable. Very large numbers of the Khoikhoi and San welcomed the new world they encountered, with its opportunities and advanced technology. But the brutality of the process, the fracturing of lives, the destruction of security, and the final enslaving of a whole people made this an interaction of a most painful kind.

The very starkness of the process enables us to see more clearly than we might otherwise something important about the nature of human affairs. If we stand back for a moment and consider the meeting of white and Khoisan in power terms, we will see that the same realities which determined human outcomes 1½ million years ago in South Africa, continued to operate. Here were two peoples in

19

competition for limited economic resources. Those with superior organization and technology won out; the others died or succumbed to servitude and absorption. Nothing could be simpler – nor in human terms more dreadful. Khoisan independence died because their economies were too fragile; because their way of life had not permitted social and political institutions to form which might have given them a chance of coalescing and uniting against the alien onslaught. It died because in the end there was no real escape: by the time it was clear what was happening their society was so eroded it could not restructure itself adequately to ensure their survival as a distinct people. Some San live on as a reminder of what was – but not as a salvation.

But we should not fall into the trap of arguing that because the power contest conformed to patterns which we can trace much earlier in human existence in South Africa, it was therefore inevitable or logical or justifiable that the whites should respond to the Khoisan as they did. Human society is certainly subject to many animal imperatives, but of course we are not beasts. What distinguishes us precisely is the self-awareness and imagination which allows morality and 'humanity' to operate. The whites had choices, and we must judge their choosing by our own standards. The Khoisan mastered the new technology of the gun at once, but the whites set about denying it to them because they wished to keep them vulnerable. Nothing in nature says this is right; this is not some iron law that is being obeyed. This is political policy, which is a quite different matter.

It is against this background that we can begin to examine some of the issues of race which have become so intrusive in modern South Africa. Let us consider first the question of white superiority. In what did it consist? White racists continue to believe – in their hearts, at least – that it consisted in an innate, biological superiority of race, a superiority not only of know-how but of a wider greatness which they think of as civilization. The Europeans' encounter with the Khoisan does not support this. There was clearly no moral or behavioural superiority. There was nothing very civilized in their conduct. There was indeed only a technological and organizational superiority, deliberately denied the Khoisan.

But did that technological superiority itself not stem perhaps from some innate quality of race? It seems implausible. Anatomically there was not much to choose between white and Khoisan. Their

20

brains were identical. For the early part of their existence, Khoisa-noid peoples evolved at roughly the same rate as human beings elsewhere. But at some indeterminate point thousands of years ago, a technological difference did set in.

Was this the product of race? No one can provide definitive answers to these most profound questions. But since beliefs about them continue to exert an extraordinary influence in human affairs, it is no use simply denying them. If we cannot supply answers, possibilities and alternatives to the racist view can be provided.

In Southern African, the San and later the Khoikhoi found an environment which ensured their survival. There was land and food in abundance; the climate was benign; their stone-age technology gave them everything they needed to assert their dominance over all other life. There was, in short, no incentive for them to develop at a faster rate than spontaneous discovery would produce.

It was not so in Europe. It was a different continent, with a different terrain, flora and fauna, and climate. It was not so benign. Human beings needed to develop new skills to survive. They evolved different social institutions. The Mediterranean was not a vast ocean, but an easily navigable sea. Europe was connected through the Near East to Arabia and Asia. Contact was relatively easy; knowledge and ideas could be pooled. Technology and organization could develop its own momentum. It was not so on the remotest tip of Africa, a self-supporting territory largely separated by enormous oceans from other worlds. Invention, in short, may have worked differently because it was a different place.

But if the racist view of the contact between European and Khoisan is open to doubt, so is the view that conflict must inevitably have arisen *because of* white racism. The white settlers at the Cape no doubt thought of themselves as superior to the Khoisan. They looked down on them. But these were different times. In that age, Europeans still owned slaves and the pressure for emancipating them was at least a century into the future. It is against this background that their attitude to the Khoisan must be judged. The Dutch came to the Cape espousing the idea that the Khoisan were free people, whose rights and independence must be respected. They tried to honour this view. Economic pressures drove them to violate it, but they clung tenaciously to the myth. Even when the Company had set up its own colonial judicial system, complete with courts and magistrates, they maintained the idea that the Khoisan

21

were equal with whites, able to sue and seek protection in the same way. They may have been hypocritical, but it was by no means thoroughgoing racism.

From the very start, Van Riebeeck entertained Khoikhoi as honoured guests at the fort. He brought up Khoikhoi children in his own home, and the Company financed and blessed the marriage of his famous protégée, Eva, to a Danish surgeon. Mixed marriages, though they were very much the exception rather than the rule, were not by any means uncommon, and the couples lived normally among the settlers. Miscegenation was widespread, and white fathers often brought up the offspring of such liaisons in their own homes. In the cosmopolitan port of Cape Town, people of all races met and socialized together. Even on the frontier farms, white bachelors regularly sought the company of non-white women, and were in many ways closer to their societies than their own. A recent study by the distinguished Afrikaans academic, J. A. Heese, published amidst much controversy in South Africa, provides evidence to support his argument that literally hundreds of the most prominent Afrikaans families have either intermarried with non-white peoples in the past, or have non-white blood in their veins.

In addition to this, the Dutch tried actively to promote a class of free blacks at the Cape – mainly ex-slaves and Christian converts. There was such a population, and they enjoyed substantial rights, even occasionally being accorded the same title as white settlers – *burgher*, or citizen. So race relations between the early settlers and the Khoisan peoples with whom they first came into contact were not quite what they are often believed to have been. Discrimination was certainly not as institutionalized as it was to become in modern South Africa. The whole pattern of intercommunal living was qualitatively different.

We should be quite clear what is being said here. The Dutch settlement in the Cape was not a non-racial paradise in which all people lived freely as equals. Europeans enjoyed the highest status, privileges, and freedoms. People of other races were discriminated against and could only with difficulty attain the same position as whites. But seen in its historic context, it was a much more fluid society than modern South Africa. Racism existed, but in a much less virulent form than it does today. In many ways it was little different from other multiracial societies of the time.

Attitudes and ideas, many of them contradictory, exist and are juggled together in people's minds. They change and are adapted. Some are discarded; new ones are taken up. Which attitudes are built on and elaborated, and which are eroded and then jettisoned, is not a random process. It is linked closely to other processes. In many multiracial societies, the dominant race becomes progressively more tolerant and liberal. Racial fusion takes place. In South Africa the impulses towards progress and reaction existed side by side. In the end, reaction won out. It won out not because there was some special inborn racism in those Dutch, German, and French people who found themselves at the Cape – itself a racist notion – but because an accident of birth had given them membership of a group with special technological advantages. Given the kind of competitive economy they practised, self-interest made adherence to that group their most rational and profitable course as individuals. That group was a racial one, though in other societies it might have been primarily religious, regional, or tribal. Since the economic conflict with other peoples could not be resolved without violence, fierce attachment to this group was the key to economic triumph. The whites acted brutally to preserve their interests, as people usually do, but they felt the need to find some justification for it in their own minds. Few individuals – and certainly not whole peoples – have the stomach for brutality and even genocide if they believe themselves to be acting cold-bloodedly and cynically. They need an excuse.

The rationale, which had to make killing, dispossession, and enslavement tolerable, needed to find a way of diminishing other peoples' rights and claims. And so, those racist attitudes and ideas which were in play together with other instincts and notions, came more and more to the fore, to justify behaviour and ease consciences. They became slowly crystallized. The process ebbed and flowed. Alternative sensibilities never quite died out, even in the modern era. But the balance tilted profoundly – and in the process the Khoisan paid the price.

Meanwhile white South Africa was about to come up against other peoples and powers. This time the results would be rather different.

3

BLACK, BOER, AND BRIT

If the eighteenth century brought a decisive settlement of the relationship between the Cape settlers and the Khoisan, it also brought the settlers into contact with new peoples – the Bantu-speaking black farmers of South Africa, and the British. This would present challenges of a different order.

In the Eastern Cape, Khoisan lived in the area between the Gamtoos and Fish Rivers, with Xhosa immediately to the east. The demarcation was not quite as clear as this, but as a general picture it is broadly correct. Throughout the eighteenth century, white settlers periodically took themselves through this territory to establish contact with the Xhosa. The major reason was trade. The Xhosa, like the Khoikhoi, owned cattle – and the white farmers, as Khoikhoi sources of livestock dried up, were anxious to purchase elsewhere. The Xhosa, with long-established links to the interior, were also a rich source of desirable commodities, like ivory. Moreover the Xhosa were friendly. They, too, had had contact with whites before: many a shipwreck victim had found shelter among them, and many refugees from Company justice had found sanctuary there.

The latter half of the century saw the by now inevitable expansion of white settlement, increasingly in an easterly direction, and as the Dutch began to settle among these remaining Khoisan, it immediately created new turbulence. The Khoisan, like their brethren in the Western Cape, resisted these incursions into their territory. But it also brought the Europeans into much closer contact with the Xhosa. Inevitably cattle-rustling ensued, and disputes quickly broke out over grazing and hunting rights.

The VOC was anxious to ensure its position as the sole outlet for white enterprise. Its commandos were also busy trying to deal with the San in the Northern Cape, and it did not want wars on another

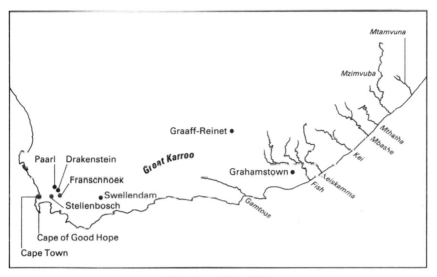

The Cape 1652–1870

front. So, alarmed by this new disturbance, it forbade cattle trading between white and black, and tried to prohibit white settlement east of the Gamtoos. In the long run, it failed, but its attempts to assert control over more remote settlers produced the first significant white resistance to its authority. By now the settlers had lived in South Africa for more than a century. They were beginning to develop their own sense of identity. New towns were constantly being established: small, rustic affairs, with their sprinkling of Dutch houses, their churches, and the Company *drostdy*, from where its local official, the magistrate, oversaw the administration of Company rules and regulations. The Eastern Cape settlers resented this attempt by men in distant Cape Town to tell them how to run their affairs, and towards the end of the eighteenth century formed a *Kaapse Patriotte* (Cape Patriots) movement, which demanded more representation for settlers on the Company's policy-making and judicial bodies. In 1795, indeed, this led to the declaration of two short-lived 'republics' in the more easterly magisterial districts of Swellendam and the recently established Graaff-Reinet. Meanwhile, fighting with the Xhosa, raid and counter-raid, continued.

Unexpectedly, an entirely new force intervened, when in 1795 the ruling House of Orange was expelled from the Netherlands, to be succeeded by the Batavian Republican government. William of Orange fled to Britain, and asked Britain to seize control of 'his' Cape possessions. The British, after encountering brief resistance, did so, and British rule was established at the Cape. So, a new element was injected into the already complex mix of peoples now inhabiting South Africa. And the introduction of a British presence was to have a profound impact on the country – an impact which would survive long after they had gone.

At first the British adopted a relatively uncontroversial policy towards the settlers, seeking to reassure them and maintain harmony. *Burgher* representation in Cape Town was improved. But already, signs of a different sensibility were emerging. From the beginning of the nineteenth century, British missionaries – most notably from the London Missionary Society – settled among the non-white people of South Africa, and immediately condemned their treatment at the hands of the settlers. By this time, too, the movement to emancipate slaves and colonial peoples was reaching a highpoint throughout the British Empire. Missionary voices articulated these novel ideas for the first time in South Africa.

British rule was, however, not yet consolidated at the Cape. The Treaty of Amiens of 1803, in which the British made their peace with the new authorities in the Netherlands, handed the Cape back to the Dutch. By now, the Dutch East India Company had collapsed under the weight of worldwide economic competition from rival trading powers, so government at the Cape was assumed by representatives of the Batavian Republic.

It spelt the end of the Cape as the fiefdom of a chartered company, and its start as an overseas colony of a European nation-state. Batavian rule did not, however, last long. Three years later, with the outbreak of the Napoleonic Wars, Britain, which had begun to appreciate the Cape's strategic positioning midway to India, decided to reoccupy the Cape for fear it would fall into French hands, and its presence there was confirmed by treaty at the end of the Napoleonic Wars, in 1815.

British colonial overlords, usually upper-class, ex-India hands, were now being installed in the Dutch *Tuinhuis* – or Garden House – in Cape Town, the ruling mansion with its charming garden, today still in use as the South African President's office. One can image the extraordinary contrast between the English and the raw Dutch *burghers* in far-flung little settlements that they now had to govern.

The British occupation opened the way for British traders and businessmen to move into Cape Town. Their experience, coupled with the ending of the stultifying VOC monopoly, produced a flourishing agricultural and commodity trade, and South Africa rapidly became tied in to the world trading system. It soon became apparent to the British governors that the major irritant in this important and prospering little colony was going to be increasing Dutch occupation of the eastern frontier, and the bitter disputes it was giving rise to.

The settlers' successes in expanding hitherto had strengthened them economically as a group and led to an increase of population. Both these factors encouraged them to seek more land and cattle, which their pastoral economy needed if it was to grow. The eastern extremity of the colony – and Xhosa resources – seemed the most fruitful avenue of advance. But the Xhosa were different from the Khoikhoi. They practised settled intensive farming, as well as pastoralism, and their density on the land and extra resources made them better able to put up military resistance. At the same time it seems probable that their own population was growing, so like the Europeans they were also land-hungry, a condition intensified from early in the nineteenth century by their adoption of maize farming, which depleted the land more quickly than their previous crops, and by pressure on their own eastern border, where other Bantu peoples were bearing down on them.

Black and white met head-on, therefore, with similar needs, pushing against each other from opposite directions. The Xhosa – who were not only more settled than the Khoikhoi, but had cohesive social structures – were more aggressive and better able to defend themselves. This head-on collision produced a situation in which between 6 and 9 wars were fought over a period of 100 years, depending on precisely how one defines a war.

British policy on this most central issue was, in many ways, self-contradictory. For a considerable period they extended the VOC's policy, which had been in essence to keep white and Xhosa apart. To that end they established successive neutral zones on the border between white and black, which were supposed to remain unpopulated by either side. But because the British came from a great mercantilist empire, they wished also to allow a measure of free exchange between the two, and instituted regular trade fairs on the white side, to which bona fide Xhosa were allowed to come, subject

27

to an authorized 'pass' – a device the British borrowed from the VOC, who had introduced it in regulating white-Khoikhoi contacts. In doing so, they breathed new life into a regulatory mechanism which has proved peculiarly persistent in South Africa and which, in modern times, has come to have an increasingly repressive and dishonourable history. In any event, these practices undercut the policy of separation and rendered it futile by allowing economic forces to perpetuate interaction.

The neutral buffer zones were not, therefore, effective, and conflict over land and stock continued alongside trade. In this conflict, the British made a pretence of being even-handed, but in reality came down repeatedly on the side of the white settlers. This was inevitable, for the growing British trade at Cape Town depended on the Dutch farmers beyond it, and their interests were bound to be put first.

So, in 1812, for instance, British troops, in trying to separate the contesting parties, drove 20,000 Xhosa eastwards across the Fish River. But they made no concerted effort to stop white settlers moving into the gap, which had the effect of moving the locus of conflict further east. When that conflict became intense again, the British once more moved the border of the Colony eastwards, thus eating further into Xhosa land – and used their troops to enforce it. This pattern was repeated constantly, with the result that the Cape Colony expanded steadily eastwards until eventually, by the end of the century, all the Xhosa area had been incorporated and the Cape border met Natal.

It is by no means clear that the white settlers would have had the power to effect this encroachment by themselves. The Xhosa, with their greater concentration than the Khoikhoi and their more robust social structures, as well as their growing acquisition of the gun and horse, were formidable opponents and certainly a match for the settlers. It was British troops who, being used to bolster white land claims, tipped the balance. The British were, therefore, not only party to the dispossession of the Xhosa – they were actually the agents of their loss. The British played this role in relation to many other black people in South Africa and therefore bear a major responsibility for their subjugation – and thus for the shaping of the modern South African conflict.

In regard to the Khoikhoi living within the defined area of the colony, it would be too much to accuse the British of being responsible for their gradually losing their land. From the moment *trekboers* settled among them in the Eastern Cape, the same fate which had befallen Khoikhoi elsewhere was probably inevitable. It should be said that even before their traditional economy had been eroded, many Khoikhoi – and indeed Xhosa – were attracted by the prospect of working in the white economy. The British, strongly believing in the value of a modern wage-earning economy, positively encouraged the Khoikhoi to take up work on white farms in the buffer zone. In doing so, however, they facilitated and accelerated the process of their becoming effectively enslaved as impotent low-wage labourers. The colonists complained bitterly to the British authorities about 'vagabonds' – their code word for the free movement of increasingly landless Khoikhoi around them. To allay this, a Proclamation was issued in 1809 by the Governor, Lord Caledon, requiring the Khoikhoi to have fixed employment, and passes when travelling – and subjecting them to arrest if they could not produce them. This inevitably put pressure on dispossessed Khoikhoi to attach themselves to white farms.

Yet, despite favouring the Dutch for their own self-interest, the British were not the same breed as these subjects. Whereas the *trekboers* were by now firmly wedded to a frontier economy, with all the inequities of status for different peoples that entailed, the British came to South Africa from a world trading empire with much more liberal ideas about the desirability of free exchange of all kinds. Such an outlook, implying a powerful attachment to the notion of a free market in labour and goods, would have a much more egalitarian thrust, and involved the belief that the economically most profitable course was to allow all peoples, irrespective of race or other social differences, to seek employment in a fair and properly regulated system. And where impediments or unscrupulous practices existed, the British believed a start should be made in removing them.

Their attitude to non-white South Africans, and the whole framework within which they viewed what was desirable in South Africa, was therefore quite different from the settlers'. It was, putting it crudely, a conflict between liberal capitalism and quasi-feudalism. This can be clearly seen in the fact that in 1808, as a result of the growing emancipation sentiment throughout the Empire, further trading in slaves was prohibited at the Cape. This not only conflicted with the settlers' deeply ingrained assumptions about how the world should be organized – it dealt a fundamental blow to their

29

economy which, even in the frontier areas, still relied to a considerable extent on slave labour. The 1809 Proclamation regulating Khoikhoi movement was seen by the British as merely introducing order into a disorderly situation, but the other side of it was a desire to see the Khoikhoi properly protected. So the decree also imposed novel obligations and restrictions on white employers, designed to ensure the better and fairer treatment of non-white employees. These impositions were regarded by the settlers as unwarranted interference, and were not at all well received. There was as yet no open breach, but two quite different economic approaches were beginning to collide.

Some indication of the growing differences concerning non-whites, and growing settler independence of mind, can be seen, however, in incidents such as the short-lived Slachters Nek Rebellion of 1815 when the farmers baulked at the British use of Khoikhoi troops to arrest a white man. Although it was smartly put down by the British and was no more than a hint of the fundamental divergence between the two European forces, it was a portent. For the clash of views was soon to play its part in precipitating one of the most convulsive events in white South African history, and would contribute, too, to a mighty conflict almost a century later.

Taking a broad view, then, the British presence not only failed to arrest the process of white conquest of the land, it actually brought it about. But the British liberal tradition would cause the introduction of hindrances to the way in which settlers might have implemented that conquest if left to themselves, and in doing so create weaknesses in their armoury. The British also brought with them, and left behind, a tradition of dissent which would withstand later onslaughts, and which would, in the end, play an important part in making available to black South Africans opportunities to end their subjugation.

That culture of dissent was given life in South Africa by a most significant event which occurred in 1820. The British soon realized that their attempts to stabilize the eastern frontier were not really succeeding. Within the very first decade of their second occupation, casting around for ways in which to make it more effective, they alighted on the perhaps not entirely surprising notion that what was needed was a substantial British presence on the frontier. Immigrants from Britain itself were encouraged to come to the Cape. Small, isolated parties began to arrive, until, in 1820, a group 4,000-

strong finally cast anchor near the modern Port Elizabeth, soon followed by 1,000 more.

Lured by free passages and the promise of free land, families from places like London, Bristol, and various parts of East Anglia found themselves in wild bush, thousands of miles on the other side of the world, surrounded by curious Dutch farmers, what they thought of as funny little Hottentots, and bellicose black warriors. No proper arrangements had been made for them. They had to borrow ox-wagons from the Dutch to get to the parcels of promised land; they had to build their own houses; and they found themselves totally cut off from all amenities. Some of them were farmers, but the savage African bush was a rather different proposition from the gentle English countryside. And many were not farmers at all: their numbers included working-class artisans, shopkeepers, and even a sprinkling of professional people. They were settled to the west of the Fish River, and it soon became clear that even the farmers were going to find it hard going. Catastrophic harvest failures, flash floods, and terrifying night-time attacks in which their houses might be burned to the ground were hazards that Colonial Office propaganda had hardly prepared them for. Without much delay, many began to drift off the land and to move to the small new settlement of Grahamstown, where, with the usual British sang-froid, they set about re-creating a little English town. There, on a frontier where such things were unheard of, they carried on much as they might have at home. Shops were set up; a little English church with a vicar and green (still extant); dressmakers, candle-makers, accountants and lawyers opened up their doors. They even set up not one newspaper, but two. The Dutch thought them most odd – and steered clear of them.

In the longer term, of course, their contribution to South Africa was great. These were to be the founding-fathers of a new English-speaking population, who today make up 40 per cent of all whites. They brought to South Africa the urban and service culture it had so far largely lacked. Most significantly of all, perhaps, they brought with them the truculent expectation of being able to speak their minds. Under men like Thomas Pringle, John Fairbairn, and Robert Godlonton, a lively, critical, and disputatious press tradition was established, which struck such deep roots in South African society that it survives even today, remaining a formidable instrument for changing political ideas in all communities.

31

The British settlers also brought with them a strong belief in representative government, a sentiment they soon began to articulate vociferously. In doing so, they ensured the gradual granting of self-rule, and added potency to the already developing hostility to central government among the Dutch, an hostility which would also shape South Africa's future.

In 1824, shortly after their arrival in the Cape, a handful of British traders also struck camp much further east on the Natal south coast, laying the foundation for the future Port Natal – Durban, as it was later to be renamed. It soon became a prosperous centre, too, and spread the British influence further across South Africa.

Whatever the future implications of British settlement, however, it did not solve the problems for which it had been conceived as a solution: the turbulence on the Cape's eastern frontier. Indeed, it added to the congestion, putting even more pressure on the land. The skirmishing continued unabated, with 12,000 Xhosa launching a major attack in 1834 across the Keiskamma River, to which the frontier had by this time been moved. There was widespread burning and destruction of white property, and the seizure of cattle. Once again, it was British troops who subdued the Xhosa, driving them back and taking 60,000 of their cattle in reprisal.

By now the settlers of Dutch origin had been living in the Cape for something approaching 200 years. They had gradually begun to lose all affinity with the Netherlands and were already thinking of themselves as a distinct people in Africa, if not of Africa – a process reinforced by the final removal of Dutch government in Cape Town. They came to be called simply 'Boers' – farmers. With their growing sense of a separate identity, they also became more rebellious against what they saw as alien authorities. Eventually they decided they had had enough.

Although the British were helping to consolidate the white hold on Xhosa land, tension and insecurity continued. The British proved reluctant to legitimize the Boers' large farm claims. They were anglicizing government and the civil service. Most important of all, they were behaving in an unsatisfactory way towards South Africa's non-white peoples. Not content with using Khoikhoi as armed troops, they had also, in 1828, established equality for them under the law, phasing out their passes (though retaining them for Xhosa), and tightening up employers' obligations, even going so far as to insist that contracts should not exceed one year in length,

32

thereby destroying the labour stability the Boers had come to expect as of right. In 1834 slaves throughout the Empire had finally been emancipated. Compensation was paid only in London, which involved hiring collecting agents who took large commissions. The emancipation affected the frontier Boers less than their co-linguists in the Western Cape, but it was taken as symptomatic of the general British attitude. In short, in the conflict between British liberal capitalism and Boer pastoralism, the British were imposing changes which were profoundly threatening to the Boers' economy. And although they enjoyed good personal relations with the English settlers, it must have suggested to them that this British dominance was beginning to take on an unpleasantly permanent character. They decided to leave.

Starting in 1835 and coming to full fruition in 1836, there was a mass, wholesale emigration by Boers into South Africa's interior. The process, which continued thereafter at a lower rate for several years, led to the exodus of 14,000 people over a decade and reduced the Dutch-descended population of the Cape by about 20 per cent. This extraordinary uprooting and movement has become known as the Great Trek, and its greatest significance lay in its achieving the penetration by Boers of the rest of South Africa and their gradual establishment there, a process that will be examined in the next chapter.

Meanwhile, on the eastern frontier which the *trekkers* were now vacating, land congestion was hardly eased. Conflict continued. Eventually the British abandoned attempts at formal segregation and starting in 1835, tried instead to pacify the area by signing treaties with Xhosa chiefs and attempting to co-opt them into policing their own people. The British did not, however, really understand the political structure of Xhosa society, in which there was little central authority and a great deal of local autonomy.

When this strategy also failed because the chiefs were unable – and also to some extent unwilling – to control the turbulence, the British decided to go further. Following another major outbreak of fighting in 1846-7, the British Governor and High Commissioner, Sir Harry Smith, formally annexed the area between the Keiskamma and Kei Rivers as a separate colony called British Kaffraria. The chiefs became salaried British agents, 'advised' by white magistrates. It stopped neither the turmoil nor the inexorable white pressure on Xhosa land.

In 1856, the Xhosa staged what was seen by whites as an act of irrational folly, but which can more properly be seen as a desperate attempt at final resistance – not unlike the the response of the *kulaks* to pressure from the Soviet authorities in post-revolutionary Russia. The Xhosa, responding to a vision by a young woman seer, Nongqause, believed themselves instructed by the spirits of their ancestors to destroy their cattle as a way of ridding themselves of the alien white invaders. In a few short months, nearly 20,000 cattle were killed, and in the ensuing catastrophic starvation, perhaps 20,000 Xhosa died. As an act of defiance, it failed. In fact, it hastened the disintegration of the traditional economy by forcing thousands – perhaps as many as 30,000 – to seek employment among whites and scattering many others into the interior to find alternative means of support.

None the less, it was not the death-knell of the pre-European Xhosa way of life. Many did survive, and cattle stocks were slowly replenished. Though greatly weakened, resistance to white encroachment continued, as did British attempts to subdue it by force. The colonial borders kept moving eastwards. In 1858 they were extended to the Mbashe River; in 1878 to the Mthatha. Finally, in 1894 the whole of Pondoland – the area between the Mthatha and the Mtamvuna – was annexed and incorporated into the Cape Colony, into which British Kaffraria had now been absorbed. The subduing of the Xhosa had finally been achieved and the process of taking control of all their territory completed.

In those areas where the hilly terrain made it unattractive for whites to settle – chiefly the area east of the Kei, known as the Transkei – the agricultural and pastoral way of life of the Xhosa survived on into the modern era, slowly being influenced and modified by the external white economy. But in the rest of the Cape Colony, the earlier Xhosa way of life disappeared under the impact of lost land and stock, a process consolidated by British guns. The Xhosa there became a class of low-wage workers on white farms, and in the now thriving towns and cities.

The Cape became prosperous. Those English-speaking settlers who remained farmers struck gold with the importation of merino sheep, and a profitable wool industry developed. Cape Town continued to burgeon as a port. More and more new towns were set up, and the Cape, though it remained a long way behind the developed world, began to take on the appearance of a modern society.

Self-government came to the Cape in 1853. In 1872 full responsible government was granted, though the British Governor remained a powerful figure. The fledgling colony had finally been pacified. In keeping with British ideas, the franchise was non-racial, but voters were required to meet a property qualification, a more acceptable way in British eyes of limiting non-white participation in government.

The British rulers and the English settlers continued to dominate Cape life into the twentieth century, though the remaining settlers of Dutch origin made their peace and carved out a prosperous niche for themselves. The remnants of the slaves and the Khoikhoi, fused into the Coloured community, enjoyed an intermediate status as skilled artisans or semi-skilled workers. The Xhosa became the lowly under-class. Apart from the eventual disappearance of British government, and a more equal relationship between the English and Dutch descendants, the structure of Cape society has not altered that much even now.

What has altered once again though, is the nature of racism. Throughout all of the nineteenth century and a good part of the twentieth, there was a more relaxed relationship between people of different races in the Cape, though it did not disguise the pattern of power and dominance. But the British influence, building on some of the cosmopolitan inheritance of the Dutch era, ensured a fluidity, and an acceptance of the possibility of an improvement of the position of non-white people.

From the very start of their occupation of the Cape, British officials treated the leaders of non-white communities with courtesy and formal respect. Inter-racial sexual liaisons and intermarriage continued to take place among a minority of people – but remained by no means uncommon. British governors supported and advanced the idea of multiracial schools and education. Mixed schools were to be found throughout the colony, and as late as 1891, a third of all white schoolchildren still attended multiracial schools. The Theological Seminary at Stellenbosch – a bastion of Dutch Calvinism – admitted non-white students, and multiracial hospitals were established, particularly in the Eastern Cape. Some black people found their way into artisan and even professional jobs. Blacks could, and did, own property. Towards the end of the century, even with a restricted franchise, between 15 and 25 per cent of the Cape electorate was black, and Coloureds formed about 30 per

35

cent of voters. They played no leading role in Parliament itself, which was dominated by the English and Dutch. But it is worth remembering that even within living memory, a different kind of South Africa still existed – with a potential quite other than the one which has been realized.

The reasons why that potential was snuffed out lay largely beyond the Cape: in the hot, dusty interior of South Africa, where some old, and some new, conflicts were being played out, in a greater blood-letting than even the Cape had seen.

4

THE STRUGGLE FOR MASTERY

As the Boers trekked away from the Cape in the late 1830s, they abandoned the only European structure of government existing at that time in Southern Africa. The hinterland beyond the Cape Colony consisted of a vast escarpment, gently running from 6,000 feet above sea level in the Southern Transvaal to the coast in a series of downward-rolling grassy plains. A long chain of mountains rising to 15,000 or 16,000 feet and running north to south through the modern Lesotho – the Drakensberg, or Dragon Mountains – divided it into two. This huge interior, extending about 1,000 miles north, was not a country as such: it was a territory in which some areas were ruled by established black chiefs and in which some were ruled by no one or were disputed by different groups. European explorers and traders had already ventured there. Some *trekboers* had already, indeed, taken their families and a small number of dependants to settle in these inland regions. But it was largely a journey into the unknown.

It is a measure of Boer discontent that they were prepared to exchange a degree of settled existence and prosperity for such uncertainty and potential danger. They moved off in long, slow parties of covered ox-wagons, taking their cattle and horses with them, their families and mainly Coloured servants hanging on from the wagons as best they could. The Bible went with them, and the odd roving *predikant*, or preacher. They took plenty of ammunition – and kept their rifles close beside them. As they built their camp-fires at night, and sang their songs, their fierce attachment to religion helped to calm their fears. But no doubt the ever-ubiquitous brandy bottle played its part too – though the history books are silent on that point. And as they lumbered away into the interior they found themselves having to cross, and re-cross, huge mountain ranges, suffer extraordinary discomfort and disease and, in due course, fight and fight again for their very survival. It did nothing, of course, to soften or refine an already highly insular, conservative frontier culture: it simply made rough and ready folk even tougher.

Afrikaner mythology has elevated the Great Trek into the central miracle of their existence as a people. It was not, in truth, a unique or unparalleled movement. But none the less it did require an exceptional sense of purpose, determination, and courage – and it was an epic in many ways heroic. It is even more extraordinary when one considers that it was this small band of wandering displaced Dutch people who, as everyone now knows, were ultimately to emerge the victors in a vicious and absolutely fundamental battle which was just then beginning to take shape. In that battle they would have to fight not only the other peoples of South Africa, but the greatest empire in the world, too. It was the struggle for mastery over all of South Africa that was beginning, and it is in this chapter that we shall be discovering how they achieved it.

A considerable part of the difficulties they met arose from the fact that the established pattern of black settlement in the interior had recently been shattered by a tumultuous upheaval known as the *Difaqane*, a word meaning 'forced migration'.

The *Difaqane* had had its origin in Natal. There, at the start of the nineteenth century, profound changes had taken place, changes whose causes remain obscure even today. They began in the area between the Pongola and Tugela Rivers, an area which had been slowly becoming more and more congested, and in which there came to be an increasing shortage of sweetgrass for cattle-grazing. This may have been a major factor in the transformation which now occurred. Ivory hunting and trading may also have been a factor, for as it became ever more lucrative, control of elephant herds and the securing of free passage through this congested region to the major export centre at Delagoa Bay became vital.

Whatever the precise reasons, the fact is that at the start of the nineteenth century the delicate equilibrium between relatively small, autonomous black kingdoms or chieftaincies in the area had been violently disturbed, and the people had become slowly welded into much larger political units with new paramount overlords. Dingiswayo of the Mthethwa had begun the process. He had reorganized the military basis of his chiefdom, doing away with the *ad hoc* conscription of his men into local units in times of trouble and substitut-

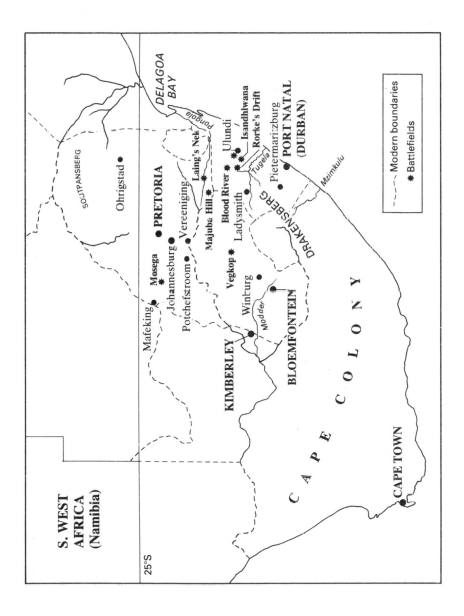

S. WEST AFRICA (Namibia)

25°S

SOUTPANSBERG

Ohrigstad

DELAGOA BAY

Pongola

Mosega

PRETORIA

Johannesburg

Potchefstroom

Vereeniging

Laing's Nek

Majuba Hill

Blood River

Ulundi

Isandhlwana

Rorke's Drift

Tugela

Pietermaritzburg

PORT NATAL (DURBAN)

Mzimkulu

DRAKENSBERG

Vegkop

Ladysmith

Winburg

Modder

BLOEMFONTEIN

KIMBERLEY

Mafeking

C A P E   C O L O N Y

CAPE TOWN

- - - - Modern boundaries
✳ Battlefields

ing a system of a permanent standing army, with regiments – or *impis* – organized by age rather than kinship. This was a unique institution in a society which had never had standing armies, and it had had the effect of breaking down local attachments and making the men much more loyal to Dingiswayo personally. With this strengthened military force, he had begun conquering other chiefdoms and to absorb them under his banner.

When he died in about 1818, Shaka, of the Zulu, one of the smaller kingdoms Dingiswayo had subsumed, had stepped into the power vacuum, and greatly expanded the process of conquest and absorption. He was, indeed, one of the great figures of South African history, and a military genius. He did away with sandals for the warriors, forcing them to fight barefoot, which gave them greater speed and mobility. He replaced the inefficient system of throwing spears over the enemy's shields with the famous short, stabbing *assegai*, which forced contending armies into closer hand-to-hand combat and gave his men a novel technological advantage. He forbade the warriors to marry, cementing their allegiance to him, and imposed an iron discipline on them. He also developed a new strategy of warfare, in which the regiments attacked in two 'horns' on the enemy's flanks – a pincer movement – and wrapped them up from the sides and rear. As a result of his pioneering militarism, the *impis* had been turned into a ferocious fighting-machine, the like of which had never been seen, and who were feared and dreaded wherever the pounding thud of their massed battalions had shaken the ground. It also meant the Zulu kingdom had now become paramount in Natal, welding previous separate kingdoms into one great new nation under his authority.

But in this process of military conquest, great turbulence had ensued. Refugees began streaming out of Natal into the rest of South Africa, where they came into conflict with other settled peoples. A vast knock-on effect was set in motion. Sometimes the newcomers tried to conquer the people they came into contact with; sometimes they were absorbed; sometimes they had to keep moving, and the wave of collision and instability moved on further. It was this extraordinary tide of change which had put so much pressure on the Cape Xhosa from their eastern and northern borders. It was this tide that the Boer trekkers were now to run into.

The first *Voortrekkers*, or frontier pioneers, came to settle in the northern section of the area that was later called the Orange Free

State. Across the Vaal River was Mzilikazi of the Ndebele, a power-ful military figure whose people had previously lived in Natal. Mzilikazi had been an important lieutenant of Shaka's, but had des-erted, leading his people through to the Transvaal. Deeply fearful of Shaka's wrath, he was very suspicious of these new arrivals, who seemed to threaten him from his vulnerable southern flank. A series of engagements inevitably followed.

At Vegkop, in the modern Orange Free State, in October 1836, the *Voortrekkers*, under their leader Andries Hendrik Potgieter, were able to beat off an attack by Mzilikazi by forming the *laager* which was to become such an important part of Afrikaner mythology and which has come to be almost a symbol of the Afrikaners' attitude towards the world around them – the defensive drawing together of ox-wagons into a circle and using them as a barricade from within which to fight off attackers. They could not stop Mzilikazi, however, from driving off nearly all their cattle and sheep. For a few months it was touch and go, but eventually the *Voortrekkers* felt strong enough to take him on directly. They attacked him at Mosega in the Trans-vaal, and then, several months later – in a series of engagements in the Northern Transvaal – drove him out of the Transvaal altoge-ther, across the Limpopo. There, beyond latter-day South Africa, Mzilikazi's Ndebele people – close relations of the Natal Zulus – fin-ally established themselves and have come to be a major and signifi-cant section of the modern state of Zimbabwe. By this action the way was cleared, to some extent at least, for *Voortrekker* penetration into the Transvaal.

By now, however, more *trekker* parties had arrived in the Orange Free State and Potgieter's dominance was challenged by the arrival of senior Dutch figures like Gert Maritz and Piet Retief. Amidst con-siderable acrimony, Maritz and Retief prevailed on the *trekkers* to move south-east into Natal rather than north into the Transvaal as Potgieter wanted. Across the huge Drakensberg mountain range the *trekkers* dragged their wagons – a journey of extraordinary hardship and peril – and then on down into Natal.

Retief recognized that if the *Voortrekkers* were to have any security in Natal they would have to come to terms with Dingane, Shaka's half-brother who had assassinated him in 1828 and taken the Zulu kingship for himself. Retief went on ahead to negotiate the conces-sion of a tract of Zulu land from Dingane, and appeared to be suc-ceeding. Dingane himself was in a very difficult position. He respec-

41

ted white people but was understandably fearful of the power their guns gave them. While the white presence in his territory had been confined to isolated groups, he had treated them generously. But the arrival of such a large contingent, apparently determined to settle permanently in the Zulu kingdom, represented a grave threat to the integrity of his domain.

On the morning of 6 February 1838, during a final ceremony to mark the hand-over of land to the *Voortrekkers*, Retief, his seventy-one companions, and their thirty Coloured servants were brought to watch a ceremonial dance at Mgungundhlovu, Dingane's capital. As they were watching the colourful ritual, Dingane suddenly raised his hand and gave a signal to his warriors. The entire *trekker* party found itself surrounded and overpowered. They were dragged away to the execution hill outside the town, and there they were bludgeoned or impaled and left to die.

A great torrent of blood-letting now ensued. Ten days later, Zulu *impis* fell upon the most easterly of the *Voortrekker* camps and virtually annihilated everyone. Two months later, they descended on the British encampment at Port Natal, with whom, until now, Dingane had had good relations, and razed it to the ground.

The remaining *Voortrekkers* were in a dire predicament. Potgieter, who had been slighted when his advice on the direction of migration had been rejected, upped and took his party to the Transvaal, amidst bitter allegations of cowardice. Maritz died. The *Voortrekkers* were alone in a hostile, alien wilderness, leaderless – and awaiting a final onslaught.

The situation was saved by the arrival from the Cape of a new trekker leader, Andries Pretorius. On 16 December, having only just arrived and receiving news of an impending Zulu attack on the remaining *Voortrekkers*, Pretorius *laager*ed the wagons on the banks of the Ncome River. There, in a battle of unparalleled ferocity and intensity, the *trekkers* not only beat off a huge Zulu onslaught, but inflicted 3,000 casualties on them. The Ncome literally ran red with blood – and the victors re-christened it Blood River, a name which still appears defiantly on South African maps today. *Trekker* forces then sacked Mgungundlovu, forcing Dingane to flee. They lent their assistance to Mpande, one of his and Shaka's half-brothers, who was eager to seize power himself. Together they broke Dingane's forces within a month. With Mpande now installed as the Zulu king with their support, the *trekkers* were able to settle between the

Mzimkhulu and Tugela Rivers, leaving the area north of that to Mpande. The *trekkers* had not broken the power of the Zulu, but they had made the king their vassal and had forced acceptance of their presence.

In their new lands, they settled down to the quieter life of pastoral farming which they had left behind in the Cape, and decided to set up an independent Boer republic – the first of any significance. They called it the Republic of Natalia, with a *Volksraad* – or People's Council – elected only by white people, and with Pretorius as military Commandant-General. Its capital was founded at Pietermaritzburg, a name commemorating Retief and Maritz, and it remains to this day the capital of Natal.

The murder of Retief and the victory at Blood River has come to be celebrated by modern Afrikaners as the central event in their history. It occupies pride of place in the Voortrekker Monument on a hill overlooking the modern capital of Afrikanerdom, Pretoria – named after Andries Pretorius. A hole in the roof is specially constructed so that on 16 December precisely the sun falls directly on a memorial to those early *trekkers*. The night before the battle, the Boers had vowed that, if delivered, they would build a church on the site to the glory of God, and would keep the anniversary forever as a holy day. The church they built to honour that vow still stands. Every year the memory of Blood River is rekindled by a public holiday which was once known as Dingaan's Day, but is now renamed the Day of the Vow. The central place of Blood River in modern Afrikaner mythology is simple to understand. Its potency lies in its unmistakable symbolism: that blacks cannot be trusted; that they are out to kill every white person they can lay their hands on; but that *Voortrekker* courage, skill, and weaponry is the sure guarantee of survival and victory. It speaks nothing, of course, about Zulu fear and the struggle to maintain *their* identity.

The fledgling republic was, however, a fragile creation. Pretorius re-established relations with Potgieter, and Potchefstroom, around which his Transvaal *trekkers* were now settled, was loosely incorporated into Natalia, together with Winburg in the Orange Free State, where another section of *trekkers* still remained. But considering the difficulty of travel and the unforgotten animosities, links were tenuous, and unity existed only in name. Natalia was also chronically under-financed. Moreover, the Boers' newfound security quickly evaporated when large numbers of black refugees from

43

Shaka's era began flocking back in the comparative peace of Mpande's reign.

The Boer Republic, trying to control the influx, planned to drive some black communities south towards the Cape's eastern border – at a time when the Cape British were still trying to pacify the Xhosa. The British decided to send a military contingent to Port Natal to prevent the Boer Republic adding to their problems. The port itself (subsequently known as Durban) was also becoming a significant commercial centre, as more and more British traders established themselves there. After a year or so of uneasy relations between British troops and the Boer Republic, the British, in 1843, decided to annex the whole of Natal to bring the unruly Boers back under their control. The Boer Republic had lasted barely four years.

It was a bitter blow for the *trekkers*. They could hardly believe their bad luck. They had, after all, left the Cape precisely to escape the British. Now, after everything they had been through, they were to become British subjects again. They despaired. The small Republic could not fight off the British presence in Natal. What were they to do? It says much about the vehemence of their anti-Britishness, and their determination, that rather than submit, the majority of them wearily got their ox-wagons out again, and started the long trek all the way back over the Drakensberg. Their first foray into self-government had ended in collapse.

As a result Natal became the most purely English part of South Africa. More British traders arrived. Later in the century English settlers followed. In the lush, fecund, sub-tropial climate, a rich living was to be had. Sugar plantations started up. Durban began to rival Cape Town. The English brought cricket and drama societies and roses and other such trappings of their native culture. Towns arose with names like Glencoe and Colenso and Ladysmith. Pietermaritzburg, the Boer capital, began to sport Anglican churches and garden parties. Even today, it maintains its quiet air of self-confident English provincialism. Apart from the bougainvillaeas and the poinsettias, one might almost be in Dorset.

For the *trekkers*, however, there was to be no such easy tranquility. There now followed a period of continual movement and wandering, of argument, personal rivalry, and disunity. Some went to the Free State; most to the Transvaal. Potgieter, at Potchefstroom, pointed out in relation to the Natal adventure that he had told them so. This irritated them. They bickered and quarrelled. Never at ease

with others, Potgieter wandered his lonely way round the Transvaal, establishing a new settlement at Ohrigstad in the Eastern
Transvaal, where more Natal refugees then set up home. After another quarrel, Potgieter went off and founded yet another settlement, at Soutpansberg in the far north, in whose remoteness he
seemed a little happier. The various Boer settlements each declared
themselves a republic, but none had real authority, and attempts at
unifying them never really succeeded.

Then the dreaded enemy struck again. The British, in fact, had
never accepted the possibility of Boer independence, for under the
Cape Punishment Act of 1836 – passed as the Great Trek was getting under way – the British had decreed that the *trekkers* were still to
be subject to British law as far north as 25 degrees S. In 1848 the new
British Governor and High Commissioner, Sir Harry Smith, annexed the area between the Vaal and Orange Rivers as the Orange
River Sovereignty. Some Boers accepted this, but those at Winburg,
led by Pretorius who had joined them from Natal, tried unsuccessfully to resist. Once failure was apparent, Pretorius quit, and went
to Potchefstroom.

Pretorius realized the only way of keeping the British at bay was
to do business with them. The other Boers would not support him,
so he went off independently and persuaded the British to leave the
Transvaal *trekkers* alone. By the Sand River Convention of 1852,
Britain agreed that they should have self-government.

Armed with this achievement, he went back to Potchefstroom and
declared the Transvaal a new South African Republic, with himself
as President and an all-white *Volksraad*. Among those who assisted
in drafting the Constitution was a young Boer commando who was
to play a fateful role in the republic's future, one Paul Kruger. The
various outlying Boer settlements resisted the authority of the republic for some years, but finally, by 1860, they had all accepted it.
Boer sovereignty over the Transvaal was finally established.

Meanwhile the British, in keeping with their decision to allow the
Transvaal Boers their independence, decided to end the annexation
of the Orange River Sovereignty. Their initial desire to exert authority over the *trekkers* had largely been an attempt to reduce interior
instability which periodically created knock-on effects on the Cape.
Their real interest, in other words, was the protection of that most
important colony. The fractiousness and rebelliousness of the Boers
made it difficult to control them. The British judged it was probably

45

best to leave them to themselves. So by the Bloemfontein Convention of 1854 they ceded the area between the Orange and Vaal Rivers to the Boers living there, and it was at this time that it was formally named the Boer republic of the Orange Free State – the name the region retains to this day. Josias Hoffman became its first President. The *trekkers* had finally succeeded in establishing two independent republics for themselves beyond the sovereignty of the British.

We should remember, however, that these interior states bore little resemblance to modern countries. Their white populations were tiny: in the mid-1860s the Free Staters totalled no more than 35,000: the Transvaalers 30,000. The republican Boers lived in small, scattered communities. They continued to practise pastoral farming and compared with the Cape, which by now had a modern trading economy with large urban centres and distinct classes of professional and business people, artisans, and skilled labourers, they were still rudimentary, stagnant, and relatively poor economies. Their distance and isolation made their people inward-looking, constantly bickering among themselves and unwilling to yield even to their own political institutions, which were consequently weak. Divided and disunited, surrounded still by a much larger number of black people, they were able to defend themselves against them when the need arose, but they had never really been strong enough decisively to crush black power in Southern Africa. So, for most of the time it was live and let live, with large numbers of black people maintaining their autonomy and well able to resist settler encroachment.

To the north of Natal, which became a British Crown Colony in 1856, for instance, the Zulu kingdom remained a formidable political and military authority. To the east of the Free State, the outstanding Sotho statesman Moshweshwe, had welded together his own Sotho people and remnants of the *Difaqane* into a powerful and cohesive group, who had proved able to withstand assaults not only from other black groups but from Boer and British alike. With great diplomatic skill, he was later able to win British protection and lay the basis for the modern independent country of Lesotho. Surrounded and completely land-locked by South Africa, it remains an enduring testament of how he preserved his people's freedom in the face of the white onslaught. To the south-west of the Free State, along the Orange River region, the Griquas also maintained their independence. They were people of mixed race, incorporating what remained of the Northern Cape Khoisan, interbred with earlier white *trekboers* and some Bantu groups. They spoke Dutch and kept their independence, both by their horsemanship and their successful acquisition of guns. To the west of the Free State and the Transvaal, a number of Tswana chieftaincies were well entrenched, having fought repeatedly during the *Difaqane* and the Boer arrival to maintain an independent foothold for the future. In the Northern Transvaal the Venda people remained strong, and in the east the Pedi were a powerful force from whom the *trekkers* were obliged to keep their distance. In the south-east of the Transvaal, the Nkosi and Dlamini clans were fusing with Natal refugees to create the Swazi nation, which despite future vicissitudes was also able to maintain its independence right into the modern era.

A rough balance, therefore, existed in the interior of South Africa in the mid-nineteenth century between Boer and black. The Boers had carved out a niche for themselves, but it was precariously based. They had scored victories over some black people – but they were not strong enough to defeat and subjugate them all.

What the future might have brought is now academic, for the course of South African history was suddenly wrenched off its pivot by one of those extraordinary, unforeseeable developments which frequently intervene without warning in human affairs. This remarkable occurrence fundamentally altered, and decisively settled, the future of the entire territory we now know as South Africa, and, just like the arrival of white men, it came in an astonishingly innocent guise.

It was children at play in one of the most backward, God-forsaken corners of the land who were the agents of this amazing intervention. For as they played in the desert sands just south of the Orange River in 1867, they found a 'marble' to use in their games. It turned out to be nothing less than a diamond – and a diamond of extraordinary size and purity.

When the British Colonial Secretary laid one of the early finds on the table of the Cape Parliament a few months later and said: 'Gentlemen, this is the rock on which the future success of South Africa will be built', he was stating nothing less than the truth – for the country would never be the same again.

The discovery of diamonds breathed life into the tiny, arid settlement of Kimberley, for when it became clear that the deposits in the

47

surrounding area were on a scale virtually unprecedented in the world, it became the focal point of intense activity. This sleepy and benighted corner of South Africa was transformed. Diggers poured in from every corner of the globe. Within a few years, 45,000 people were engaged in excavation – considerably more than the entire white population of the Orange Free State – and Kimberley became the second largest concentration of people in the country virtually overnight. The 'Big Hole' – quite literally an enormous excavation dug by prospectors in the centre of the city and the largest man-made hole in the world, still gapes in the midst of modern shopping centres as an enduring reminder of this extraordinary development in South Africa's history.

In political terms, the significance of the discovery was to bring Britain back into the equation, and further to poison an atmosphere already rancorous. The diamond area lay between a number of rival authorities whose precise boundaries had never been clearly delimited. Sovereignty over the region now became of critical importance. Five separate groups leapt to claim it: the Tswana chiefdoms of the Tlapin and the Rolong, the Griquas under Nicholas Waterboer, and the Free State and Transvaal republics. Under the Keate Arbitration of 1871, it was awarded to Waterboer. Waterboer, aware perhaps that this inheritance, with greedy eyes being cast on it from all directions, was bigger than he could manage, asked for British protection. In 1871 Britain annexed the area, known as Griqualand West. In 1873 it became a Crown Colony, and in 1880 it was incorporated into the Cape. The Free State, which had a strong legitimate claim to the diamond area, was furious, and the payment of £90,000 compensation by Britain, only intensified their feeling that they had been cheated.

The discovery of diamonds had profound economic significance as well, and quite transformed South Africa's material future. It soon became clear that the largest deposits required deep-shaft mining, and the basis was therefore created for major industrialization in a country which had so far been very little developed. It was probably inevitable that the Cape would dominate in this process, being the only region with the capital and business base fully to exploit the new resource. Between 1876 and 1881, a new financial star came to prominence – Cecil Rhodes, a Briton who had settled in South Africa at the age of seventeen. Under his wheeler-dealering the thousands of individual diamond claims were subsumed into a huge

(1) Jan van Riebeeck, leader of the first
Dutch settlers, 1652

(2) Andries Pretorius, *Voortrekker* leader

(3) Dutch ships at the Cape, Table Mountain in the background

(4) San (bushman) rock painting, showing cattle

(5) Zulu men, late nineteenth century

(6) British coverage of the Zulu War, 1879

(7) Cecil Rhodes

(0) President and Mrs Kruger on the
verandah of their Pretoria home

(9) The British inheritance. The South African Parliament, opened 1885.
Queen Victoria still stands guard. To the right is the site of the original
Dutch gardens

(10) Gold mining, 1888

(11) Early Johannesburg

mega-corporation: De Beers Consolidated Mines, and after a protracted, blood-thirsty battle, he wrested sole control of it from
another famous financier, Barney Barnato. De Beers quickly established a monopoly of the world diamond market – a position it
retains today, more than a century later – and it made Rhodes a
fabulously rich man. The extraordinary economic metamorphosis
brought not only industrialization, but an unprecedented European
migration, the arrival of thousands of black workers from all over
the country, a vast inflation of land prices in the area, and a booming
market for food and consumer goods. It precipitated great infrastructural development, too, particularly the construction of railways.

Britain's interest in the interior of South Africa, apparently given
up when they had agreed to the independence of the Boer republics
in the early 1850s, now resurfaced with a vengeance. Their earlier
reasoning came to the fore again: South Africa was a crucial strategic staging-post on the route to India. It was vital to secure this
stepping-stone, and to make sure it did not fall into the hands of
colonizing rivals. The stability and prosperity of the Cape hinged on
developments in the interior. Hegemony over the whole region was,
therefore, vital. But, of course, it was really the desire to keep the
diamond fields in British hands – and the Boers at bay – that rekindled their enthusiasm. The British Colonial Secretary, Lord
Carnarvon, resuscitated earlier ideas of federating the country, and
tried to persuade the various white-dominated regions of its advantages. It foundered on local antagonisms. The Cape was jealous of
its wealth; the Boer republics deeply hostile to the British presence
with its concomitant economic power and more liberal race policies.
Carnarvon failed.

Whipped up into a paroxysm of imperialist fervour, he decided
that what he could not achieve by persuasion, he would have to
achieve by force. Carnarvon did not yet know it, but what he
thought would be a simple affair, was to turn, in fact, into a protracted, costly, and bloody business.

The first stage in the British campaign to federate the country by
force was to incorporate the Transvaal. British troops simply marched into Pretoria in 1877, and annexed the South African Republic.
Carnarvon chose a moment when the Boers were weak and exhausted after a campaign against the Pedi in the Eastern Transvaal, a
campaign in which, much to their surprise, they had been driven

49

into retreat by the Pedi. Consequently, they were unable to put up much resistance.

The next step was to subdue the Zulu kingdom, north of Natal, which, under Mpande's successor Cetshwayo, remained far and away the most powerful military force in the region. Cetshwayo had rebuilt the Zulu military machine and re-formed the *impis*. He had pursued a policy of peaceful pragmatism towards the British in Natal, enjoying a harmonious relationship with the Secretary of Native Affairs, Sir Theophilus Shepstone, but remained a potentially formidable threat.

Moreover, the British, in all their dealings in South Africa, saw the Boers as the alternative local power with whom they had the greatest common economic interest, and who had, potentially at least, the greatest capacity to destabilize the British presence. They therefore wanted not only to subjugate the Boers, but to keep them on the British side as well. They felt they needed their co-operation and goodwill. Now, in the area around Blood River, the Transvaal Boers had been making encroachments, claiming the land as theirs. Shepstone, the man in charge of the Transvaal annexation – and in a complete reversal of his previous policy – decided that by conquering the Zulu, not only would they demolish a potent threat, but they could win the Boers over by settling their land-claims, and by laying to rest their suspicion that the British were soft on the blacks. He persuaded the new High Commissioner for South Africa, Sir Bartle Frere, that Britain should act against the Zulu. When Cetshwayo refused to agree to an ultimatum demanding that he disband his army within thirty days, 13,000 British troops commanded by Lord Chelmsford invaded Zululand in January 1879.

Things did not go quite as the British had expected. On 22 January, the Zulu *impis* struck the central column of the British expedition at a site called Isandhlwana, and wiped out 1,600 men, with only 55 British troops in the column surviving. Later 4,000 Zulu who had taken part in Isandhlwana went on to attack a British supply base at Rorke's Drift. After ten hours of hand-to-hand fighting, the 150 British troops, *laager*ed in the base hospital, beat off the attack by the exhausted *impis*, who had been on the move for six days, had not eaten for four, and had fought two battles within a day.

The shock to British morale at the devastating blow inflicted on them by men with spears at Isandhlwana was enormous. To compensate they elevated the defence of Rorke's Drift into one of the great legends of British military history. Eleven Victoria Crosses were awarded to men who had taken part – far and away the highest total for a single military action. Even today the gruesome romance of this campaign lives on – with films like *Zulu* and *Zulu Dawn* raking in a small fortune at British box offices.

Despite their extraordinary achievement in inflicting such ferocious damage on a technologically superior force – testimony to the courage and strength of the Zulu fighting machine – Cetshwayo's *impis* could not not stave off the day of reckoning. Over the next few months the British were reinforced and the inexorable power of their guns ensured their penetration through the picturesque but alien Valley of a Thousand Hills, through mile after mile of inhospitable grass-covered uplands, into the very heart of Zululand. On 4 July they finally broke the Zulu army in a battle at Ulundi, Cetshwayo's capital. Today, more than 100 years later, it has been restored as the Zulu capital, but it remains a remote, benighted place. A few hundred yards from a building which sports itself as the world's smallest Holiday Inn, a handful of graves surrounded by thorn-bushes contain the remains of the British who died, and nearby a single plaque speaks eloquently of the destruction they wrought on one of the greatest military powers in African history:

IN MEMORY OF THE BRAVE WARRIORS WHO FELL
HERE IN 1879 IN DEFENCE OF THE OLD ZULU
ORDER

The British, now in control of the Transvaal and having broken the power of the Zulu, turned their attention next to the Pedi under Sekhukhune, in the Eastern Transvaal, whom the Boers had failed to subdue. This was a further step in breaking remaining power-blocs which had the potential to threaten the British hold over South Africa, and a further attempt, too, to win over the Boers by flattening their enemies and showing Britain's toughness with blacks. A massive assault was launched on the Pedi in November 1879 – and brought to a successful conclusion.

In these actions, the British, for their own imperialist reasons, had done the Boers' work for them. By the start of 1880 the delicate balance of power between Boer and black had been decisively changed by the British intervention. The Zulu and Pedi had represented

51

two of the most important remaining bastions of black strength, and in shattering their military capacity, Britain was denying black South Africa the ability to resist future attack by the Boers. In perpetrating this, then, Britain became responsible for much later unhappiness in South Africa and played a central role in shaping the violent years to come.

Nor did it avail them. The Boers, far from being won over to the idea of a British-dominated South African federation, took fright at this dramatic escalation of British aggression. Heartened by the valiant resistance of the Zulu, they decided they were not going to submit. On 8 December 1880 they unilaterally declared the South African Republic in the Transvaal restored, with Paul Kruger as President. It marked the start of the first Anglo-Boer War.

Under General Sir George Colley, the British were provided with new evidence that subjugating South Africa was a costly and traumatic business. Colley tried to storm Boer encampments at Laing's Nek, guarding the route to Natal from which British reinforcements might come – and was sharply repulsed. He then occupied nearby Majuba Hill, and was ignominiously humiliated when the Boers stormed and captured his position in broad daylight, virtually annihilating the entire British force.

Gladstone decided enough was enough. The Pretoria Convention of 1881 signalled a British defeat. The Transvaal's self-government was restored. It turned out, however, to be no more than a breathing space in the protracted see-saw of relations between the two white powers.

British imperial ambitions in South Africa hardly had time to fade before they were greatly intensified, despite all the setbacks, by yet another unforeseen development, this time of a magnitude besides which even the discovery of diamonds paled into insignificance. In 1885 gold was discovered on the Witwatersrand, a huge reef running about eighty miles west to east about forty miles north of the Vaal River, with modern Johannesburg at its centre. As exploration got under way it became clear that the deposits were of an unimagined volume, and that a literally inestimable fortune lay beneath the Southern Transvaal veld. The precise scale of the discovery can be gauged from the fact that a century later the Rand gold-mines still provide a significant part of South Africa's gold exports which themselves constitute about two-thirds of the Western world's total gold supply, and that by the mid-1960s the revenue yield from the Rand mines had already exceeded £6,000 million.

The discovery of diamonds turned out to have been a mere dress rehearsal for a much more lavish production. A similar pattern of development followed with breath-taking speed, only on a considerably larger scale. The Southern Transvaal saw a phenomenal industrial expansion; cities grew up over night; commerce and markets mushroomed where nothing had existed before. Roads, railways, the telegraph and telephones – modernity had suddenly arrived.

Foreign immigrants poured in. No proper census was taken of the *uitlander* (foreigner) population, but within four years the gold-mines were employing 100,000 people. The population of Johannesburg, which had been a farm before 1886, reached 166,000 by the turn of the century, and it seems probable that the *uitlanders* were by then outnumbering the total male Boer population in the South African Republic.

It is difficult to underestimate the contrast between this dynamic new industry and the sleepy, sparsely populated Boer settlements flung out hundreds of miles all around it. The Boer capital, Pretoria, barely thirty miles away, could have been on another continent. It represented the largest concentration of Boer people, yet it was a hick village by comparison. Paul Kruger's one-storied bungalow ran alongside the main road surrounded by trees, and there of an evening the State President was to be seen sitting in his top hat on the *stoep*, or wooden verandah, chatting to any passing Boer who had a complaint or an opinion to voice, while Mrs Kruger, in her full-length black skirt, waited in attendance on them, serving coffee from the can by candlelight. Today a national museum, Kruger's house sits incongruously dwarfed by huge glass-and-cement skyscrapers, but the juxtaposition gives a clear symbolic impression of the position he and his Boers must have found themselves in. For even as the ox-wagons were creaking into the open plot of ground which passed for Pretoria's main square so that the Boers could attend communion at the Dutch Reformed Church, the ragbag collection of Johannesburg shysters, hucksters, prospectors, adventurers, and sharp-eyed English businessmen – gold-diggers, in short – were flinging up mining industries, modern office buildings, electricity poles, railway stations, hotels, taverns, and even brothels complete with imported French dancing girls. One can just imagine what Paul Kruger – who refused to believe the earth was round – made of it all. Even today Pretoria, despite inevitable modernization, retains its quiet, tree-lined provincialism as though it cannot quite bring itself to slough off that final hint of manure in the air, and as an almost conscious reproof to its fast, flashy, hard-nosed neighbour half an hour's drive down the motorway.

President Kruger and his people did not like it a bit. The goldmines brought revenue and government patronage over lucrative contracts and concessions. But the process of industrialization was out of their hands. They did not have the know-how or the personnel to carry though this expansion. Suddenly, in their midst, were all these foreigners; suddenly Johannesburg, a town full of immigrants and dominated by English capital, was overwhelming their state. With their inefficient pastoral farming, the Boers could not meet the profitable, but insatiable, demand for agricultural produce and goods. New immigrants, and those speaking English, benefitted most.

Kruger's attitude to the *uitlanders* was therefore one of guarded hostility. He did his utmost to limit their power. He decreed that they could only become citizens of the Republic if they had lived there for ten years, and meanwhile denied them the most basic civil rights. Dissatisfaction grew.

Meanwhile, Britain and English South Africans, seeing the earth opening up before their very eyes and disgorging truly fabulous riches, became obsessed with the desire to bring this treasure trove under their own control. Rhodes, barely able to contain himself, quickly added the giant of the Rand gold corporations, the Goldfields Company, to his already impressive collection of money-spinners built around De Beers, thereby becoming a man of quite exceptional wealth and power. Being nobody's fool, he saw that the path to even greater economic success lay through politics. In 1890 he became the Prime Minister of the Cape. Casting his eyes further afield to north of the Limpopo, he persuaded the British to put Bechuanaland, the modern Botswana, under a protectorate, both in order to secure an access route to it from the Cape, avoiding the Transvaal, and to stop any further advance by the Germans who had recently colonized South-West Africa (the modern Namibia). Then, armed with a Royal Charter for his South Africa Company, he took it upon himself personally to organize the subduing of the Ndebele and Shona peoples who lived beyond South Africa, thereby giving himself further mineral riches and Her Majesty a new colony bearing his name.* He then installed his confidant, Dr Jameson, at Harare (later Salisbury) to protect his interests.

Rhodes was a man with a vision. He dreamed of a British empire which would extend from the Cape to Cairo. It would be for the greater glory of Queen, country, and British civilization – but it would also have the incidental advantage of allowing the exploitation of who knew what other wonderful secrets Africa might be harbouring in her soil.

But first, a little local difficulty had to be sorted out. The foundation of this great empire – South Africa – had to be consolidated. As long as the Boers remained in charge of large sections of it, there would be a mismatch between their interests and his. Rhodes recognized that the Boers were implacably hostile to any British presence, so he conceived the idea that South Africa should become a self-governing federation, with Britain remaining in the background as a remote, but ultimate, guarantor of the country's defence.

So he tried to persuade the Transvaal of the desirability of economic federation with the Cape. Kruger was having none of it, for he had little difficulty in spotting what Rhodes hoped to keep hidden from him: that in this self-governing federation, English South Africans would contrive to make sure that it was they who really ran the show.

Like Carnarvon, twenty years before, Rhodes reached the inevitable conclusion: if the Boers were too pig-headed to see sense, they would have to be forced to do so. In 1895 he decided to topple the Transvaal government. On the pretext of defending the *uitlanders* in their struggle to achieve political and civil rights in the Transvaal, his colleague Dr Jameson launched an armed raid on the Transvaal from Bechuanaland, which was to signal the start of an uprising by the Johannesburg *uitlanders*. The Boers caught wind of this plan, and surrounded and captured Jameson on the first morning of the military expedition.

Britain stepped in. The British High Commissioner at the Cape, Sir Alfred Milner, needing little encouragement from Rhodes, persuaded the Colonial Secretary Joseph Chamberlain that the threat

* In fact Rhodes had the rare distinction of having not one, but two countries named after him, for Northern and Southern Rhodesia became separate states.

to British subjects and interests in the Transvaal was too great to be ignored. Tough action was needed. British troops in the Cape were accordingly authorized to station themselves near the Transvaal borders. Kruger and the Transvaalers were in a dire predicament, the worst they had ever been in. In October 1899 Kruger demanded that British troops be removed. The deadline expired on the 11th, and the troops had not been withdrawn. The Orange Free State decided to support the South African Republic, and together they declared war on the British Empire.

The Second Anglo-Boer War commenced – and it was to be a very different affair from the first. The Boer War, as it was simply known, was a momentous event for both sides. For the British, who confidently expected everything to be over in a few months, it turned into a great trial of their imperial strength. As battle succeeded battle, this remote struggle on the other side of the world gripped the British public's imagination, and a war psychosis pervaded the entire nation. Defeats turned into national disasters: victories occasioned celebrations in the streets. For South Africa, it represented something greater still. The British has assisted the Boers is subduing South Africa's non-white peoples. They had tipped the balance decisively, and had been instrumental in writing black South Africa out of the country's political future, at least for the foreseeable future. Two forces now vied for control of the territory: British liberal capitalism and Boer pastoralism. The Boer War was the contest to decide which would win ultimate control. It was, therefore, fundamental to South Africa's entire future. For the British and their English-speaking supporters economic control was the prize. For the Boers, their very survival as a distinct people seemed at stake, and in the process of fighting this huge engagement, a national identity was forged where previously local attachments had been paramount and a sense of community diffuse and ill-defined.

In the early stages of the war, the Boers took the British by surprise. Without standing armies, the farmers came together on horseback, their guns, with which they had learnt to be crack shots, at the ready. A large detachment poured into Natal and besieged the main British troop concentration at Ladysmith. Another force moved towards the Cape and surrounded British forces at Kimberley and Mafeking. At the beginning of 1900, Lord Roberts arrived in South Africa to take charge, with Kitchener as his number two. British troops moved up the railway to the Modder River, and relieved

Kimberley on the way. Rhodes provided a celebratory banquet of champagne, peaches, and grapes. Around the Modder, the Boers were well dug in in trenches, and after protracted fighting, which provided the British with a useful training for the First World War, they succeeded in breaking through. The Boer General Cronje and a large commando were forced to surrender, and the British cut off the southern Orange Free State. With the Boers in Natal stranded, the British broke through another major Boer entrenchment in Northern Natal. Ladysmith was relieved and the Boers in that area mopped up. Bloemfontein, the Free State capital, fell in March 1900, and Mafeking was relieved, where Lord Baden-Powell, who was given to dressing in women's clothing in amateur theatricals, had been keeping up the morale of his troops by entertaining them, and had created the forerunner of the Boy Scouts in his Cadet Corps. By June, Pretoria was also in British hands. President Kruger, so long a doughty stalwart in defence of his people, fled to Delagoa Bay, and thence to exile in Europe. He never saw South Africa again and died, his spirit broken, in Switzerland in 1904.* By September 1900 British sovereignty had been declared over both the Orange Free State and the Transvaal. The Boers began to trickle back home. Amidst congratulations, Lord Roberts returned to Britain.

But the British had underestimated the Boers. A substantial element decided to fight on. Using Natal and the friendly support of Boers in the Cape as their base, the commandos improvised a guerrilla war. The British had taken control of the towns and cities, but unlike the conventional wars they had fought to date, this did not give them control of the country. The Boers harried them wherever they went, attacking their supply routes, disrupting their operations.

A new strategy was needed, and Lord Kitchener devised one. Boer women and children were rounded up from their farms and brought together in prison settlements, which the British called concentration camps. It was a new device in warfare, and one of which the twentieth century would see more. 26,000 of the women and children died from disease and hunger. Their abandoned farmsteads were burnt to the ground in a scorched-earth policy, and the crops destroyed so that the guerrillas would be denied supplies. Kit-

---

* Proof of his enduring legacy, however, can be seen, for example, in the naming of the South African gold coin, the Krugerrand.

chener then divided the country up into grids which were fenced off and policed at regular intervals by blockhouses, many of which still dot the South African landscape even today. The grids were systematically swept and Boer prisoners sent into exile, St Helena being turned into a major prisoner-of-war camp. Bit by bit, the policy gained ground, and the Boer strength was gradually eroded. After a number of peace feelers had been put out, the Boers finally surrendered.

On 31 May 1902, after nearly three years of war, the Peace of Vereeniging was signed. In the course of the conflict 80,000 Boers had fought, of whom 6,000 had died; 500,000 had fought on the British side, of whom 22,000 had died. Even at the close of the war, the Boers had still been able to field 21,000 *bitter-einders* – those who had fought on to the end.

Rhodes did not live quite long enough to see the surrender, but he died in the arms of a friend shortly before it, secure in the knowledge that Britain had won. Even then, though, his fertile imagination was far from satisfied. With his last breath he gasped out: 'So little done; so much to do.' He was buried at a site he himself had chosen in the Matopos Hills in Rhodesia, so that he could look out for all eternity on the empire he had fashioned.

The Peace of Vereeniging was not the closing chapter. Under the terms of the treaty, the Transvaal and Orange Free State became British colonies, but limited self-government was pledged in the near future. Generous financial assistance was promised by the British to aid rehabilitation of the war-torn societies, and in deference to their sensibilities Dutch was guaranteed as an official language alongside English.

The new closeness between the Boers which had been engendered by the war provided the basis for a sense of identity and interest which went beyond the individual colonies. The concept of South Africa as a larger spiritual home gained ground, promoted by the establishment of a customs union between the Cape, Natal, the Free State, and the Transvaal, and by the final achievement of an integrated railway system.

Following the implementation of responsible government in the two former Boer republics in 1907, a National Convention met in 1908 to lay the foundations for a new unified country. In addition to their new-found feeling of unity, the Boers realized that, within South Africa as a whole, they would constitute a majority of the white population. Suddenly the idea of integration which the British had been advancing for half a century no longer seemed so threatening.

On 31 May 1910 the Union of South Africa came into being, as a self-governing dominion within the British Empire. Its first Prime Minister was Louis Botha, who had been a distinguished Boer general in the recent war, and in his Cabinet sat Jan Smuts and Barry Hertzog, two other renowned Boer generals. Botha and Smuts, in particular, had played a skilful hand, persuading the Boers that having lost the war, they could win the peace. They had exerted themselves to establish a *modus vivendi* with the British, demonstrating by their general attitude that British economic interests, if left in Boer hands, would not be harmed. The war had shown Britain that the cost of imposing their authority on the Boers was fearsomely high. With an implied guarantee that British interests would be safe, it was hardly worth hanging on to South Africa to face Boer rebelliousness again in the future. So, in the greatest irony of all, Britain, having achieved what it had set out to do, effectively withdrew from South Africa for good.

It left behind a powerfully entrenched set of economic interests, a substantial English-speaking population of British origin, and a muted liberal tradition of dissent. More importantly, having tilted the political balance between Boer and black decisively in the Boers' favour, it left behind a government in their hands, with the fate of black South Africa dependent on it. In all the deliberations about union, South Africa's black majority had been excluded. Boers in power over a newly unified country; black South Africans crushed and completely defenceless: that was Britain's fateful legacy after a century of involvement in South Africa's affairs.

If we look back in terms of fundamental conflicts of interest, we find that Dutch and Khoikhoi had had to contest with each other for economic resources, because those economic resources were scarce. The superior technology defined the group: the Dutch had guns; the Khoikhoi did not. Because of the competition between them there was no incentive for the Dutch to admit the Khoikhoi to their group. Special attachment to the notion of African-Dutchness justified this in their minds. In the end, they won. The arrival of the British found a similar battle between Dutch and Xhosa unresolved. The British could not team up with the Dutch because their interests, although they overlapped also diverged, but it was too costly to take them on.

59

Dutch co-operation was more valuable than the Xhosa's, so they tried to buy it by fighting the Xhosa for them. The Dutch took fright because if they had been overwhelmed by the British, most of them would have lost their way of life. So they set off on their great migration. The British kept discovering economic reasons to try and win their co-operation, but the incentive for the Boers was never strong enough. In the process of trying to win them over, the British did the work of subjugating their rivals – the blacks – for them. In the end, it came to a showdown between Britain and the Boers. In all this long process British individuals justified their economic interest by attachment to 'Britishness' (like Rhodes) and the Boers justified theirs by attachment to 'Boer-ness'. In the final battle, the Boers put up a good performance and played their hand skilfully thereafter. The two powers struck a bargain. The Boers would guarantee the British a continuing share of the cake, and the British would leave them to run the show, to make of the rest what they could.

Racism was not the underlying cause of all this: economics was. But it was the cement that had kept the Boers together. If, after the Boer War, most Boers had been satisfied that their economic interests were reasonably catered for, they might have eased up on the blacks. But most felt they had not yet had their fair crack of the whip – and it was this that they would now seek.

In doing so, racism against blacks would be required to play an ever more vital role. The next decades would see that process work itself through – with fearful consequences.

5
THE TRIUMPH OF AFRIKANERDOM

When, in 1910, the separate regions of the Transvaal, the Orange Free State, Natal, and the Cape came together to constitute, for the first time in Southern African history a unified nation-state, the shape of that country, which was later to become infamous throughout the world, was already to a considerable degree formed. Nations are like people, however: their past gives them a distinctive personality, but contains the seeds of change. Whether their existing complexions are reinforced or whether that potential for change is brought to the fore depends in part on the innate balance between them, but also, in part, on the conditions they meet in the material world. As South Africa stood on the brink of nationhood, it was always likely that the attainment of white supremacy, coupled with the bitter previous relationships between Boer and black, would see the evolution of a racist and profoundly repressive political system. It was by no means, however, inevitable. It was the accident of its material circumstances that confirmed South Africa's pre-existing tendencies, and which helped to shut the door on an alternative course of development.

South Africans of all races, as they left behind membership of disparate political units, could not fail to experience the sudden thrill of nationhood, and the question of who precisely constituted that nation and what its internal character was to be, was subject to some measure of generosity, and by no means unambiguously resolved. It was reinforced by the profound economic transformation gripping the country, as it moved into an era of wide industrialization and experienced the construction of a modern economy. The shattering of earlier ways of life, the upheaval and movement of people, and the formation of new patterns of existence created turmoil, but also flexibility, contributing to the sense of a new nation being born, and allowing the possibility at least of the break-up of prior loyalties and political attachments.

The first few decades of South Africa's nationhood, then, saw a groping towards a definition of itself in which a certain fluidity of racial, class and social alliances were experimented with – a fluidity which subsequent events have buried from view, and which strikes us now as surprising. At moments in those early years, it seemed possible that working-class whites and blacks might work together or that peasant blacks, Coloureds, and Indians might join against the richer middle class of all races. These trials of association, this testing of the inner dynamics of the new state, were always tentative and short-lived. Circumstances conspired to rigidify the nascent country into racial categories, but as South Africa tries today to un-learn its past and gropes towards another new definition of itself, its people may take heart from the fact that their forefathers once knew a different kind of South Africa.

Under the constitution agreed by the all-white National Conven-tion, the former colonies were in future to be known as provinces. There would be an elected Parliament sitting in Cape Town consist-ing of two legislative chambers – a lower House called the *Volksraad* or House of Assembly, and a Senate – and a Cabinet which was drawn from them and answerable to them would govern the country. The British Governor-General was largely a figure-head, acting on the Cabinet's advice. It was, essentially, Westminster re-created on the southernmost tip of Africa. Only in the Cape Prov-ince were non-white people allowed to vote – an arrangement which reflected the historic experience of the different provinces – though even then only if they met certain property qualifications, and without themselves being eligible to sit as Members of Parliament. In Cape Province too they were allowed a qualified vote for, and the right to sit on, the Provincial Council. In many quarters it was assumed that voting rights for the rest of the non-white population would follow in due course, though not for the foreseeable future. In the meantime, the Cape non-white franchise was entrenched by re-quiring at least two-thirds of both Houses sitting together to change it – a protective device also guaranteeing the status of English and Dutch as the country's official languages.

The first Government was formed by the South African Party (the SAP), which, although it had some English support, embodied the

Boer leadership which had come to prominence during the recent war against Britain. Not only was the Boer general, Louis Botha, the first Prime Minister, but the two other famous generals, Smuts and Hertzog, were extremely prominent in the Cabinet. Their concerns as a government became apparent at once. Even before the end of the nineteenth century it had been evident that people, both black and white, were being driven off the land, that a process of urbanization was taking place, and that it was producing great hardship and difficulty. It was this problem they tackled first.

The traditional rural white economy was being destroyed by modernization. Railways, for instance, had displaced rural whites who had worked as horse- and ox-transport riders, and it was also eating into farming land. Game was being destroyed. The Boers' system of subdividing a farmer's property on his death equally between all his children led to ever smaller plots of land, growing-congestion, and increasing agricultural unviability. Many poorer Boers had been slowly driven into becoming *bywoners*, or tenant share-croppers on other white people's farms. Perhaps as much as a quarter of all rural Boers before the Boer War fell into this category. But as modern farming methods took hold, farmers increasingly rid themselves of this feudal encumbrance. The Boer War added greatly to the problem. Not only did it result in the destruction of huge swathes of Boer farm land, but it created bitter feelings between many land-owners and their *bywoners*. One of the secrets of the Boer War only recently highlighted is that after the apparent British success midway through the conflict, many of the Boers who started to trickle back from the commandos, unable to pursue their rural life during the period of the scorched-earth policy, had little alternative except to join the British – most notably through the locally recruited National Scouts. Their main work had been to mop up Boer resistance. Indeed, at the end of the war, virtually one-fifth of all Boers still fighting were actually fighting on the side of the British. In most cases, these people – contemptuously referred to by those who had fought on as *hensoppers*, 'hands-uppers' – were the poorer share-croppers and newly landless. After the war, the more independent Boers, who had tended to fight to the end, were understandably unforgiving towards them and refused to shelter them on the land as they had once done. At the same time, the development of large-scale mining and industrialization held out the promise of new opportunities and the lure of regular wages.

A flood of 'poor whites' was therefore engulfing the towns and cities. The same processes of modernization were also driving rural blacks off the land and attracting them to the towns and cities, in their case greatly aggravated by the incursion of whites into their traditional farming and grazing lands. Those who had lost their own lands but remained in the rural areas tended to live much like the white *bywoners*, becoming squatting share-croppers for white overlords, but increasingly squeezing out their white competitors by working harder, and for lower wages. Gradually, many also began to resort to the eminently practical solution to their landlessness of banding together and buying up unviable white farms, thereby engendering even worse hostility from dispossessed whites.

The intense pressure of increasing landlessness and urbanization brought black and white into direct economic competition, on the land but more especially in the towns and cities. It was inevitable that a Boer government, in trying to resolve conflicting demands, would give priority to whites. Thus was born the infamous Natives Land Act of 1913, conceived as a measure to be reviewed later, but which in fact crystallized into thoroughgoing racial segregation, giving it a foundation in theoretical territorial separation. The Land Act set aside about an eighth of South Africa's surface area as 'native reserves', making black squatting on 'white' land illegal and outlawing black purchase of land anywhere except in the reserves. It did not apply to the Cape, since this would interfere with non-white people's property rights on which their vote depended, but it had particular force in the Transvaal and the Orange Free State. It was an Act whose cruelty and brutality could not morally be defended, even on the grounds of white survival. Thousands upon thousands of black squatters were evicted. At first, not even realizing the true legal position, they went cheerfully, confident of finding other white farms to work on. Gradually, as the reality dawned on them, they were consigned to wandering the veld in increasingly desperate droves. Those who had purchased land legally were evicted without recourse. The reserves, far from being the best or most fertile land, quickly became over-farmed, over-peopled, undernourished and incapable of supporting the large majority of the population they were supposed to house. The Land Act did nothing to stop black landlessness or the flood of blacks to the towns and cities, as some of its more disingenuous supporters claimed it would; it simply added calamity to hardship. Nor, incidentally, has this ended. As the Land Act came to be the basis of all subsequent political development, the processes described still continue today.

With the stream of impoverished whites and blacks pouring in to the urban areas, there was fierce competition between them for the better-paid jobs in the still developing mines and accompanying industries. Botha's Government therefore also passed a Mine and Works Act in 1911, the effect of which was to reserve skilled and semi-skilled work for whites (in the Transvaal and Orange Free State). This approach — graced with the term associated especially with General Hertzog of a 'civilized labour policy' – now added to territorial discrimination another layer of injustice in the workplace and began the process, successively extended, of deliberately retaining the best-paid jobs for whites and forcing non-white South Africans to remain trapped at the bottom of South African society as unskilled labourers.

Despite their apparent efforts to ensure white people, and particularly impoverished Boers, a privileged place in South Africa, Botha and Smuts, though still enjoying considerable Boer support for their war-time distincton, were already under suspicion from many of their own people. Anxious to consolidate the nation's independence by not confronting Britain or English-speaking South African interests, and largely dependent on an English-speaking bureaucracy, they were at pains to conciliate and assist English-dominated big business, especially the mining houses, and to reassure Britain at every turn of their loyalty. Indeed, one of the purposes of the Land Act was to guarantee the English-owned mining companies a ready reserve of labour, for despite the influx of people to the cities, the mines had frequently found their labour-supply fluctuating. The Land Act, by putting blacks in a more dependent position, ensured a constant pool of workers, especially as the notorious Pass Laws, codified by the Urban Areas Act of 1923, prohibited the free movement of blacks, thus allowing whites to channel them for their own economic purposes.

In adopting this pro-English posture, Botha and Smuts were treading on dangerous ground. For many of the impoverished Boers came to see them as traitors to the Boer cause and as insufficiently sympathetic to their needs. Their frustration was mirrored among a small intelligentsia in the Cape, and in alienating the poorer Boers, Botha and Smuts provided a context in which these two forces could slowly come together and fuse into a new Boer nationalism – with

65

the greatest possible significance for South Africa's future.

During the nineteenth-century development of the Cape into a modern sophisticated mercantile society, a class of urbanized people descended from the Dutch who had not trekked off into the interior had come to constitute a shackled intelligentsia. Finding commerce, law, and the civil service dominated by English-speakers, they tended to become teachers, clergymen, and journalists, from which positions they found further upward mobility blocked. Their resentment against anglicization of the levers of power began to produce a new, more intellectually based, Boer nationalism. Though they came from a Dutch tradition, they began to establish a distinctive Dutch-South African identity for themselves. They called themselves 'Afrikaners', or people of Africa, and they found a potent, and safe, way to give this identity shape and character through the birth of a linguistic and cultural movement. Educated Boers had continued to speak High Dutch and had learned English. Indeed, as late as the 1930s many of the leading Boer families spoke English at home and had become more familiar with it than Dutch itself. But among poorer, less-educated Boers, English remained a remote, alien tongue and their own lingua franca had long since deviated from classical Dutch into a readily identifiable local dialect. The Cape intellectuals, from late in the nineteenth century, began to establish a new nationalist identity by seizing on the cultural weapon of this dialect, called 'Afrikaans', associating themselves with it, and seeking to establish it as a legitimate tongue in its own right. But Afrikaans was not just a white language. It was the language of the Coloureds, too, and the means of communication between Boers and their black servants. The Afrikaans language movement therefore also involved stripping it of its non-white associations and elevating its status beyond a *kombuistaal*, or kitchen-language.

As the language movement was striving in the early part of the twentieth century to give Afrikaners a distinctive 'white' culture of their own through the refinement of Afrikaans – in poetry, literature and journalism – the political leaders of the impoverished northern Boers gradually began to associate themselves with the nationalism implied in the language movement, to use the intellectual base of that movement as a method of giving poorer whites a sense of their own unique identity, and of rallying them politically. It was a process which took two or three decades to reach fruition, but it began even as the Union was being born.

Hertzog was the man within the Boer leadership who was most susceptible to this new nationalism. He was not an Afrikaner sup-remacist. He believed in a 'two-stream' policy – that Afrikaners should be equal with the English. But in articulating Afrikaner grievances and promoting Afrikaner nationalism, he became the un-witting agent of Afrikaner supremacy. From the very outset of the first Cabinet, he argued that the recognition of Dutch and English as official languages should include the right of parents to have their children educated in Dutch rather than English. He also cam-paigned vigorously against the somewhat ambiguous residual rights retained by the British crown over South African foreign policy – most notably on the question of whether South Africa was auto-matically obliged to fight a British war. His general stance led to his falling foul of Botha and Smuts, and he was ousted from the Cabinet in 1912 over anti-British remarks he had made and which his col-leagues deemed disloyal and unwise. At the beginning of 1914 he founded an alternative political organization, the National Party (NP). It was a fateful moment, for the organization was to have the most profound impact on twentieth-century South Africa.

The strength of Afrikaner anti-British feeling and republicanism, and the very real importance of the nature of the constitutional link between Britain and South Africa was soon put to the test. Later in the same year, when the First World War broke out, 10,000 Afrika-ners joined an armed rebellion which refused to support the war ef-fort. Led by famous Boer War generals like De Wet and Beyers, it provoked a national crisis, especially when the Government exec-uted one of the rebels, an army officer called Jopie Fourie, and put the rebellion down by force. The sight of an Afrikaner Government taking this kind of action against other Afrikaners for the sake of a 'foreign' power they had only recently been fighting created bitter divisions, and greatly fuelled support for the newly formed National Party. Smuts's distinguished role as a member of the British War Cabinet, still commemorated in London by his statue in Parliament Square, served only to identify him further with British interests.

At the same time as a new Afrikaner nationalism was stirring, and Botha's Government began to respond in the land and employment fields to white pressure, black South Africans began trying, to find a new way of fighting the forces which were threatening them. Armed resistance had been broken in the nineteenth century, with a short-lived Zulu revolt, the Bambata Rebellion of 1906, having been its last forlorn stand. Now, other methods had to be tried. The political leadership of black South Africa passed in the early twentieth century to the small educated black élite. They tended to be Christians, educated by missionaries, who had achieved positions for themselves by exploiting what openings there were for them in white society

In the late nineteenth century, small groups of such people had banded together in the various colonies to press unsuccessfully for greater civil rights for black people. They had come together in 1908 to try to represent black interests at the National Convention, with a similar lack of success. Now, in the newly unified country, they gave birth to a national body. In 1912 they formed the South African Native National Congress (SANNC), to be renamed in 1923 the African National Congress (ANC). Like the National Party, with whose birth it broadly coincided, it was to have a critical importance in the country's figure. This early period can therefore be seen in retrospect as the crucial moment when both parties to the current South African conflict first came into existence.

The leading members of the SANNC were Dr Pixley Seme and the Revd John Dube from Natal. Their aims were to try and unify all black people, to fight to remove racial prejudice, and to promote civil rights for all. Their approach was conciliatory towards whites, supporting petitions and deputations. They steered clear of explicit political demands, believing perhaps that they could gradually extend the qualified Cape non-white franchise, as talk at the time encouraged them to believe. At first, indeed, they were divided over whether segregation was a bad development, some believing they could use any space accorded blacks as a foundation from which to build, though within three years this debate had been resolved against segregation. Their stance was summed up in the words of the Revd Dube, their first President, who said that Africans were approaching the government 'not with *assegais* but respectfully as loyal subjects, with the intention of airing their grievances and removing the obstacles of poverty, prejudice and discriminatory legislation'. But their efforts were also to prove unavailing.

The First World War helped to broaden the South African economy by spurring the development of secondary industry, and as black and white urbanization continued relentlessly, bringing workers up against the harsh realities of industrial life, a rapid process of unionization took place in the late 1910s and early 1920s.

68

Whites found a formidable weapon in the Mineworkers' Union, already heavily Afrikaner. In the light of the long years of enforced black passivity which were to come later, it is interesting to note that blacks, too, evolved powerful workers' organizations. Perhaps the most notable was the Industrial and Commercial Workers' Union (ICU), founded by Clement Kadalie in 1919, which was responsible for several years of sporadic rural unrest in the twenties. By the late 1920s, indeed, its membership stood at little short of a quarter of a million. On the Rand in 1920, no less than 71,000 black workers came out on strike.

But during this whole period of industrial ferment, the divisions between white and non-white workers had still not solidified completely. Multiracial trade unions still existed, and even periodically joined together, or tried to join together, with white and non-white unions for occasional displays of cross-racial worker solidarity. These experiments, however, never took root, for just as they were being attempted, white workers were gradually discovering that their best method of self-improvement was to promote a government explicitly committed to protecting their interests against workers of other colours. So the shutters were slowly being brought down on multiracial co-operation.

An important landmark, which helped to align white workers behind Afrikaner nationalism and to turn them against co-operation with non-whites, was the white mineworkers' strike on the Rand in 1922. It was triggered when the mining houses announced that they were going to bring blacks into semi-skilled positions, a course of action which would have threatened white workers, already dominant in those jobs. The strike developed into a major trial of strength between Smuts, who was now Prime Minister, and white workers, and Smuts resorted to using troops to put down what had become a small-scale rebellion. The outrage which greeted this tough action was enormous. It greatly aggravated incipient tensions between black and white, and simply confirmed the Afrikaner workers' view of Smuts as a lackey of English business and a traitor to the Afrikaner cause. Even though he promoted an Apprenticeship Act in 1922, which ensured that only whites could be trained for semi-skilled jobs, the damage was done.

The English-led Labour Party, which though workerist was essentially concerned only with white workers' interests, threw its support behind Hertzog's National Party, and in the aftermath of the 1922 strike, the two together won a notable victory at the polls in 1924, throwing Smuts out of office and bringing in a so-called Pact Ministry under Hertzog. None the less Afrikaner worker-power was still divided between loyalty to Smuts and its own self-interest, and was still tentative and not yet consolidated as an independent political force. In this fluid situation it is remarkable that Hertzog, the founder of political Afrikaner nationalism, actually bid for Coloured and black support in the run-up to the election. He had proposed ending the industrial colour bar for Coloured workers and even extending the franchise to Coloured people in the Transvaal and Orange Free State. As a result of his overtures, the mainly black ICU withdrew its moral support from Smuts's SAP, and the ANC (as the SANNC was now known) actually went so far as to urge the black electorate in the Cape to vote for a change of government, i.e. for the National Party. Considering later events, this must rank as one of the all-time great ironies in a country which saw many others, but it does serve to illustrate how different a country it still was from the South Africa of today.

The unsettled relations between the races can be seen too in Hertzog's early attitude to the Indians. The Indians had first arrived in South Africa in the 1860s, when they were brought as indentured labourers by English sugar farmers in Natal to work the crop for them, because the Zulu had proved reluctant to do what in their society was 'women's work', especially under the appalling conditions on the plantations. Over the years, their numbers had been boosted by a class of Gujerati traders, who had begun spreading further afield from Natal, particularly into the Transvaal.* The plantation-workers had encountered much hostility from the Natal English, who resisted 'Coolies' being allowed political rights, and the merchants had upset white small business people. South Africa's Indians had, therefore, always faced discrimination, despite the campaigning efforts of a young Indian lawyer who had spent twenty years in the country working on their behalf – Mohandâs K.

---

* The Orange Free State Republic had stopped them from establishing themselves in that area by the simple device of passing an ordinance making it a crime for an Indian to settle there. When, under changed circumstances in 1985, the South African Government ordered that this law be scrapped, consternation broke out – but it went ahead. Not many Indians have yet availed themselves of this dubious new privilege.

Gandhi.* Hertzog, in his first ministry, though, showed a pragmatic attitude to the Indians, and, in particular, scrapped the law which had forbade Indian workers' wives and children from joining them in South Africa, also allowing those who were already illegally there to be accepted as South African citizens.

This National Party stance towards non-white people did not last long, however. The pressures of urbanization continued to mount and Hertzog's attachment to Afrikaner nationalism, though it had not yet produced a full commitment to total segregation, meant he was bound to put white workers first. The promises to the Coloureds came to nought. The apparatus of discrimination, as a response to his white constituents, continued to be elaborated under Hertzog. Under the Wages Act of 1925, blacks lost the right to strike. The Mine and Works' Amendment Act of 1926 put the final seal on the prevention of black or Indian advance to higher grades in the mining industry. The Native Administration Act of 1927 was supposed to improve the allocation of land to black reserves but actually consolidated territorial injustice and separation, while also introducing a new repressive note by making it a criminal offence to incite hostility between 'Natives' and Europeans – a swipe aimed at union and multiracial political organizations.

None the less, white ambiguity on the question of race relations remained unresolved even into the late 1920s. In 1928 Smuts tried to persuade Hertzog privately to consider 'a common franchise all over South Africa, based on occupation and income or salary which was to apply to all, black and white alike' but whose qualifications were to be high enough to exclude the bulk of the black population. It seems that for a time Hertzog appears to have been attracted by this proposal and considered it seriously before abandoning it on the grounds that the time was not yet ripe.

Throughout this period the development of a modern Afrikaner identity proceeded. In 1918 Afrikaners had made their first foray into capitalism with the establishment of Santam and Sanlam in the

---

* The few remaining relics of Gandhi's stay in South Africa have not fared well. Despite protests, the government pulled down the Old Jail in Vereeniging where he had first worked out his strategy of *satyagraha*, or non-violent resistance, during a prison spell. And in 1985 a centre set up near Durban to perpetuate his philosophy was burnt down during black-Indian riots. A granddaughter still lives in South Africa though.

Cape, financial institutions founded to try to begin to break Afrikaner dependence on English money by providing them with their own insurance and investment houses. The same year had seen the creation of the forerunner of the *Broederbond*, or Fraternal League, a secret society dedicated to promoting Afrikaner advancement into key positions of power and influence. In 1929, it also took the lead in setting up the *Federasie van Afrikaanse Kultuurverenigings* (Federation of Afrikaans Cultural Unions) which in its turn became a potent, overt umbrella body for propagating the Afrikaans language, culture, and identity.

The effect of this growing Afrikaner nationalism made itself felt in the political arena. Northern Nationalists led by Hertzog were responding to it when they fought to get Afrikaans recognized as an official language in its own right. A prime mover in this was Hertzog's Minister of the Interior, Education and Public Health, Dr D. F. Malan – significantly from the Cape – who finally succeeded in 1925 in getting the constitutional definition of Dutch extended to embrace Afrikaans. This was a great triumph: with its recognition as an official language, Afrikaans came of age and quickly superceded Dutch, which rapidly disappeared from South African life, while Afrikaans continued to grow and flourish into a fully formed modern language. This recognition had another extremely important effect: it opened up all public services to Afrikaner work-seekers who had previously been disqualified by unfamiliarity with Dutch or English. Afrikaner employment by the state became very significant as a way of mopping up economic discontent. During the life of the same government, state enterprises like the Iron and Steel Corporation (ISCOR) were created, providing thousands of jobs. In foreign policy, too, Afrikaner nationalism was making an impact. Hertzog had always made it a central plank of his political platform to continue the struggle to assert South African independence of Britain. In 1926 and again in 1931 (after winning a second term of office in 1929), he continued his drive to free the country of its remaining imperial constraints, and in the process established full control by South Africa of its foreign relations, a development marked by the setting up of the country's Department of External Affairs in 1927.

Although the creation of a hegemonistic, exclusivist Afrikaner identity took time and co-existed for a couple of crucial decades with broader conceptions of the national interest, black South Africans, who were increasingly bearing the brunt of this development, saw the danger signals and strove desperately to find an appropriate response to it. But they were still considerably hampered by the lack of a national identity among blacks, who had until only recently owed political allegiance to fragmented authorities, and the much looser ties between them required a longer period in which to weld the same kind of unity their white fellow-citizens were groping towards. None the less, nascent forces of precisely this kind were now detectable. Recent scholarship has shown that, in the 1920s, the ideas of Marcus Garvey, a black American who sought to repatriate black people in the United States to Africa, gained ground in South Africa. Garveyism there took the guise of an 'Africa for the Africans' message, and millenarian hopes that black Americans would come to liberate them from the white yoke reflected a similar Africanist aspiration to the cattle-killings of 1856 when the Xhosa had believed that, in slaughtering their livestock, strangers (sometimes identified as Russians whom the British were then fighting in the Crimea) would come to liberate them. These ideas, which represented an early form of black consciousness, were reflected within both the ICU and the ANC, and may have been an important mobilizing force in the rash of black strikes and black rural discontent in the 1920s. Garveyism remains, even today, an important influence in the world, particularly in helping to create black self-awareness, for as recently as the 1970s his ideas provided a central strand of thought in Rastafarian movements in the Caribbean and Britain. But in South Africa these ideas were too diffuse, and lacked a coherent organizational framework in which to provide a fundamental challenge to a white supremacy of growing virulence. The ICU began to disintegrate at the end of the 1920s under personal and regional rivalries, and the ANC remained too much of an élite and apologetic organization to be able to harness the kind of black militancy which would have been needed to counter growing Afrikaner nationalism. None the less this Africanist impulse should not be forgotten. It was to resurface later in an important way, and its longevity suggests it will continue to have a significant role in South Africa's future.

But its comparative failure in the 1920s and the lack of black organizational success meant black South Africans were becoming trapped in their low status, stripped of any leverage to change it, and lacking in the means to galvanize themselves before it was too late.

Coloureds and Indians, with whose worker and political bodies a certain degree of co-operation had taken place, failed to rally behind them. Hertzog's softly-softly approach to these intermediate groups, though it discriminated against them relative to whites, allowed them to retain certain privileges denied blacks. The Coloureds, for instance, were not required to have passes and he had consolidated the previously insecure status of Indians as South African citizens. The late 1920s therefore came to be the critical moment at which multiracial alliances on a sufficiently large scale might still have been possible and might have thwarted the permanence of white domination. But the moment was lost.

Of course it was never so clear to the South Africans of that time. The ambiguity of race relations still held out the possibility of change. Indeed, gradual reform probably seemed inevitable to rational people. But they reckoned without the intervention of external forces. Such a force was now to descend on South Africa – and one whose legacy South Africans are still, more than half a century later, living with. It was the Great Depression.

The Depression is often under-rated as a critical factor in the development of thoroughgoing racial segregation in South Africa. The basis for racial segregation and the engine of Afrikaner nationalism which was driving it forward was, as we have seen, already in place by the end of the 1920s, and no doubt this dynamic would have continued to make itself felt in South Africa. But that was not the whole story. The development of capitalism in South Africa was to show, from the 1970s onwards, that expansion and prosperity brought in their train greater psychological security for whites and an inevitably strengthened position for black people. Should South Africa have experienced steady economic growth from the 1930s onwards it is reasonable to argue that racial liberalization – as we have seen not extinguished even then – might have set up a stronger counter-dynamic to segregation and produced a different complexion to a country which was still in its formative years.

The Depression, however, intervened. It considerably aggravated rural poverty and the process of urbanization as small-holders and farmers were driven off the land by collapsing commodity prices. It produced poverty among whites of an intensity and dramatic quality which so etched itself in their memories that it is still regularly spoken of with horror. Middle-aged university-educated men resorted to digging up roads; white women and children begged in the streets; the soup-kitchens set up by Afrikaner charities could barely cope with the massive queues. In 1930 a fifth of the entire white population was living below the bread-line. It can be no surprise that this greatly fuelled Afrikaner determination to find a way of keeping their own people on top. It is no accident, for instance, that it was during this period that a young Dutch-born Afrikaner, Dr Hendrik Verwoerd, then a social psychologist at Stellenbosch University, first began turning his mind to politics as he wrestled with the problem of the 'poor white', conceiving in the process solutions which would make a great impact on the country in the future. The position of black South Africans was even more disastrous. The reserves became prisons of starving people; as more and more fled to the cities in defiance of the law, they found little comfort there, and did not even have the fall-back of the soup-kitchens which Afrikaners organized for those they saw as their own. It was a grim, horrific picture, in which all the pre-existing economic competition between black and white was greatly intensified. Most important of all, it meant that in political terms the government of the day, committed to improving its supporters' position, was quite unable to deliver its promises. The Depression thus guaranteed that whites would turn elsewhere for protection, with fearful consequences for whole generations of South Africans.

In 1933, faced with the economic crisis, Hertzog, in keeping with his belief that English and Afrikaner should work together as equals, entered into a national coalition with Smuts's SAP, a coalition formalized when their two parties merged together the following year to form the United Party. Dr Malan felt unable to support the Fusion, as it was called, and broke away to form a new *Gesuiwerde* (Purified) National Party. In 1935 it committed itself to full republicanism and Afrikaner supremacy.

There is a clear pattern here, which remains relevant today. Throughout Afrikaner history, leaders have been produced who canalize and articulate Afrikaner nationalism. When they appear to sacrifice Afrikaner hegemony in the interests of broader co-operation, they are jettisoned and new leaders emerge to continue the fight for supremacy. Smuts and Botha were such men – Boer nationalists. When they compromised for the sake of Boer-English relations, they lost the support of their own people. Hertzog, while he promoted Afrikanerdom, was their hero, but when he, too, attempted co-operation with the English, he fell by the wayside.

Malan had no intention of following them. It will be worth remembering when we come to consider current South African developments that modern leaders of Afrikaner nationalism, like P. W. Botha, grew up in the era of the Fusion split. They know the lesson of Afrikaner history, and it has never ceased to haunt them.

In 1934, however, the United Party had an overwhelming Parliamentary majority, and the new National Party only twenty seats. The Fusion government, responding to the intensified economic competition of the Depression, continued the remorseless drive towards protecting white workers. The territorial enslavement of black South Africa was further consolidated through the Native Trust and Lands Act of 1936, and the Native Laws Amendment Act of 1937 strengthened the Pass Laws to control the black influx to urban areas even more tightly. It was also decided, albeit after much debate and controversy, that blacks in the Cape would now be prevented from voting with white people for common white candidates. They would in future be placed on a separate voters' roll and would elect three white representatives of their own. 10,000 black voters were affected, and a century of mixed voting was brought to an end.

Just as Smuts had discovered, however, the betrayal of Afrikanerdom was not to be forgiven that easily. The 1930s saw the *Broederbond* in close alliance with the Gesuiwerde National Party, and they now plunged themselves into an all-out fight to capture the soul of Afrikanerdom. Malan succeeded in wresting control of much of the old National Party from the Hertzogites. An Afrikaner railway union, *Die Spoorbond* (Railway League), was set up in 1933 to promote Afrikaner employment in this branch of public service and to break the grip of English-controlled unions. The *Volkskas* (or People's Treasury) bank was established in 1934 to promote Afrikaner capital. A great battle for control of the Afrikaans press ensued with the new National Party again winning control. In the process they set up the *Transvaler*, the most powerful Afrikaans medium in the populous Transvaal, with the ubiquitous Dr Verwoerd, turning up like a bad penny, as its editor. In their battle for hearts and minds, he was to prove a consistently powerful ally. Afrikaner nationalism was also invigorated by events like the reenactment of the Great Trek and the construction of the *Voortrekker* Monument in 1938, the centenary of the event. Finally the establishment of an *Ekonomiese Volkskongres* (People's Economic Congress) in 1939 led to

a well co-ordinated programme to rally Afrikaner economic resources independently of English institutions.

Another turn of the nationalist screw came with the outbreak of
the Second World War. Smuts favoured support; Hertzog, in keeping with his record, opposed South Africa's participation. Smuts
narrowly won the vote in Parliament, and Hertzog crossed the floor
to rejoin Malan. The cause of Afrikaner nationalism was strengthened, in this world war as in the first, by the call to sacrifice themselves for the old enemy, the British. A pro-Nazi, fascist organization, the *Ossewabrandwag* (Ox-wagon Sentinel), recruited anti-war
activists in a para-military campaign against the state, and among its
members interned as a result was a man who would also make his
mark on the future – one John Vorster.

Hertzog's reconciliation with Malan's brand of Afrikaner nationalism was not to last long. At a meeting of the party in 1940 in
Bloemfontein, Hertzog's home town, it became clear that they placed a greater priority on Afrikaner supremacy than on co-operation
with English South Africans. Hertzog's lifelong ideal was spurned.
He was now a man who could find no political home. He had written
himself out of South Africa's politics. With the prescient words 'Let
us do nothing which is unworthy of the *volk* or which will lead to its
downfall', he walked out of the hall – and political life. Two years
later he died in obscurity.

Perhaps the development which finally stoked up Afrikaner nationalism to its most full-blooded form was the direction of internal
government policy during, and immediately after, the war. Smuts,
who was busy fighting the good fight abroad as a newly appointed
British Field-Marshal, left the running of the country largely in the
hands of the Deputy Prime Minister, J. H. Hofmeyr, a Cape liberal.
Segregation slowed down. This was largely because the war nec-
essitated further rapid industrial growth, and with white workers
away fighting, the economy was more dependent than ever on black
labour. Welfare provision for blacks was considerably improved;
there was a go-slow on enforcing the Pass Laws, which had anyway
only really been systematically implemented from 1938. The possibility of recognition for black trade unions – never illegal, but
never formally acknowledged either – was held out, though, like so
much else, not in the end implemented. The Native Representatives
in Parliament, through vigorous organization and passionate argument, ensured that the case for black rights remained forcefully put.

Immediately after the war Smuts also legislated to give Indians five white Representatives in Parliament, the first time they had been offered a foothold in the legislature, though it was actually intended as a sop for having further restricted their property rights. None the less, during these years it seemed as though non-white South Africa might be achieving a new status for itself in the the country's political life.

It was another of those moments of promise when a different kind of South Africa from the one that was emerging seemed possible. It was an illusion, of course. With the return of demobilized white workers at the end of the war, economic competition resurfaced. Black confidence, which had manifested itself during the war in a spate of strikes, and had been bolstered by the organizational support of the South African Communist Party (SACP), was a serious threat to big business and Afrikaner nationalists alike.

On 26 May 1948, the National Party under Dr D. F. Malan emerged as the largest single party in a general election and together with a remnant of Hertzogites formed the first government ever to consist only of Afrikaners. It was a profound shock to Smuts, who had failed to appreciate the undercurrents in his own community. He retired to his farm at a place called Irene, near Pretoria, where he died a deeply disillusioned man in 1950. Later, his successors, with the kind of grace they were to elevate to an art, renamed Irene Verwoerdburg.

Malan's Nationalists stood for a new brand of white supremacy: Afrikaner domination through total racial segregation. The ambiguities of inter-racial life between the wars were to be brought to an end. The majority of National Party supporters had spent the war fighting Nazism. Now they were to erect a system of racial brutality exceeded only by those they had recently helped to conquer. 'Separate-ness' was what they called it – apartheid.

It was a word they were to stamp not only on South Africa, but on all the world.

6

APARTHEID AND RESISTANCE

The coming to power of Malan's Nationalists in 1948 marked the start of a distinct new period in South Africa's history. Until the twentieth century the Boers had been a dispersed, fragmented people, who had lacked a fully formed sense of their own identity. They had seen both blacks and Britain as a threat to themselves, but they had had no clear long-term strategy for dealing with them. The Boer War gave them a much sharper image of themselves as a distinct people, and left them in political control of the country. But they had not yet quite made up their minds what kind of relationship they were to have with English and black South Africans. It was during the inter-war years that this was decided, and it was economic hardship, especially the Great Depression, which was the critical determining factor. Afrikaner economic advancement became the supreme goal, and this required action on two fronts, which were opposite sides of the same coin.

In the case of English South Africans the Afrikaners were prepared to let them continue enjoying economic success, as long as they did not try to restrict Afrikaner advance. In the case of black South Africans, the economy could not provide a marked increase in living standards for them without retarding whites. The English, therefore, had to have their links with the great imperial power overseas snapped off once and for all, so as to leave them captive to the Afrikaners; the blacks had to be subdued, subjugated, rendered impotent and, if possible, written out of the equation altogether.

Republicanism − severing the tie with Britain, and apartheid: these were the twin goals which the Gesuiwerde National Party had clarified beyond ambiguity for Afrikaners; these were the two traditional impulses which the new Government was now in office to bring to full fruition.

Many white voters, however, had only shortly before been fighting a British war, and opinion was too evenly divided on the imperial question to allow immediate progress on that issue. But weary from the recent conflict and from rationing, and newly returned home from the battlefields, they were hungry for jobs and prosperity. They had no such qualms about apartheid. The Government set to it with gusto.

The basic building block of segregation had to be the classification of all people in South Africa into racial groups. This was implemented by the Population Registration Act of 1950, which assigned everyone to such a group. To ensure that this neat ordering was not muddied by natural impulses, they were outlawed. Under the Prohibition of Mixed Marriages Act (1949), it became impossible to marry across the colour bar, and an amendment to the Immorality Act in 1950 made sexual relations between people of different races a crime. Of course, by these Acts, Malan and his social engineers were trying to impose an over-rigid tabulation on reality. There were, in South Africa, distinct agglomerations of people of different racial types, but no race was 'pure' since races never are. And between even those who conformed to the notion of a pure racial type was a vast spectrum of people who did not fit easily into any category. The Acts therefore set in train a process of separating people into different 'races' which frequently involved splitting up members of the same family and segregating them. It also created a situation where individuals could at any point be 'reclassified' into new racial groups, often with the most devastating personal consequences. The fact that thousands of people were affected by these Acts is evidence of the extent to which South Africa had actually become a multiracial society, despite substantial earlier segregation.

An instructive story of the consequences of this new separating was that of a young girl called Sandra Laing, who was at school in the Eastern Transvaal in the 1960s. Her parents were Afrikaners, and she attended the local Afrikaans school. After objections from some parents that she 'looked Coloured' she was reclassified, and forced to quit her school. Her parents' shame, in a small, rural community, was complete. After much protest, she was made 'white' again – but nine schools refused to take her. Though 'white' she was no longer accepted. Inevitably she came to identify with black people and soon after eloped with a black vegetable seller. Her

(12) Pretoria's Church Square, late nineteenth century. The Boers have come by ox-wagon to attend communion

(13) British troops driven back into Ladysmith during the Boer War siege, 30 October 1899

(14) Boer soldiers during the War

(15) The first South African Cabinet, 1910. The Prime Minister, Louis Botha, is seated in the centre. Jan Smuts stands far left, and Barry Hertzog second from the right

(16) A black man shows his 'pass', which regulates all his movements

(17) A delegation of the South African Native (later African) National Congress visiting London in 1914. Their president, the Rev. J.L. Dube, is in the centre

(18) The first Prime Minister of the modern National Party, Dr D.F. Malan, with his family at their Stellenbosch home in June 1948, shortly after his appointment

(19) Delegates arrive at the Congress of the People, Kliptown, 1955, with placards stating ideas to be incorporated in the Freedom Charter

father repudiated her. She and her lover, living in defiance of the law, were condemned to wander the segregated ranks of South African society, unable to find acceptance or a place for themselves. Eventually they separated. Today she lives in an obscure rural black settlement, a displaced person with a fractured identity, and a special victim of apartheid. She has never seen her parents again. At least, however, she is alive. The suicides of many similar victims have regularly filled the columns of South African newspapers.

The next step for Malan's Government was to try and ensure that blacks remained in their 'reserves' and only came to 'white' areas when they were needed for work. A good deal of the groundwork had already been laid by inter-war governments, but under the dynamic Dr Verwoerd who was installed as Minister of Native Affairs in 1950, an elaborate control mechanism attained its full reach.

Building on the division of the country into 'black' and 'white' areas which earlier Land Acts had effected, the Government now decreed that the only blacks who would be entitled to stay permanently in 'white' urban areas – though without the rights normally accompanying residence – were those who had been born there, who had lived there continuously for fifteen years, or who had worked for the same employer for at least ten years. These 'Section 10' rights, as they came to be called, were jealously guarded by those who had them – a small fraction of the total black population. New powers were taken, and enforced, to clear black 'squatters' off 'white' land, and send them to the reserves. Over the years tens of thousands of black people were to be forcibly removed and dumped, often in the middle of nowhere, where the lack of sustenance, housing, work, and sanitation was to exact a dreadful toll, thus adding to the extraordinary poverty, malnutrition, and disease in the midst of the most prosperous country in Africa. These forced removals – 'resettlement' was the official term – reached their peak in the late 1960s and early 1970s, but the legal framework was consolidated by Malan's Government. They also gave more authority, and rewards, to Government-selected 'tribal' chiefs in the reserves to make sure they policed blacks in those backward and impoverished rural areas.

Control of black people's movements was increased by tightening up the Pass Laws and extending them for the first time to women. In putting through the legislation the Government displayed its frequently recurring desire to persuade itself and others of its own good intentions. It showed that in writing of Newspeak in *1984*, George

Orwell had understood a frightening but real human capacity for manipulating reason and meaning. The Bill was called the Natives Abolition of Passes Act (1952), and it subjected blacks to punishment if they did not have a new document called a 'reference book'. It was the introduction of this new document which allowed them to claim they were abolishing 'passes', though in practice, of course, there was no difference.

In the 'white', and especially urban, areas, the Government was determined that full segregation would also prevail. The Group Areas Act of 1950 was the infamous basic statute which allowed the Government to decree which areas were allocated to whom. Those entitled to live in the towns and cities had to have their own separate residential areas. In the case of blacks, these were known as 'locations' or 'townships', and they were built well away from the town itself, usually surrounded by barbed wire, with box-like huts, few trees or gardens, non-existent amenities, and poor transport to their places of work. Access tended to be limited to one or two main roads, and the townships were further cut off by siting industrial development between them and the whites, precautions which later events would show to have been far-sighted.

Over the next two decades, the geography of South Africa was accordingly rearranged. Black slums which were thought to be too near white areas or occupying desirable land were simply levelled. So it was, for instance, that long-established black areas like Sophiatown in the western suburbs of Johannesburg were flattened, and their residents bodily transported to Soweto,* some miles out of the city. It thereafter became the white suburb of Triomf (Triumph – note the name). Indians and Coloureds, of course, were also affected. So it was that later District Six, a famous and picturesque Coloured quarter on the slopes of Cape Town's Table Mountain, containing fine specimens of late nineteenth- and early twentieth-century houses, was razed to the ground. Today only a lone mosque still stands amidst the wastes as a marker of this ruthless purging. The huge Asiatic bazaar in the middle of Pretoria was completely demolished and rebuilt outside the city. Attempts were made to clear many other mixed areas, like Fordsburg and Doornfontein in Johannesburg, through the lack of success was testimony to the en-

---

* Despite its African-sounding name, Soweto is simply an acronym for *So*uth *We*stern *T*ownships, i.e. south-west of Johannesburg.

durance of a continuing, if weak, desire for multiracial contact. Even the tiny handful of Chinese traders who had established themselves in South Africa were not left alone, being forced to uproot themselves and remove their children from the white schools they had traditionally attended. In all of this, it is legitimate to recall the ruthless removal of Jews in Warsaw to the Ghetto, for precisely the same process operated here. That is, indeed, exactly what these 'non-white' areas were – ghettoes.

The 'races' deemed as such by the government became well and truly separated. Every walk of life was affected: apart from residential areas and schools, public parks, shops, all lavatories, post offices, banks, sports clubs and facilities, churches, restaurants, all places of entertainment, beaches, public transport – all were segregated. In many of these areas of life, segregation had always existed to some degree – but the barriers were now rendered impenetrable by law. Only in the workplace did white and black now meet, but even there a certain irony could be noted. Every white household acquired its black maid, who would cook their food, wash their clothes, and nurse and bathe their children. In doing so, not only would she become an integral part of their daily life but enjoyed an intimacy with them denied to even their closest friends. Yet close as she was, she would remain a cipher, whose own family and children were not allowed to live with her and whose innermost thoughts remained a matter of sublime indifference to her employers.

Within a decade, then, the limited integration between the races in South Africa was being unscrambled. Within two, segregation was as complete as human beings could engineer.

Meanwhile the Government was engaged in a massive process of uplifting its own people. The public service was purged of English people or United Party supporters. The railways, police, army, civil service, Native Administration: Afrikaner National Party members found thousands of new jobs. Even the game wardens in the Kruger National Park were changed for political reasons. A spate of public infrastructural investment was undertaken. ISCOR developed a new site on the Southern Transvaal veld which brought into being an entire new town called Vanderbijlpark. A few miles south on the Orange Free State side of the Vaal, an extraordinarily ambitious new project was brought to fruition: the South African Coal, Oil and Gas Corporation (SASOL) built a huge petrochemical plant to produce oil from coal. The largest undertaking of its kind anywhere in the world, it too spawned a mushrooming town, Sasolburg, as well as two similar plants in the Transvaal later on. The thousands upon thousands of jobs created were tailor-made for an hungry Afrikaner proletariat who were at best only semi-skilled, but it also helped to create a secure foundation from which they could rise to higher skills and, later on, a better existence outside the state sector. If anyone doubts the Keynesian nostrum that public investment creates jobs and economic improvement, he need look no further than post-1948 South Africa.

Vast new gold discoveries on the West Rand and in the Western Orange Free State also created suitable new semi-skilled jobs for impoverished Afrikaners, since, owing to inter-war legislation, their trade unions had long been entrenched in the mining industry. The *Broederbond* played its part, especially in catering for the incipient Afrikaner middle class. It used its influence to assist the Government in seizing control of all education, broadcasting, and Afrikaans' communications media. It made sure that jobs all went to the boys. And behind the scenes, it became a government within a government, helping to shape all areas of policy and making sure it was implemented in all walks of life. Afrikaners had never had it so good.

The response of black South Africans to the battery of discriminatory legislation now unleashed on them was to try once more to find a way of breaking through white oppression. In the early 1940s a discernible change of mood had come over the ANC, as it had begun to distance itself from its previous position of wishing to see the condition of blacks merely ameliorated, and had now begun to think of a larger-scale transformation which would involve full black participation in the life of the country. This shift had not been clearly defined, however, and it was the formation of a youth wing, the African National Congress Youth League, in 1943 and 1944 which was to drive the movement forward into a more radical ethos.

Like their elders, the members of the Youth League tended to be mission-educated, professional young blacks, part of the small core of the black élite. Among their ranks three names were of special future importance: Nelson Mandela, from the royal Thembu line among the Transkeian Xhosa and a lawyer in Johannesburg; Walter Sisulu, his mentor who ran a small estate agency in Johannesburg; and Robert Sobukwe, a university lecturer also living in Johannesburg. The Youth Leaguers, being younger and of a more self-confident generation, took a more robust view than their elders,

84

being solidly committed to full democracy in South Africa, which implied majority rule. Alongside this belief in traditional Western liberal values, there also ran a strong current of 'Africanism', which, while it did not mean the expulsion of whites from South Africa, clearly involved the complete freeing of black people from white domination, and the ending of their neo-colonial burden.

The Youth League's moment came after the failure of older black political leaders to unify and work out a strategy in the face of the Nationalist onslaught in 1948. Blacks saw quite clearly the threat that the new Government posed to their interests, and a group of leaders ranging well beyond the ANC came together in Bloemfontein in October of that year to issue a call for African unity. Apart from the ANC led by Dr A. B. Xuma, the African Democratic Party also participated – a small, vaguely Trotskyist organization which none the less worked with white liberals – as well as the All-African Convention (AAC), led by Davidson Jabavu. Jabavu, the son of a distinguished leader of black opinion in the Cape, had been an important figure in setting up the AAC in 1935 to oppose Hertzog's removal of Cape blacks from the common voters' roll. The AAC had aspired to be a national umbrella body to co-ordinate resistance, and the ANC had been a member of it. But the AAC had followed a moderate and conciliatory line, wishing to concentrate on extending any specific rights blacks already had rather than to support a broader call for general civic rights. The ANC, especially as opinion hardened within its ranks, had consequently maintained its distance, and, to some extent at least, had actually become a rival to the AAC.

The negotiations for new unity broke down in 1949 with the AAC wanting a multiracial alliance, and the ANC favouring a black-only strategy. In the wake of this failure, and with the Nationalist threat now becoming reality, the ANC Youth League proposed, and got adopted, a Programme of Action for the ANC. This marked a clear change of tactics. Instead of deputations and petitions to the Government, the Programme of Action called for strikes, boycotts, and a campaign of civil disobedience, though of a strictly non-violent kind. It was to be passive resistance. In accepting this new approach, the ANC was beginning to recognize the impotence of trying to work within the existing political establishment and was now seeking to bring extra-Parliamentary pressure to bear on it.

Despite clear evidence of an 'Africanist' tendency within the ANC

– that is to say a belief that black South Africans should rely only on themselves, and not work with other racial groups – such an app-roach was, in reality, not general within the organization. The deli-cate balance between this view and an opposing belief in cross-racial alliances was soon tilted decisively in favour of wider co-operation. The circumstances of the day made it a rational outcome, for black South Africans needed all the help they could get.

So it was that this period saw a consolidation of the ANC's re-lationship with the white-dominated South African Communist Party (SACP), a relationship which had previously been close, but somewhat uneasy. The Communist Party had been active through-out the 1920s and 1930s in black industrial action, though generally in a supporting role rather than in its own right. It had inevitably become intertwined with black political movements, though, as a small party of white intellectuals uncompromised by the need to keep an electorate sweet, it was always much more ideologically coherent and sharply focused than they were. It was the difference between its clearly radical stance and the frequently confused posi-tion of black organizations which accounted for a certain tension be-tween them. Such differences also existed between the ANC and the Communists in the late 1940s, the Communists's fundamental ob-jective being to produce a total transformation of the entire econ-omic system, whereas the ANC's central objective was to change the relative position of black and white. But because of the Govern-ment's determination to prosecute thoroughgoing segregation, and its ruthlessness it enforcing it, the ANC desperately needed the Communists' organizational expertise. Thus, ironically, Afrikaner nationalism closed the gap between them and forged a closer link than ever, with three Communists now sitting on the ANC execut-ive.

The SACP was not long, however, for this world. The Nationalist Party, having noted the involvement of Communists in black in-dustrial militancy and now observing its links with a newly aggres-sive ANC, took quick action to eradicate it. A Suppression of Com-munism Act was passed in 1950, outlawing the Party, which disban-ded itself shortly before the legislation came into effect. The party continued to operate underground, however, and many individual members simply joined the ANC, thus continuing unbroken their inter-relationship.

It was not only towards white radicals that the ANC now turned.

86

It also sought support from Indian South Africans. Paradoxically, part of the impetus for doing so was provided by the outbreak of ugly communal attacks by blacks on Indians around Durban in 1949 – an indication of black anger as discrimination bit. Indian traders had come to carve out a comfortable niche for themselves, often by doing the job whites shunned of supplying the black townships. In a situation where blacks could not take on the white authorities, the Indians, who lived near black townships, were an easier target. This development, which cost 142 lives, dramatized the danger of non-white energies being dissipated among themselves, and encouraged the ANC to draw closer to Indian political organizations, most notably the South African Indian Congress (SAIC), which was strong in the Transvaal and Natal.

Until now, political leadership within the black population had resided almost exclusively in the hands of a tiny educated élite. The existence of numerous small parties in the inter-war years, trying to play the constitutional game, had shown that black South Africans were evolving a political awareness. But the lack of ideological agreement, and the regional fragmentation of these parties showed also that the process of developing a strong sense of national identity among blacks, rallying them around a clear set of goals, and finding an effective means of challenging white power was only in its infancy. Until the mass of black people could be rallied around common objectives, until strong links were forged between the black élite and the black community at large, no real impact could be made.

It was the achievement of the ANC's Youth League that, if it did not produce wholly clear goals for black South Africans generally, it did at least provide the tactics which would enable black leadership to begin to win popular black support.

The ANC Youth League's Programme for Action became translated in 1952 into a seminal Defiance Campaign, led by the ANC and supported by the SAIC. Its first manifestation was a mass protest by blacks over all the country on 6 April 1952, the 300th anniversary of Van Riebeeck's landing at the Cape. Thereafter, blacks throughout South Africa embarked on a campaign of deliberately throwing away their passes, or inviting the police to arrest them for not having them. This activity, which went on for several months, was accompanied by a flouting of public segregation, with blacks occupying 'White Only' benches in public parks and white railway waiting rooms. This eruption of urban black militancy created considerable alarm in white circles. 8,000 people were arrested during the campaign, and the police took tough action to break up protests. By the end of the year it was clear that repression had taken the steam out of the movement, but for large numbers of black people it had been an experience which had awakened their political interest. The ANC had suddenly found its ranks being swollen by new recruits – its membership reportedly reaching 100,000. It marked the beginning of mass participation in the political struggle.

The Government responded to these events by taking tough new powers to crush civil disobedience and repress black political activity. For a while, it looked as though they had succeeded in eradicating black opposition. But, as events were to show, although black political organizations had to some extent disappeared from view, they were still alive and exploring yet new ways to try and meet the Nationalist drive for complete domination.

And the Government, while happy enough about having put the lid on the situation, was not complacent. The wave of protest had shown that militancy was growing among blacks. Something would have to be done to counteract the *swartgevaar* (black danger) in the longer term. Their first step was to try and 're-educate' blacks so that they would accept their menial status in life and not entertain unhelpful expectations. Dr Verwoerd put it candidly:

> Education must train and teach people in accordance with their opportunities in life. . . . It is of no avail for [the Bantu]*
> to receive a training which has as its aim absorption in the European community. . . . There is no place for him [there] above the level of certain forms of labour.

To that end, 'Bantu' education was now put under the direct control of Verwoerd's Department of Native Affairs, and among other provisions, it was decided that in future all blacks would be taught at high school level in their masters' languages – English and, significantly, Afrikaans. Later, in 1959, with characteristic manipulation of meaning, the Extension of University Education Act was to

---

* 'Bantu' came to replace 'Native' early in the 1950s as the official word for a black person. It was an attempt to persuade blacks of the government's goodwill, since 'Native' had become a pejorative term.

restrict black admission to established universities to the point where it became effectively non-existent. Four 'university colleges' for blacks were set up instead in the reserves, under the control of carefully selected Afrikaner rectors, whose task it was to ensure that blacks were trained for a status consonant with Dr Verwoerd's pronouncements.

The need to adjust black expectations to what the Government regarded as appropriate continued to be demonstrated. As the steam had gone out of the Defiance Campaign after 1952, the ANC had taken the lead in trying to find a new way to rally popular support. Professor Z. K. Matthews, a leading figure in the ANC hierarchy, is popularly credited with having been the person who first suggested a 'Congress of the People'. The idea was to take the widest possible soundings of non-white opinion in South Africa, to get every area to choose their representatives, and then, for all the delegates to come together and, on the basis of their findings, to construct a charter setting out non-white South Africa's basic goals and aspirations. It was to be a kind of mini-Parliament for a people without such an institution.

By the very nature of South Africa, this could not have been a truly democratic exercise, and since the ANC took the lead in organizing it, it was bound to be shaped by their activists. None the less, an extensive canvassing of non-white opinion did take place and on 26 and 27 June 1955, 3,000 people met at Kliptown, just outside Johannesburg, to draw up the document known as the Freedom Charter. In addition to the ANC, the South African Indian Congress was also represented, as was the recently formed South African Coloured People's Organization, the South African Congress of Trade Unions – an ANC-dominated confederation which had about 30,000 members – and the small white liberal organization, the Congress of Democrats. In addition, therefore, to representing a reasonable cross-section of black opinion, it also had the support of representatives of all race groups in South Africa.

For many years after it was adopted, the Freedom Charter remained a half-forgotten declaration, reduced to semi-obscurity by the conditions of political repression and by changing times. Recently, however, as events in South Africa have moved into a new phase, the Freedom Charter has been taken off the bookshelves, dusted down, and re-examined. As white business, for instance, has come to see that it may have to reach an accommodation with the country's majority, it has become a not uncommon curiosity to find company executives hauling a well-thumbed copy out of their brief-cases and quoting from it by rote. This new status for the Freedom Charter stems from the fact that it remains the closest thing to a statement of principles by non-white South Africa, and the most significant encapsulation of their aspirations.

The charter begins with these words, which constitute its central tenet:

> We, the People of South Africa, declare for all our country and the world to know: that South Africa belongs to all who live in it, black and white, and that no government can justly claim authority unless it is based on the will of the people; that only a democratic state, based on [that] will, can secure to all their birthright without distinction of colour, race, sex or belief.

The charter further states that 'every man and woman shall have the right to vote for and to stand as a candidate for all bodies which make laws'. It does not spell out *how* the voting and governmental system shall be constructed, but it is quite clear that simple, straightforward majority rule, with every citizen voting equally and with appropriate guarantees for minority rights, is the cornerstone of its philosophy. The strong emphasis throughout on complete equality for every citizen shows that the Africanist strain of black thought had been completely jettisoned in favour of full multi-racialism. In that sense, it represents an uncontroversial, classically liberal prospectus. In the economic realm, however, a more socialist approach is evident. The charter speaks of the country's 'mineral wealth', banks, and 'monopoly industry' being transferred to the 'ownership of the people as a whole' and of the land being 'redivided among those who work it, to banish famine and land hunger'. It must be said, however, that the reference to nationalization is vague and would not be out of place in, say, contemporary France. The reference to land reform is also imprecise and qualified. The details are obviously meant to be pragmatically worked out, and it can by no stretch of the imagination be regarded as a revolutionary doc-ument.

None the less, in the context of South Africa in the mid-1950s, even these sentiments, and more especially the popular mobilization which lay behind its drafting, were profoundly subversive to Afrik-

90

aner nationalism. The Kliptown meeting was broken up by the police. In the following year, 156 people who had been associated with the congress, including the increasingly prominent figure of Nelson Mandela who, as a 'banned' person had not attended the meeting but had been consulted about the content of the charter, were arrested. There followed one of the longest and largest trials ever seen in South Africa, which only ended in 1961, a full five years later, with all the defendants being acquitted.

From the Government's point of view, things were going well in the mid-1950s, despite Kliptown. As near total a segregation of the races as was humanly possible was being successfully accomplished, and black protest, though vexing, was incapable of stopping it. One annoying detail remained unresolved, however, and continued to niggle. Malan's Government had decided that the integrity of apartheid would be compromised if the Cape Coloureds were allowed to remain on the voters' roll with whites. To continue to accept it would be to encourage the notion in some people's minds that the Government was not fully committed to segregation. They had, therefore, fought a ferocious battle to try and remove this irritant. They had been hampered by the unfortunate 'entrenched clause' in the Constitution, which required the consent of two-thirds of both Houses of Parliament sitting together to be changed. Determined opposition from the successors to Smuts and Hertzog in the United Party, and the traditional independence of the judiciary, which refused to sanction any bending of the rules, had hampered the Government throughout a long and bitter battle. In 1954 Malan retired and his successor as Prime Minister, J. G. Strijdom, the leader of the National Party in the Transvaal, immediately determined to get to grips with this problem. In 1956 he finally achieved this long-cherished goal. By enlarging the Senate and changing its structure, the Government finally gerrymandered the required number of votes. The Coloureds were removed from the common voters' roll and, like the blacks in 1936, were in future to vote separately for four white representatives. Later, in 1969, they were to lose even that.

Despite the unbroken chain of success in implementing apartheid, however, Verwoerd – supremo at Native Affairs and undisputed architect of the whole segregationist edifice – had long recognized that some kind of provision for the articulation of black political aspirations would none the less have to be found. The wave of protests and growing international condemnation of South Africa

91

made it more urgent to develop black institutions which could be held up in answer to criticism. Given the policy to which Afrikaner nationalism had committed itself, though, such channels could only be provided in the reserves. Verwoerd was not yet sure what form they would take, but when in 1956 a massive study of the reserves was completed – the report of the Tomlinson Commission – he began to elaborate in his mind the idea of turning these areas into a number of separate 'homelands' or 'Bantustans' which could be flatteringly represented as mini-statelets and in which blacks might be allowed some measure of self-determination. When Strijdom died in office in 1958 and Verwoerd finally took over as Prime Minister, almost his first achievement was to guide the Promotion of Bantu Self-Government Act through Parliament (1959). It was this Act which laid the foundation for the subsequent 'homeland' policy.

The reserves were to become eight tribally based entities in which government-sanctioned tribal chiefs would officiate over a slow evolution towards internal democracy. This was suspect enough, but the real purpose of the policy was to end all remaining black involvement in the 'white' Parliament and to create a system in which all urban blacks would be taken as being members of a designated 'homeland'. They would then be allowed to enjoy 'full' political rights there, including the right to vote. The Government called this system 'separate development' in an attempt to get away from apartheid, which had become a virtual obscenity outside white circles, and as it was progressively implemented over the next decade, they tried to argue that it was nothing worse than appropriate local decolonization. By abolishing the white Natives' Representatives in Parliament, the Act put an end, for the foreseeable future, to any possibility of black and white evolving together politically. And the policy in general had the effect of turning urban blacks into 'foreigners' in their own country. They were gradually turned into citizens, not of South Africa, which was by definition white, but of their 'homelands', which in very many cases were areas they had never had any connection with and, indeed, which they had often never even seen. Meanwhile, it destroyed what few remaining rights or privileges they had in the areas where they lived and worked.

The overwhelming majority of whites were fairly content with this policy, but it did play a part in splitting the opposition United Party. About a fifth of its more liberal MPs broke away in 1959 to form the the Progressive Party, English-dominated and opposed to apartheid, though favouring only a limited form of multiracialism. It had eleven MPs at the time of the breakaway, but in the 1961 election, only one retained her seat: the formidable Helen Suzman. Significantly, she represented the richest constituency in the country – the luxurious Johannesburg suburb of Houghton – which showed both how economic security created more relaxed attitudes and how those with the greatest personal stake in the future recognized most clearly the country's best long-term interest.

For blacks the full impact of the homelands policy was yet to come. But meanwhile the weight of white domination, dispossession, and daily humiliation was keenly felt. The mid- and late-1950s saw a spate of violent peasant protests in rural areas, generally those where black resistance to white conquest had traditionally been fiercest, for example among the Zulu in Natal, the Pedi in the Eastern Transvaal and the Xhosa in Pondoland. The late 1950s also saw spontaneous explosions of urban anger, with sporadic riots, protests, and strikes. But black political organization had not yet fully recovered from the aftermath of the Defiance Campaign, and the treason trial kept their leaders busy with other concerns. The unrest never, therefore, succeeded in coalescing and making any major impact. And as black activists regrouped and rethought their strategies, perhaps the single most important division, a division which had always been there, opened up within black politics.

In November 1958 Robert Sobukwe led a walk-out from an ANC conference and, the following March, together with a minority, but sizeable, dissident element in the organization formed a new body called the Pan-Africanist Congress, or PAC. The PAC was not to survive as an active force within South Africa for very long, though it continues to function in exile today. But it did represent a fundamental, and enduring, strain of black political thought, and therefore, despite its short appearance in South Africa, it is right to see it as the progenitor, and guardian, of a major South African phenomenon.

The immediate cause of the breach with the ANC was dissatisfaction resulting from the comparative failure of an ANC-organized stay-at-home during the 1958 white election. But the rift between the ANC and the PAC had been long in the making, and this was merely the catalyst which precipitated an inevitable parting of the ways. The PAC adherents saw themselves as the torch-bearers of

93

'Africanism'. They believed that the people of Africa, who tended to be black, had been hijacked by white colonizers, and that the priority in political struggle should be for Africans to liberate the African nation from foreign oppressors. The definition of who was African and who foreign was always ambiguous. They did not see themselves as black racists and explicitly supported non-racialism, but they believed that even white liberals tended to have a vested interest in white domination and that white Communists were the advocates of an alien, non-African philosophy, and therefore not truly African either. In effect, virtually all whites were 'non-African'. Since Africans could not trust non-Africans, they would have to free themselves by their own efforts – and in practice this meant that black South Africans should work alone.

The PAC believed the ANC had repudiated the true cause at the Congress of the People. The participation of 'non-Africans' there and the emphasis on minority rights was the evidence. The result, they felt, would be the diversion of the nationalist struggle into supporting alien battles, and the failure to achieve true liberation. They called themselves Pan-Africanist at a time when decolonization was triumphing in Africa* on a wave of similar ideas which visualized all Africa as one nation – hence 'Pan-African'.

It will be readily apparent from this that a powerful motive in breaking with the ANC was dissatisfaction with the influence of the South African Communist Party, which in turn stemmed from more conservative economic ideas. For example, when the ANC had formally adopted the Freedom Charter as its programme in 1956, Sobukwe had dissented from the clauses referring to nationalization. The precise rationalization chosen to articulate this difference of view, however, set up a contradiction. If nationalization does not follow from a belief in liberating the nation from foreigners, nothing does. In time, therefore, the PAC came to adopt a more radical economic stance, a stance even more apparent in its modern successors, and given their opposition to collaboration with other race groups, a less pragmatic and conciliatory ideology, which created the sense of stronger militancy.

The ANC-PAC split now fostered a new wave of organized black unrest, as the two organizations were galvanized into action to out-

---

* The Gold Coast, for instance, the first black African colony to achieve independence in the decolonization era had only become the Republic of Ghana in 1957.

94

flank each other. 1960 was the year which saw their rivalry unleashing an unparalleled explosion of protest. In fact, 1960 was a very bad year for the Government altogether.

Its difficulties began virtually with the arrival of the New Year, for in early January there was a major riot, one of the worst the country had ever seen, in the black township of Cato Manor near Durban, with nine policemen being murdered after a liquor raid. Shortly after that, the British Prime Minister, Harold Macmillan, arrived in Cape Town at the end of a trip through Africa, and addressing the South African Parliament, gave notice that the countries of the world would not tolerate apartheid, and warned soberly that the direction South Africa was opting to follow would cause it to collide head-on with 'the winds of change' which were sweeping the continent. They were prophetic, but wasted, words. None the less, the full implications of what they had committed themselves to suddenly began to sink into white South Africa. There was no turning back, but the long, lonely years of ostracization unexpectedly opened up before them. Macmillan's words, pooh-poohed at surface level, struck deep, and sent a chill through white hearts.

Just as unsettled nerves began to calm, the force of Macmillan's message was dramatically brought home. The ANC had called for mass demonstrations against the Pass Laws at the end of March. On the 21st, to draw their thunder, the PAC called their own nationwide protest. At Sharpeville, a black township forty miles south of Johannesburg, a crowd of 20,000 without their passes offered themselves for arrest at the local police station. The officers on duty panicked: 69 black people were shot dead, many in the back, and 180 injured. A profound shockwave engulfed the country. Whites trembled, for they feared the start of a general uprising. The Sabre jets which screamed over the densely populated Witwatersrand as they swooped down to Sharpeville, the Saracen armoured cars which rumbled through the streets of the nearby town of Vereeniging only heightened the atmosphere of war. World protest erupted around South Africa's ears. Foreign capital took flight from the country, and the currency reserve was more than halved. The leader of the ANC, Chief Albert Luthuli, publicly burned his pass. On the day of the Sharpeville funerals, blacks all over the country stayed away from work. South Africa had never seen anything like it. Apartheid had met its first real challenge, and the trial of strength had come upon it unforeseen.

95

On 28 March, the government banned both the ANC and the PAC. 18,000 people were summarily arrested. As further riots and demonstrations throughout the country greeted this action, a State of Emergency was declared. White civilians were hastily conscripted into the Army. Black townships were sealed off, curfews were imposed, political literature was seized, and activists detained. A few days later a white man walked up to Dr Verwoerd as he was addressing the country's premier trade fair and shot him in the head.

Verwoerd survived, but black civil protest expired for an entire generation. For the massive wave of repression, the cordoning off of the townships, and the systematic sweeping of the black community silenced their collective voice, and the draconian powers which the Government was constantly to upgrade over the forthcoming years made sure it stayed that way for many years by creating a true police state. With lucratively paid informers riddling the townships, ordinary black people did the only thing they could: they kept their heads down and their mouths shut.

With the crisis over and the challenge successfully beaten off, Verwoerd took heart. The basic blueprint of segregation had now been turned into reality and triumphantly defended. The interference of Macmillan had highlighted the feeling that the time had come for the other fundamental requirement of Afrikaner nationalism to be met: the final severing of English South Africa from its increasingly remote defender on the opposite side of the world. The shock to whites during the recent emergency had had the effect of drawing them closer together, and memories of the Second World War were fading fast. On 6 October 1960 a referendum was held of white voters, in which they were asked whether or not they wished South Africa's remaining links with the British crown – in effect only the symbolic office of Governor-General – to be severed. Fifty-two per cent said yes. 31 May 1961 was set as the date for the establishment of the Republic of South Africa. Two months before it came about, Dr Verwoerd attended the Commonwealth Prime Ministers' Conference in London, and when it became clear that black Commonwealth leaders would quit the organization rather than allow an apartheid republic to remain inside it, he announced that South Africa would leave.

In truth this was the ultimate moment of victory for Afrikaner nationalism. After nearly two centuries of living with the British threat to their way of life, the deep desire to be free of the imperial shackle was finally to be realized. Six decades after the Boer War, the Afrikaners' heroic struggle was finally to be vindicated. The sweetness of the re-creation on an enlarged scale of the earlier Boer Republics was made more glorious still by the total severance from the Commonwealth. Cecil Rhodes, lying buried in mountains to the north of South Africa in a country which would bear his name only a little longer, would have turned in his grave at this destruction of the cornerstone of his imperial dream. Verwoerd returned to a hero's welcome at Johannesburg airport, named after Jan Smuts. As he addressed the cheering crowds, he may have reflected that he had finally stamped on all his enemies. For by his deed he had also irreversibly undone the Anglo-Afrikaans reconciliation Smuts had devoted his entire political life to achieving, and thereby crushed out the last vestiges of what Nationalists saw as *volksverraad* – the betrayal of the Afrikaner people. The celebration at Smuts's airport of the end of his vision was more thrilling to Afrikaners even than Republic Day itself. Indeed it was probably the happiest moment his people will ever know.

What a terrible irony there is in this. One can hardly fail to be moved by the tragedy of this endless shattering of great men's dreams. Shaka had forged a majestic kingdom such as Southern Africa had never seen before, a kingdom which had collapsed in the face of an almost unimaginable onslaught within half a century of his death. Kruger had fled the Republic which he had helped build, defend, and rule, to watch it die from his distant exile. Rhodes had expired believing he had established a British empire in Africa which would succeed in stretching from the Cape to Cairo. Within living memory of his death, it was turned to ashes. Hertzog ended his days in the contemplation of his own ruin and the cold comfort of the wilderness. Smuts, too, died a broken man. His fate – that of discovering in the final days of his mortal existence that the people he loved, for whom his entire life had been sacrificed, repudiated everything he stood for – was perhaps the cruellest of all. Happily he was present only in name when Verwoerd received his people's acclamation for the final act of desecration.

Speaking in his curious, high-pitched voice, the charismatic Verwoerd must himself have believed that he had somehow found a formula finally to make this recalcitrant country succumb to a man's will. As he stood in the octane-filled air alongside the tarmac on the

97

flat, open veld, he, and millions like him, believed white supremacy was now invincible. Little could he have known the terrible death that awaited him, and the even harsher destiny of becoming a pariah among his people within two decades of his demise, a destiny to be delivered him by the silent vigil of the 'kaffir boys', as black men were derogatorily known, whom he had condemned to purgatory, and for whom he believed no place could be found above 'certain forms of labour'. Perhaps, when the long conflict of South Africa's people is finally resolved, a man or woman will in the end see South Africa bow to their dream. Only a vision which brings justice to all can achieve this ultimate triumph – but whether it can be devised or whether, even then, the order of things will defeat it, only the future can tell us.

But in 1961 victory, rather than defeat, seemed Verwoerd's destiny. Not only had he presided over the final vanquishing of the British, black resistance to apartheid had been crushed. In fact it was not yet dead, but such was Verwoerd's power that the point of maximum danger had now been passed.

The ANC's Chief Luthuli was banished to Natal after the 1960 disturbances and also 'banned', which meant that nothing he had ever said or written could be publicly quoted. By this device he was rendered a non-person. Robert Sobukwe was sent to Robben Island, a fortress off Cape Town, where he was to remain for many years, before being released to die at home in Kimberley. In the ensuing power vacuum, black South Africa, rather than giving up, kept trying to find the way to break through white supremacy.

In that quest they were, for the moment, to fail, but the search was to produce the man who, though he would not be there to discover the secret, would, by his example, provide the rallying point which would ultimately unlock the hidden door of success. He was Nelson Mandela.

In March 1961 those black leaders who remained at large came together in Pietermaritzburg to reconsider their strategy. Mandela who, following the Defiance Campaign of the early 1950s, had been almost continuously banned, was able to be present as his latest banning order had just expired. In the decimation of their ranks after Sharpeville, he looked the most promising of the surviving activists. They elected him leader of something called the National Action Council. Having failed to shake white domination by civil disobedience, black South Africa now entrusted Mandela with spearheading a new constitutional initiative. Borrowing the imagery of post-Boer War South Africa, they called through Mandela for a new National Convention – this time between white and black, rather than white and white. They hoped thereby to negotiate peacefully a new and just dispensation for all South Africa's people.

The time was out of joint. Verwoerd, basking in the glow of the achievement of Afrikaner republicanism, did not even deign to reply. Had he but known, had white South Africa but known, that this was the last brief time of asking, their response might have been different. A time would come when history would reveal this had been the last possible moment in which white South Africa could have dictated the terms for the future and ensured a peaceful resolution of the country's deep malaise. But lulled by Afrikaner triumphalism into a false sense of security, the precious instant slipped through their fingers without them even realizing it.

Mandela was not the man to deny the obvious. He disappeared quietly into hiding and bade farewell to all prospect of peace. In the long history of South Africa it was no more than a second, but a second of the gravest significance. Black South Africa's protracted attempt to win concessions by non-violent means had always been doomed. In August 1961, without ritual or ceremony, and unannounced, it was laid to rest. Mandela, his close intimates, and, unknowing, black South Africa, resumed the path of their forefathers, and took up arms. It was the start of war, a long, drawn-out civil war in which thousands of South Africans would die and the country's future be changed utterly.

In November 1961 Mandela founded *Umkhonto we Sizwe*, the Spear of the Nation, an underground armed movement. Its leaders elected to go for a strategy of hitting instalations rather than of killing people. Sabotage was their tactic. Beginning on 16 December 1961, the anniversary of the Battle of Blood River, and continuing for the next two years, *Umkhonto* began bombing electricity pylons, post offices, Bantu Administration buildings, jails, and railway lines. They were later accused of a couple of hundred attacks, though only twenty were admitted. The precise scale of the operation may never be established.

At the same time, the ANC's political organization took itself into exile abroad. Under the leadership of Mandela's close friend and legal partner, Oliver Tambo, who came from the same region of South Africa as Mandela, the Transkei, offices were set up in

99

London and various African capitals. Over time, meeting rejection from Western governments, a close financial and diplomatic relationship was developed with the Soviet Union and the Eastern bloc. In January 1962 Mandela slipped the country and toured the world with Tambo as they planned the foundation of the new operation. Among those he met were Hugh Gaitskell, Jo Grimond, Julius Nyerere, and Kenneth Kaunda. It was a brief taste of freedom. After six months he returned to South Africa, and was quickly re-arrested. He was now forty-four and it was to be the start of a long confinement. He joined other black activists on the bleak, windswept Robben Island, just visible from the wealthy white suburbs lining Cape Town's beaches. There he was thrown together again with Robert Sobukwe, and we are told that, as they broke stones together during many years of hard labour, they rediscovered the friendship and unity which political life had temporarily severed.

Sobukwe's PAC went on without him to draw the same lessons as the ANC, and it followed the same route. In 1962, PAC elements set up an armed underground organization. Its name, *Poqo,* is an interesting example of how men from different worlds but in similar circumstances see themselves in the same way. It meant almost exactly the same as the Irish phrase *Sinn Fein* – ourselves alone. *Poqo* differed from *Umkhonto* in that it saw its role as being to foment insurrection and accepted the need to kill. In that way it had much more in common with the Kenyan *Mau Mau*. It was implicated in violent riots in the town of Paarl in the Cape, during which eleven policemen and police informers were murdered – a noteworthy portent of the future. It also set up hit-squads which failed to assassinate the Government-installed chief of the Transkei 'homeland', Kaiser Matanzima, and inspired considerable fear among whites when it murdered a group of white workers at the Mbashe River in the Cape in February 1963.

The PAC also set up an external operation. With Sobukwe in prison, its acting leader, Potlako Leballo, went into exile and supervized the creation of an overseas political presence. With the Eastern bloc supporting the ANC, its main protector was Communist China.

The activities of *Umkhonto* and *Poqo* alarmed white South Africa, but having contained the Sharpeville wave of unrest, the Government little doubted its capacity to deal with these new threats. They were right. Under the tough-minded guidance of Verwoerd's new

Minister of Justice, no less a person than the former *Ossewabrandwag* general, B. J. Vorster, the police took swingeing powers to break the movements. It was, indeed, the period when South Africa's police state began to move into the phase of greatest control over all South African life. Publications, theatre, entertainment, the radio – all were brought under the strictest scrutiny. White military service was extended. House arrest was introduced, with an elderly white liberal, Mrs Helen Joseph, being the first to be made an example of. The right of the police to detain people for up to 90 days in solitary confinement and without charge was introduced, to be extended in 1965 to 180 days. Sabotage and terrorism were legally defined so as to give the police power to detain and interrogate pretty much whom they pleased. In 1963 more than 3,500 people were detained, and many of them brutally tortured. One who died while in police custody was accorded the added distinction of being 'banned' after his death, in order to prevent statements he had made when alive from being quoted. By these means, the first modern foray into armed resistance was fairly easily crushed, and white South Africa reassured.

The Government's greatest success was in smashing *Umkhonto*'s headquarters on a farm in Rivonia, near Johannesburg and arresting all the major figures who had continued its work without Mandela, most prominent among them being Walter Sisulu. In 1964, Mandela, who was in prison for inciting strikes and travelling without valid documents, was brought back from Robben Island to stand trial with the others for sabotage. In the *Voortrekker* capital of Pretoria, he, one white man, and seven other black men were found guilty and sentenced to life imprisonment. Mandela's wife, Winnie, was not there to see it. She had been restricted to the municipal area of Johannesburg. Outside the court women carried a banner which said: NO TEARS: OUR FUTURE IS BRIGHT. Mandela himself made the following statement to the court:

> During my lifetime I have dedicated myself to this struggle of the African people. I have fought against white domination, and I have fought against black domination. I have cherished the ideal of a democratic and free society in which all persons live together in harmony and with equal opportunities. It is an ideal which I hope to live for and to achieve. But if needs be it is an ideal for which I am prepared to die.

He went back to Robben Island to serve out his life sentence.

Later the same year, the police infiltrated the South Africa Communist Party, which had continued to function secretly, and arrested its remaining leaders. Among them was Bram Fischer, one of the most distinguished Afrikaner advocates, who had recently defended Mandela at his trial. Fischer represented the cream of Afrikanerdom and was the son of a Judge-President of the old Orange Free State Republic. His exposure as a Communist dedicated to the overthrow of white rule was more shocking to white South Africa than *Umkhonto*'s conspiracy. To add insult to injury he slipped bail and, with the entire nation's police force looking for him, continued to live in the suburbs of Johannesburg under the ironic name of Mr Black. In November 1965 he was finally discovered and imprisoned. There, according to Hugh Lewin, a white political prisoner, the peculiar bitterness he inspired in fellow-whites caused him to be singled out for special punishment by the Afrikaner guards, punishment he bore uncomplainingly. A few weeks before he died of cancer in 1975, he was released into the custody of his family. After his cremation, the authorities insisted that his ashes be returned to them on the grounds that they were state property. Afrikanerdom, riding high on the wave of victory, was not in a mood to be reminded of darker questions. There was to be no mercy for traitors to the cause. Vengeance was theirs.*

By the mid-1960s their triumph was complete. The first 'Bantustan' – the Transkei – had received limited self-government in 1963. Forced resettlements of black people to their 'homelands' began to occur regularly. The South African economy had recovered from the aftermath of Sharpeville and was now entering a period of high growth, rapid expansion, and soaring living standards for whites. The spectre of black resistance had apparently been exorcized. Apartheid was working better than anyone could have imagined. White and black children were growing up for whom it seemed the natural order of things. Nearly everyone forgot there had ever been any other way of life; nearly everyone believed it could not but be so for all the future.

In the midst of this white sunshine, a bolt of lightning struck

---

* Even the National Party could not bury legends though. Such was the martyrdom of Fischer, that he was later immortalized in a fictional account of his daughter's experience during the long travail of his imprisonment – the prize-winning novel by Nadine Gordimer, *Kruger's Daughter.*

without warning. The creator and presiding genius of apartheid, Hendrik Verwoerd was gruesomely stabbed to death by a deranged Parliamentary messenger as he sat at his desk in the House of Assembly arranging his Order Papers in September 1966. Afrikaners carried his blood-spattered corpse to its final resting-place in Heroes' Acre in Pretoria. Their grief was great, but they had as yet not understood the true magnitude of their loss.

No act in South Africa's history is capable of yielding a more complete symbolism than Verwoerd's sudden extinction by an assassin. Seated in the very heart of white power, at the very pinnacle of his success, he was done to death when and where he least expected it, by a man in whose veins white and black blood ran together, for it later turned out that this employee of an all-white institution had actually had a black mother. This irony of apartheid paled by comparison, though, beside the greater significance of the act. For, in retrospect, it has become clear that Verwoerdian apartheid – that apparently invincible and immutable way of life – was a fragile child, destined to die after a short and violent existence. It had barely reached adolescence when its progenitor was struck down. With no other man can an entire social and political system be so closely identified. His vision, his force, had driven history remorselessly forward to give apartheid its breathing space. Probably not even he could have staved off the inevitability of its death. But without his extraordinary determination, his successors certainly could not. Apartheid, in other words, though it might not have survived with him, was inevitably doomed without him. In the insane fortress he had created, only a madman could have slipped through the barricades to kill him; only a madman could thus have dealt the blow which ensured the demise of his brain-child.

When they buried Verwoerd, they were burying his apartheid also. For although nearly everyone had forgotten other ways of life, although nearly everyone believed it would endure long into the future, there were men he had consigned to an outcrop of land on the southernmost edge of the continent who bore within them the memory of another world, and the unextinguished hope of a different future. Impotent then, their moment would come, when new generations looked back and rediscovered their message.

Verwoerd had thought that he had laid the ghost of black nationalism to rest. Like everyone he made mistakes, and that was surely his greatest.

7

SOWETO

By the time Verwoerd died in the mid-1960s, South Africa was a very different country from the one the Gesuiwerde National Party had taken control of in 1948. Segregation had, of course, been elevated from a customary way of life to a thoroughgoing national organizing principle, codified, elaborated in every aspect of daily existence, and ruthlessly enforced by the power of the law and the security forces. But, deeper than this, the economic and social complexion of South Africa had altered fundamentally too.

Before 1948, South Africa had been a rural country with a growing urban population concentrated around mining and heavy industry. Secondary industry had still been in its youth, and commerce the preserve of a small number of people. Some – mainly English-speaking whites – had been very rich. The mass of Afrikaners and the non-white peoples had still been emerging from their rural traditions, and were generally poor.

By the mid-1960s South Africa had become much more of an urban society. Spurred by the necessity for self-reliance during the war, by the growing wealth its mineral deposits brought it, and by the expansion of world trade and the improvement of communications after the war, the country had seen a vast burgeoning of industry and commerce, of services and the professions. It was now much more balanced as between town and country, with the towns still expanding. Most Afrikaners had now established themselves in urban areas. There, bolstered at first by employment in para-statal organizations which an Afrikaner government had opened up for them, they had begun to move out into industry and commerce, to develop, if you will, a distinct middle class. Their protected position combined with very rapid economic growth had seen their living standards soar, so that whites as a whole had come to enjoy one of the most privileged lifestyles in the whole world.

The needs of the South African economy had meant that despite the Government's attempts to restrict the number of blacks in urban areas, they had continued to flock there. By the mid-1960s almost as many were living in towns and cities as on the land. Though held down by apartheid, their living standard, too, had risen, though it remained a fraction of whites'.

Education had vastly improved, as a modern economy required. Whites were near-universally literate; black education, though much worse, had also produced a literate urban black population. Urban South Africa, in particular, through the growth of trade, travel, and communications, had become tied in to a large extent to the ideas and values of the Western world.

In a society subject to such a strong dynamic, apartheid, a regressive or, at best, rigidifying force, began to run counter to the direction of development. The stresses and strains of this contradiction were not yet clear, but were slowly surfacing. This came on top of the profound subterranean distress that apartheid, or to be more precise racism, was inflicting, not only on the non-white peoples of the country, but on the whites themselves. South Africa, for centuries a land with a rough, crude, and brutal frontier culture, had long known a harsh way of life, full of menace and violence. Urbanization tends also to create unhappy conditions of turmoil and human collision. But apartheid South Africa in the mid-1960s, even allowing for these factors, displayed a quite astoundingly high level of white neurosis when compared with similar societies like the United States or Australia. White South Africa, indeed, filled the record books with unenviable attainments: they were the highest spirit drinkers in the world; the level of drunkenness and alcoholism* was exceptionally high; white rates for divorce, wife-beating, murder, suicide, general violence and crime, drug addiction, road fatalities, and child-battering were all among the worst in the world. No one is qualified to pronounce on why this should have been and, indeed,

---

* As recently as 1981, a survey conducted at ten o'clock on a Saturday of white drivers in the tiny Transvaal town of Naboomspruit disclosed that two-thirds of all those examined exceeded the legal limit of permitted alcohol in the bloodstream. This was not, in fact, ten o'clock at night – but ten o'clock in the morning.

continues to be so. But in a country where a comparatively small minority is suppressing a much larger majority by systematic force and cruelty, where they live besieged by hatred and resentment, it can be no accident that such an appalling toll is visited on their psyches. Nor was this limited to whites: black South Africans, corralled in their festering ghettoes, frustrated and impotent to change their condition, were tearing themselves apart in similar ways: through drunkenness, physical violence, and crime. Soweto, for example, the largest urban centre in South Africa and a city in its own right of nearly 2 million, was one of the most dangerous places in the whole of South Africa, where marauding bands of *tsotsis*, or gangsters, would lie in wait to attack people as they came home on Fridays with their weekly earnings, and where the murder toll on any given weekend – usually between twenty and thirty – was the equivalent for, say several weeks in the whole of the United Kingdom

This deep malaise, then, combined with economic development, modernization, education, and exposure to outside values, was bringing apartheid into increasing conflict with the changing realities of South African life, and as it did so, many individuals began to articulate some of the underlying tensions. This was true within both the white and the black communities, and as is natural, an important vanguard was the young.

In the 1960s, young urban Afrikaners began to rebel against the conservatism and, to some extent, the racism of their elders. The process was strongly reflected in literature, particularly, and the significance of this was not lost on a people whose political identity had itself grown out of a linguistic and cultural movement. One of the brightest stars of the Afrikaner literary firmament was a young poet Breyten Breytenbach. When he left South Africa and married a Vietnamese princess in Paris, a woman regarded in South Africa as black, it sent shockwaves through the entire community.* Throughout the 1960s, many other young Afrikaners also began articulating their opposition to the prevailing ethos through literature and the theatre, and the movement became known as *Die Sestigers* (People of the Sixties).

---

* Later, in the 1970s, he went on to join the ANC's underground military wing and was captured when he returned to South Africa in disguise. He was sentenced to seven years' imprisonment and later wrote an eloquent account of the mental torment of a privileged Afrikaner seeking to express dissent, and of his imprisonment (see *Bibliography*).

The stirrings of unease which these intellectuals were giving voice to were felt within the political establishment, too. The government, now led by John Vorster, began to bend the rules of apartheid at its fringes. In doing so they were usually prompted by larger concerns of state, but they would not have done so had the climate not permitted it. Vorster, for instance, in seeking to breaking South Africa's growing diplomatic isolation, found a black African leader willing to do business with him in the person of Malawi's Dr Hastings Banda. The carrot of such a political prize overcame inhibitions, and Vorster met Banda and allowed a black Malawian diplomat to be accredited to Pretoria. Similarly, as international sports boycotts began to bite, Vorster succumbed to pressure from South African sporting bodies to allow a few halting experiments in mixed-race sport. These were tiny concessions, but in a system which relied so heavily on ideological purity, they were seen as serious deviations. Most importantly, so-called petty apartheid – like separate parks or park benches, shop entrances and lifts – began to be regularly infringed, and the Government at first turned a blind eye to it, and later began specifically to endorse it.

This created a certain muted conflict within Afrikanerdom, with die-hards beginning to resist. Two tendencies became identified at either end of the Afrikaner spectrum: the *verkramptes* and the *verligtes*, or the reactionaries and the enlightened. The institutions of Afrikanerdom, which had been instrumental in promoting Afrikaners to positions of influence and power in South Africa, reflected the strains and became subject to systematic wrangling. In some cases, open warfare broke out as, for instance, in the battle to retain control of the *Akademie vir Wetenskap en Kuns* (the Academy of Arts and Sciences). One should not overemphasize the divisions; they were still incipient and operating at the margins. But they reflected a growing divergence which was real enough. Vorster himself, though no *verligte* by instinct, was sufficiently impressed with the needs of *realpolitik* to throw his weight behind this group. Tension grew within the Cabinet itself and came to a head in 1968 when the Minister of Health, Albert Hertzog – son of Barry Hertzog – was dismissed. He went on to set up his own political party in 1969, the *Herstigte Nasionale Party* (HNP), or Re-Established National Party. It saw itself as the torch-bearer of true Verwoerdian orthodoxy and, for a while, the shades of Afrikaner political history, especially with the name Hertzog echoing down the decades, sent shivers of anxiety through the political establishment. The HNP remained very much a tiny splinter group, however, and failed to get a single MP elected, until, that is, very different circumstances came to prevail in the mid-1980s. None the less, the spectre of splinter groups breaking away and remaining in the wilderness only to hijack the body of Afrikanerdom later continued to stalk the land.

Despite the growth of a *verligte* trend, and to some extent to stop *verkramptes* deserting the Government, it continued to push ahead with the fundamentals of apartheid, even if it was prepared to concede on some minor details. In 1968, at a time when the Government had 126 seats in Parliament compared with the anti-apartheid Progressive Party's one, it passed a bill to outlaw cross-racial political contact – the richly-named Prevention of Political Interference Act – so as to debar the still-enfranchized Cape Coloureds from lending support to the Progressives, and soon after ended all political representation for Coloureds in the South African Parliament. From 1970 onwards black people were systematically stripped of their 'South African' citizenship and designated as members of whichever 'homeland' the state decided they belonged to. The 'homelands' in turn were coaxed along the road to self-government, this being a necessary requirement if it was to be claimed that blacks had their own – though separate – political rights. By 1972 the Ciskei, KwaZulu, Bophuthatswana, and Lebowa had all joined the Transkei in being accorded nominal self-government, and in 1976 the Transkei became the first of these to be granted 'independence' – an independence which hardly anyone in the world recognized as such.

Repression of dissent, of which, as Minister of Justice, Mr Vorster had shown himself a virtuoso exponent, continued unabated too. Committees of inquiry were appointed to 'investigate' the activities of dissident white student organizations, theological bodies, and research institutions. The Government took powers to deem any such body an 'affected organization', which prevented them from receiving funds from abroad and subjected them to other restrictions. These measures were particularly aimed at undermining the support they gave to political prisoners' families.

None the less, the spirit of change was abroad, and nothing dramatized this as clearly as the remarkable results of the 1974 general election, when the long-beleaguered Progressive Party finally ended its thirteen years of Parliamentary representation by the lone figure

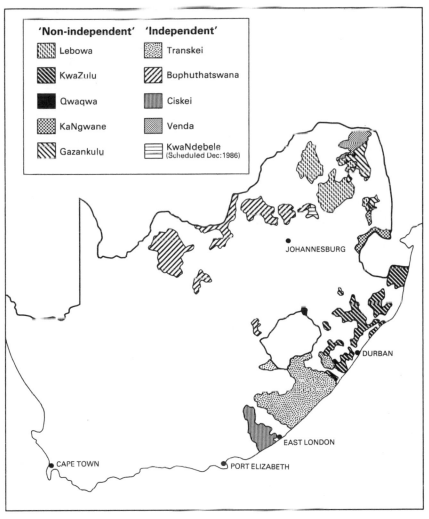

'Non-independent' **'Independent'**

Lebowa   Transkei

KwaZulu   Bophuthatswana

Qwaqwa   Ciskei

KaNgwane   Venda

Gazankulu   KwaNdebele
(Scheduled Dec:1986)

JOHANNESBURG

DURBAN

EAST LONDON

CAPE TOWN

PORT ELIZABETH

Black 'homelands'

of Mrs Helen Suzman, with the capture of an additional six seats. This, of course, was a still tiny presence, but although the seats were won in predominantly English-speaking areas, it was clear many Afrikaners had voted for this anti-apartheid party. In a country where attachment to the National Party had become synonymous with loyalty to the tribe, it was an unmistakable indication of much deeper changes.

Much more important than any of this, however, were the profound changes taking place among black people. In the dusty, fermenting urban townships, where the coal-fires in thousands upon thousands of powerless homesteads choked the air day and night, a new generation of young people had come of age. Better educated than their parents, aware of themselves as part of a broader world beyond South Africa, and growing up at a time of economic development in which the gap between whites and blacks was ever more starkly dramatized, the cream were sent for higher education to the 'university colleges' of the Bantustans. There, cut off from the local people by their background and culture, they were subjected to the iron discipline of white principals who, in what were rated as low status posts, were drawn from some of the least sophisticated and most obscurantist Afrikaans teaching circles.

Bantu Education, conceived by Dr Verwoerd as a means of bringing home to black youngsters the impossibility of their being integrated into white society, had, in that respect, precisely the effect he intended. These young black people, unlike their parents, had never known a time in which black people might be seduced into believing that slow integration and a progressive mitigation of their condition might be possible. Verwoerdian apartheid precluded any illusions of that kind. But in a more crucial respect, Bantu Education not only failed – it sowed dragons' teeth. Young blacks growing up in the changed conditions of the late 1960s and early 1970s could not fail to notice that they were the intellectual and moral equals of their white fellow-citizens, and their awareness of political currents abroad emphasizing the injustice of racism would have suggested this to them if they had. Under these circumstances they were considerably less suggestible to the idea of accepting the menial role Bantu Education envisaged for them. As they were brought together in remote and alien rural areas and as they chafed under the benighted regime of Bantustan institutions, their colleges became, not schools for subjugation but for revolt.

110

They evolved, in these tribalistic outposts, an ethos which was profoundly subversive to white power: black power. They called it the Black Consciousness Movement – and apartheid was its begettor. Black Consciousness was not an organization; it was a philosophy and a way of looking at the world, and it was taken back from the 'university colleges' to young blacks in townships all over South Africa. It spread down from older students to infuse their younger brothers and sisters. It became the outlook of an entire generation.

Black Consciousness defined blacks as anyone who was not white. In that, and in other ways, it owed more to the 'Africanist' strain of black political thinking than to multiracialism, but the definition did include Coloureds and Indians. It did not see itself as racist, but believed people should enjoy equal rights as individuals and not by virtue of belonging to a group. Multiracialism was seen as co-operation between racial groups, and was not therefore acceptable. It believed whites were too enmeshed in the system to be reliable allies. Blacks were on their own in the fight. Perhaps its greatest contribution to black politics was to engender among millions a new, powerful, passionate and, above all, confident sense of black identity. It even gave South Africa an African name, Azania, and it saw blackness as something to be proud of, to be defiant about – and to fight for. Solidarity with each other, self-reliance in the face of a ruthless enemy: these were its teachings.

The particular circumstance which gave rise to the movement was growing dissatisfaction among black students at their treatment within the National Union of South African Students (NUSAS), a body dominated by English-speaking white students and which was, in fact, fiercely opposed to apartheid. But black students, being smaller in number and less well organized, felt that they, the victims of apartheid, were not getting a proper look-in. The sense of grievance was heightened by the realities of South African life. Black students attending conferences, for example, would have to travel back late at night to outlying townships while white students had comfortable quarters nearby. Initially, black students began organizing themselves as a caucus. As they grew more confident, and angry, they asked themselves why they should bother to stay. Eventually they withdrew completely and, in December 1968, set up an alternative South African Students Organization (SASO). Its first president was a young black intellectual from near East London called Steve Biko.

111

The circumstances which gave rise to Black Consciousness, however, were in a sense unimportant. It was bound to be the case that
in an apartheid society, the barriers between black and white were
too great to provide an effective alliance. It should be seen, therefore, as an inevitable, and necessary, response if black people were
to begin anew to assert themselves.

Although Black Consciousness was not an organization *per se*, it
spawned a number of interlocking bodies and offshoots. SASO was
the first of them, and it began to set up literacy campaigns, *ad hoc*
health services, and 'black studies' groups. By 1972 a Black People's
Convention (BPC) had been established as an umbrella political
body both to co-ordinate the growing number of Black Consciousness groups and to act as a catalyst for the black community as a
whole. The interweaving of organizations gave young blacks a certain defence against detection and banning; it also gave them an enormously valuable experience of organizing themselves. In their
work, they effectively re-educated their whole generation, and
schools, both primary and high, became imbued with Black Consciousness from top to bottom.

Events moved rapidly. In 1972 Black Consciousness gave rise to a
spate of student protests all over South Africa, though as yet on a
fairly small scale. By now black workers in a South African economy
which was increasingly prosperous and increasingly dependent on
them, began to flex their industrial muscle. *De facto* black unions –
not legally recognized, but not illegal either – began to grow, though
there was little direct relationship between this and Black Consciousness. 1973 was a year which saw black industrial militancy on
a scale unprecedented for many decades, with many wildcat strikes.
As black workers began to press for higher wages and better conditions, it put heart into the students. In 1974 the Portuguese dic-
tatorship of Salazar's successor, Marcello Caetano, was overthrown
by a military coup and guerrilla armies in the nearby Portuguese
colonies of Angola and Mozambique reached the climax of their
long, and increasingly successful, push against the Portuguese colonizers. Just as it was no accident that Black Consciousness in South
Africa followed in the wake of Black Power in the United States, so
the students were strongly influenced by these external developments. Demonstrations were held in many parts of South Africa to

* Frelimo was the name of the Mozambican guerrilla movement which subsequently became the country's first independent government under Samora Machel.

(20) 21 March 1960. Sharpeville

(21) 20 March 1961. Dr Verwoerd arrives back triumphantly from London after ending South Africa's membership of the Commonwealth. He is greeted by the head of the Army

(22) B.J. Vorster, 1977

(23) P.W. Botha, shortly after becoming
Prime Minister, 1978

(24) Soweto, 16 June 1976. Note the thousands behind

(25) Nelson Mandela on Robben Island   (26) Chief Gatsha Buthelezi

(27) Police action outside the UDF's Johannesburg headquarters, May 1985

(28) Young boys in Daduza dance round the burning car of a suspected informer, 1985

(29) A lone resident of the Cape Town squatter camp, Crossroads, contemplates the devastation after days of communal fighting, June 1986

express solidarity – the 'Viva Frelimo!' rallies.* In 1975 and 1976, South Africa invaded Angola to try and prevent the Marxist Popular Movement for the Liberation of Angola, the MPLA, from taking power there, but had to withdraw when no Western powers would support them. This, too, encouraged the young students. The conditions were right for an eruption, only a trigger was needed.

It came on the morning of 16 June 1976. Several thousand black students in Soweto took to the streets to protest against being taught in Afrikaans, the language of the oppressor. The police confronted them, opened fire – and the fuse was lit. Four days of rioting followed. An official death toll of 176 was admitted, and at least 1,800 were injured. An orgy of destruction was unleashed in many townships. Schools, Bantu administration offices, beer halls, hostels, and police vehicles were set on fire. Buses and railway lines were destroyed. The violence spread. Within a few weeks the Western Cape was engulfed, and Coloured students were particularly conspicuous there. The participation of this community was a wholly new development in South Africa, but given the Nationalist Party's determined assault on their traditional rights, it was hardly surprising they should identify themselves with black youngsters.

For many months the unrest ebbed and flowed. The Eastern Cape, Biko's home ground, became involved, but throughout, Soweto continued to be the prime focus. Not only was it the most populous black town in South Africa, but its population was the most sophisticated. At the same time it was little better than a slum: hardly any part of it had electricity; its roads were mainly untarred; extraordinary congestion and the lack of anything approximating adequate housing created appalling hardship. The Soweto Students Representative Council (SSRC), linked to SASO and another student umbrella body, the South African Students Movement, and under the effective leadership of Tsietsi Mashanini who had been an important figure in the June protests, proved particularly adept at dodging in and out of sight, providing continuing co-ordination and evading the police.

The police at first responded with brute force. The daily running battles caused the casualty figures to soar. The final death toll will never be known. Certainly at least 700 died; it was probably in excess of 1,000. Hundreds of millions of pounds worth of damage was done. As tough policing began to seem increasingly counterproductive, the security forces began to withdraw, making it their priority to contain the violence in the townships and to prevent it from spreading to 'white' areas. The isolation of black residential 'locations' from towns and cities helped. Periodic forays were made into the townships to pick up and arrest whomever they could find, but by and large they began to confine themselves to heavily entrenched roadblocks on all access roads.

Most older blacks kept out of the unrest. But some did try and mediate between the authorities and the students. Some also tried to plead with the Government for improved conditions. This provided a small, but important, number of older blacks with experience of organization too. The Black Parents' Association, heavily focused on Soweto but with branches elsewhere, was a key group. In Soweto older blacks spontaneously formed a committee to represent their views to the state. It was called the Soweto Committee of Ten and was headed by a charismatic doctor whose surgery regularly overflowed with the dead or wounded, Dr Ntatho Motlana, a man who, with his erudition, BMW and car-stereo playing Bach, would, in other societies, have been a highly valued citizen, but who, in South Africa, found his pleas falling on deaf ears and closed minds.

Many parents, however, were deeply perturbed by what was happening. When the students tried to organize stay-at-homes, or mini-general strikes, parents at first responded, but became anxious about their livelihoods and so, increasingly resistant. A mood of counteraction began to make itself felt.

The students, now subject to an increasing decimation of their ranks, through death or injury, through police detentions, and through the flight into exile of many of those being hunted, found it hard to sustain the momentum. The unrest began to die down for longer periods, and when it broke out again it was less intense and lasted a shorter time. An important part was played in accelerating this process of attrition by migrant workers, most notably in Soweto. Brought from rural areas on limited contracts and segregated from permanent township-dwellers in fenced-off all-male barracks, they had little in common with the students, and when the students tried to prevent them from working – cutting off the valuable earnings they sent home to keep their wives and children alive – they went on the rampage against the students. Many of them, though by no means all, were Zulu. Since the leader of KwaZulu – the Zulu 'homeland' – Chief Gatsha Buthelezi, had always occupied a somewhat ambiguous position, being a paid employee of Pretoria but a man

114

who remained critical of apartheid, this gave rise to the suspicion that he was wielding his influence over the migrant workers to do the Government's work for them. It is a charge which is hard to sustain, but it poisoned relations between him and urban radicals for the future.

Gradually, then, the steam went out of the unrest. By mid-1977 it was more or less over. It had never been a rebellion precisely, since it had been a children's insurrection only. This, in the end, was its undoing. The movement had not built links with the broader black community and received no active support from it. Indeed, it came increasingly into conflict with it. The network of organizational structures provided a measure of leadership continuity but they were still too few in number and too flimsily based to be able to withstand the assaults inflicted on them. In the end, they became isolated, weak, and exposed.

Once it became clear to the Government that the movement was flagging, they moved in. In September 1977 Biko, its major figure, was arrested and during interrogation was beaten senseless by the police. Manacled and naked, he was driven in freezing temperatures in the back of a Land-Rover 800 miles to Pretoria. There he died in police custody. The Minister of Justice, Police, and Prisons, Mr Jimmy Kruger said of his death: '*Dit laat my koud.*' The precise meaning of the word *koud* in this context has been interpreted less cruelly by the man who uttered it, but a reasonable man could be forgiven for taking it in its normal sense: 'It leaves me cold.' Twenty-two people had already died in police custody, several of them having apparently pushed themselves voluntarily out of the tenth-floor window of John Vorster Square, the security police headquarters in Johannesburg, appropriately named after their mentor. Despite a world outcry and an inquest which though it exonerated the police, provided evidence of sickening brutality, many more have since died at their hands.

The following month, Mr Kruger banned twenty Black Consciousness organizations, including SASO and the BPC, and shut down two black newspapers, as well as banning Mr Donald Woods, an East London newspaper editor who had written favourably of Biko. Scores of activists still at large were detained. It was the end of Black Consciousness, at least in that manifestation. Its spirit still lives on, as we shall see, but in a new guise, and it remains today a minority attachment, though this could change.

115

Whatever the future, Black Consciousness played its part in changing the course of South African history. It broke the silence of black South Africa, which had last spoken politically in the early 1960s. It provided models of organization and rebellion whose implications were to be studied and which were to be implemented again in modified form in the future. Above all, it brought to adulthood a new generation of black South Africans, people who believed in their own worth and their intrinsic right to justice, people who had seen white power taken on and dented, if not dislodged, and people who had finally sloughed off all sense of inferiority. It had also given them a taste of battle, whetted their appetites, and hardened their mettle. It is thought by those unfamiliar with South Africa that the spine-chilling sentiments recently articulated by young blacks on the world's television networks are a new phenomenon. It is not so: even in 1976, twelve-year old boys were telling foreign journalists: 'We know what we are up against. This is the most powerful army in Africa. Tens of thousands of us will have to die to break its power. But we are prepared for that.'

It is the horrific and grim truth that in apartheid South Africa, a political revolution could only be made when not just groups of individuals, but whole peoples, thought in these terms. Black Consciousness enabled that precondition to be met. It liberated black South Africans psychologically and gave them the stomach for sacrifice.

Soweto was the phoney war. The next generation of young blacks would seek liberation of a more fundamental kind, and unleash the *blitzkrieg* which would start the real war.

8
WHITE FRAGMENTATION AND REFORMISM

Although Black Consciousness and the Soweto protests had a profound impact on black South Africans, white South Africans were also touched in a way that was far deeper than they realized. Of course, they saw the crushing of the unrest and the decimation of the movement as a victory for the white-controlled security forces, and for themselves in general. But behind the bravado, the shockwave had started a reverberation which was to shake the foundations of their power.

For sixteen long years, there had been no protest of any significance against apartheid from ordinary black civilians. Soweto broke the silence. The overwhelming majority of white South Africans had been lulled into believing that however unhappy blacks said they were, they could not really be that discontented, since they never complained openly. White South Africa had begun to believe that black protestations were largely rhetoric and that, more fundamentally, they were not sincere. Our blacks, as they had told anyone prepared to listen, knew which side their bread was buttered on, and were really quite happy.

Soweto put an end to that illusion and demonstrated beyond dispute that this was not so. It must be remembered that all of white South Africa, including even the *Sestiger* generation, despite their muted dissidence, had long been screened from the routine brutality of apartheid, carried out in their name behind closed doors, or in the black townships carefully removed from where they might pass by. All whites knew about it, yet because it had never intruded into their lives, they had never really had to imagine the reality of it. They had never come face to face with real black anger either. Now they had, and it began to make an impression.

The orgy of violence, killing, and destruction shocked them profoundly – and frightened them. Because there were now so many whites better educated than their parents, more affluent, better travelled, and more in touch with the values of the broader Western world, they were also more disposed to take notice. Many began to realize that they had never even seen the inside of a township; that they had absolutely no idea of what was going on in the black heads all around them. This had all been perfectly natural before and not something they had ever questioned. With Soweto it began to change.

But Soweto was worrying in another way too. Previous protests in South Africa had been short-lived affairs: indeed, they had seldom lasted a day. But Soweto had been quite different. It had initiated a wave of unrest which had lasted more than a year, something quite unparalleled in contemporary white experience. It had encompassed widely separated parts of the country. It had produced a situation in which the security forces had felt it prudent to withdraw for long periods, leaving the townships, in effect, in the hands of the mobs. It produced not inconsiderable economic disruption. It had forced political changes, like abandoning the teaching of Afrikaans in black schools. Neither Sharpeville, nor all the rumblings from *Umkhonto we Sizwe* and *Poqo*, had achieved anything like it.

Not many whites were prepared to admit it to themselves – and fewer still knew what to do about it – but the message was clear: blacks had demonstrated not only their anger, but their capacity to act on it. The turbulence had been brought to an end, but it had been far worse than anyone had expected. If black youngsters, largely unsupported by their parents, could achieve this, what might black South Africa as a whole be capable of ? The implications were far-reaching indeed.

There was one other aspect to the disturbances which white South Africa had found particularly alarming: the support given to the youngsters by the Coloureds. The Afrikaners, when carried along on the wave of Nationalistic triumphalism in the early 1950s, had been implacable in their determination to strip the Coloureds of their entrenched rights. They had known, buried deep within their inner selves, that the Coloureds were their own half-brothers, linked to them by blood, language, a shared culture, and a long common experience. Afrikaner history – the Great Trek, the Boer War, the erection of apartheid itself – bears repeated witness to a profound

118

longing in their soul for uncompromising purism. The Afrikaners, when once they have embarked on a particular course of action, want to pursue it utterly. This cast of mind grows out of their history. Their ferocious attachment to their identity as a people has ensured their success as individuals, but it has been achieved at a price. Afrikaner nationalism, like all nationalisms, must tell half-truths. It must distort and bend reality; it must attribute false motives and passions to other people; it must reinterpret experience and over-simplify. This is, perhaps, rational, for the Afrikaners' experience of compromise has frequently seemed to threaten their survival. The longing for purism is both an attempt to suppress the voice of inner doubt, which, if unstilled, would unravel their belief in themselves, and also a way of avoiding the shoddy compromises life throws up and which most other people have to make, but which the Afrikaners believe would be their undoing.

In constructing modern apartheid, the Afrikaners had felt the need to pursue the goal of racial segregation down to the last jot and tittle. Any messy inconsistencies would have undermined its ideological integrity, and left room for back-tracking. So they had executed the disenfranchizement of the Coloureds with a vengeance. And in doing so they had been motivated by the special need to deny that these people with brown skins were indeed their own kith and kin. Soweto proved that even under apartheid, people never forget the truth.

Afrikaners were horrified and outraged by the support the Coloureds had given the young blacks. Suddenly, lifelong Nationalists were heard to murmur perhaps it had been a mistake to disenfranchize the Coloureds in quite the way they had. The Afrikaans press and cultural institutions began to remind themselves of their historic relationship with the Coloureds. There was a practical political point to this, too. Coloureds, having occupied an intermediate position between whites and blacks, had always been better educated than the blacks, and consequently more skilled, with greater experience of organization and leadership. It was clear to the whites that the Coloureds could prove formidable enemies – and formidable allies for black South Africa.

However the ordinary white voters tried to shut their eyes to the lessons of Soweto, the Government of the day could not afford to do so. Even before the dust had finally settled, they began to try and find ways of dealing with the long-term threat. As far as the blacks were concerned, the Government began by making a few cosmetic changes which were designed to show a new spirit of goodwill. The hated Ministry of Bantu Affairs, whose Bantu Administration Boards had been a particular target of the rioters, was renamed the Ministry of Plural Relations. The right-wing *verkrampte*, M. C. Botha, who had presided over this key ministry was hastily ejected, and Connie Mulder, a *verkrampte* who had changed his colours, was installed in his place. Dr Mulder went out of his way to meet with Soweto community leaders who were clearly shown a new face of Afrikanerdom, for he adopted a new, markedly more counciliatory, attitude towards them, listening attentively to their complaints and promising he would investigate them sympathetically. Recognizing perhaps that many black grievances stemmed from the appalling material conditions in the townships, the Government pledged itself to bringing electricity to all of Soweto and to the general improvement of facilities.

As far as the Coloureds were concerned, the Government came up with a plan masterminded by the leader of the party in the Cape and Minister of Defence, P. W. Botha. By their own standards, it was indeed radical.

Despite their purism and attachment to legalistic tidiness, the Government had never really produced a satisfactory blueprint for the Coloureds (nearly 3 million) and Indians (under 1 million) within the greater apartheid scheme. Neither had an obvious 'homeland' which was not already allocated to the whites (4½ million), and this had been the root problem in trying to accommodate them in separate development. Now this turned into a happy accident, for the failure to provide for these two communities gave the Government the justification for a new scheme to win there.

Each was to have, in future, its own Parliament – just like the whites – and its own Cabinet, which would then represent the views of their constituents in a Cabinet council where they would be a minority. The Government believed this could be presented as eminently fair and democratic, for were not the Coloureds and the Indians being given exactly what the whites had?

It was not clear to the Government that, even allowing for changing ideas, the mainstream of Afrikanerdom would be prepared to go along with something as radical as this, smacking as it did of incipient democracy. Even though the plan was endorsed by party congresses in each of the four provinces, rumblings were clearly audible in the undergrowth. A meeting in Vienna between Mr Vorster and the American Vice-President, Walter Mondale, helped them over this hurdle, for Mr Mondale laid down the law to Mr Vorster telling him that there would have to be one-person, one-vote in South Africa. Mr Vorster returned home and called a snap general election in November 1977. On the table, requiring voter endorsement, was the new Triple Parliament scheme – but Mr Vorster's campaign theme was the terrifically popular one that he wanted white backing to show Mr Mondale who was boss in South Africa.

The National Party achieved its greatest victory ever, winning 134 seats out of 164, or more than 80 per cent of the vote. The snap election had been called, however, not simply to capitalize on white sympathy for a leader under attack from foreigners, but to make the most of the disarray in Opposition ranks, a condition which told much about the changing nature of white politics in South Africa.

Ever since it had lost power in 1948, the United Party had remained the Official Opposition in the white Parliament. It had drawn its support from those Afrikaners who had grown up in the Smuts tradition of pragmatic accommodation with the English and the world, and from English-speaking whites whose different economic position in South Africa had caused them to dissociate themselves from modern Afrikaner nationalism. Racial segregation had not really been an issue between them; the only question had been how rigidly or flexibly it should be managed.

But the United Party's Afrikaner supporters had been a constantly dwindling band, and among the whites as a whole it had become increasingly clear that the English-Afrikaans divide was no longer the issue. It was now the existence of segregation itself. As a result, the United Party had seen its support constantly eroded, and in June 1977, it had finally disbanded itself. Astonishingly, the new Official Opposition after the November election was the Progressive Federal Party, a party committed to the abolition of apartheid and to a non-racial future. Although it won only seventeen seats, it showed that white attitudes were indeed changing. Though, like the UP, it drew its main support from the more affluent English-speakers, its progress since 1974 showed it was continuing to draw some support from wealthier Afrikaners too, a development characterized by the presence in its ranks of MPs like Dr Frederik Van Zyl Slabbert, a charismatic young Afrikaner whose blue-chip credentials as a former Western Province rugby player and grad-

121

uate of the Afrikaner Oxford, Stellenbosch University, impressed even his opponents. In 1979, indeed, he became party leader.

The political arena was only the visible tip of profound and far-reaching changes which were taking place among whites. Until the 1950s, Afrikanerdom had been fairly homogeneous, and white social and economic strata fairly simple. The English had been urbanized, professional, and broadly speaking middle class. The Afrikaners had been originally small farmers. When, in the inter-war years, substantial numbers of them had been driven off the land by industrialization and the Depression, they had constituted only a semi-skilled or even unskilled urban proletariat, who had retained the values of their rural tradition. Indeed, as we have seen, their hardship in the towns had caused them to give new potency to that tradition, and had been the major factor in the rise of modern Afrikaner nationalism and in the erection of apartheid.

Apartheid, whatever else one might say about it, succeeded in rescuing its own. The absorption of many of these impoverished Afrikaners into Government service or into the vast, specially created para-statal industries created employment and economic security for them. Indeed, it remains the case even today that a staggering fifty per cent of the entire Afrikaner workforce is employed in one way or another by the state. This new-found cushion, coupled with an enormous improvement in white education, had provided a springboard for Afrikaner economic advance.

By now a new Afrikaner middle class was clearly identifiable: supervisors, white-collar clerical administrators, technicians, middle management. With government backing, Afrikaner financial institutions had succeeded in establishing an independent base and breaking the Afrikaner dependence on English money. New Afrikaner banking giants like Nedbank and the Trustbank had added their weight to older institutions like Volkskas and Sanlam, both to give Afrikaners a new commercial freedom, and to promote the growth of an Afrikaner entrepreneurial class. Afrikaners were by now successfully ensconced in light and medium industry; they were owning hairdressing salons, steak houses, and laundromats. With rising revenues but tight restrictions on the export of capital, Afrikaners had discovered the stock market. They had bought into the big mining houses, eventually taking control of conglomerates like Gencor (General Mining Corporation), enabling them for the first time to look English monied interests in the eye as equals.

122

These Afrikaners, with their soaring living standards, their new-found security and upward mobility, and their access to regular foreign travel, found the old cultural isolation breaking down, and were beginning to feel comfortable with the values of that fiendish outside world that their forefathers like Paul Kruger had recoiled from. This was bound to mean that some of the values of Western liberalism should begin to permeate the upper strata of Afrikaner society, a process much assisted by their further tying in to Western culture through the introduction of television in 1976, an initiative long resisted by Afrikaner conservatives, in large measure for that very reason. At the political level, it began to produce a convergence of view between some of the better-educated and wealthier Afrikaners, and the English.

But this middle class represented only a minority of the Afrikaner population. The farmers, urban industrial workers, and the bulk of public servants from artisans on the railways to policemen, still constituted the mainstream of Afrikanerdom. Their economic position remained much more precarious. Their improved living standards did not yet flow from an independent economic base, but from state support and the protection of job reservation. For them, the memory of severe hardship and real poverty was still alive in the experience of their own mothers and fathers. They therefore saw the new liberal ideas as a threat, and not surprisingly they remained much more resistant to them than did their better-off co-linguists.

So in addition to producing a growing identity between some Afrikaners and the English, increasing Afrikaner affluence had the much more important effect of producing within Afrikanerdom a widening ideological cleavage. Already pre-figured in the *verkrampte-verligte* tension in the early 1970s, it had reached the point, by the late 1970s, where the old monolithic *volk* was well and truly something of the past, and where the differences of interest and outlook were diverging, rather than narrowing – and this at a time of unparalleled vulnerability. None the less, it is important to realize that this new class differentiation was having the effect of stringing out Afrikaners along a spectrum, rather than dividing them neatly into two camps.

But it was unquestionable that a new dynamic was at work. It was this dynamic which produced a certain sobering after Soweto; which could be glimpsed in the 1977 election; and which provided the elbow room for P. W. Botha's Triple Parliament plan. Mr Botha soon found himself with the perfect opportunity to begin to put his reformist ideas into practice The Minister of Plural Relations, Dr Mulder, was forced to resign over a financial scandal and the shock-wave swept John Vorster from the premiership too. P. W. Botha became Prime Minister in his place in 1978.

Mr Botha represented in his own persona the modern experience of the Afrikaners. Unintellectual and dour, he had worked his way up the party machine as a bootboy with native cunning and adroitness. As Minister of Defence he had shown a healthy respect for armed might and had proved himself willing to use it ruthlessly in the abortive invasion of Angola in 1975-6. He was the living embodiment of *kragdadigheid*, a quality Afrikaners much admire and which can be loosely translated as the willingness to use force unsparingly. None the less, he was a man who admired knowledge and specialization, and was prepared to listen to experts. In his long years at the head of the country's military brass, he had been much impressed with their arguments in connection with the guerrilla war in Namibia that a conventional military victory was not possible, and that a modified political approach was necessary. He had taken their advice – and it had worked.

Namibia was the modern name for the old German South-West Africa. South Africa's control of the territory had sprung from their having captured it on behalf of Britain during the First World War. Thereafter, their presence had been legitimized by a League of Nations mandate, but in the decolonization era of the 1960s, the United Nations had terminated it and had ordered South Africa to leave. South Africa had agreed to withdraw, but in reality, wished to remain there as long as practicable in order to secure its north-western flank. Ranged against it was the South West African People's Organization (SWAPO), deriving support from the majority Ovambo tribe, and committed to guerrilla warfare against the South African Army. Mr Botha had broken with tradition in a territory where South Africa had practised its home-grown apartheid, and had formed a series of ongoing and changing alliances with minority black tribes who feared Ovambo power. This had not actually given the white authority majority support in the territory, but it had greatly broadened its base and moved the centre of gravity in Namibian political life so that the threat from SWAPO had successfully been held at bay for more than a decade. Mr Botha had had to concede a certain measure of desegration to achieve this support, but the strategy of dividing had allowed the whites to continue to rule.

These lessons had sunk in, and he now intended to apply them to South Africa. The Triple Parliaments' idea, designed to win the Coloureds and Indians to the side of the whites, was the first move in this direction. But Mr Botha had more ambitious plans in mind. He knew the nub of the problem was really black South Africa, and he knew that attempts to woo elements of that community would meet considerable resistance within the National Party.

Before he moved, then, he decided he needed more room for manoeuvre. From 1979 to the early 1980s, Mr Botha embarked on an internal purge of the party and party organs. He fought a long, bloody, but ultimately successful battle to remove die-hard *verkramptes* from control of the South African Broadcasting Corporation, perhaps the most powerful medium of propaganda in South Africa. The *Broederbond,* once the all-mighty secret power in the land, now became gripped by ideological paralysis as *verkramptes* and *verligtes* divided on whether to support Botha or not. Botha won, ousting *verkramptes* from the leadership, and installing his own men. But the *Broederbond* mattered far less now, for Botha was his own man. He purged the highest echelons of government policy-making in the same way, and where he could not, he bypassed them, by overhauling and streamlining departments, bringing in his own men – often young, well-educated, and frequently non-political academics – to advise him. He began, more importantly, to devise ways of bypassing the white Parliament where the strongest political opposition was bound to be voiced. In 1981 the Westminster model on which it had been based was ditched. The nominated Upper House – the Senate – was abolished, and turned into a President's Council, an appointed body significantly including a minority of Coloureds and Indians. Its stated function was to look into particular policy issues and make recommendations to the President, who could then lay them before the elected House of Assembly. This was in reality an elaborate device for making contentious changes look as though they were not the initiative of the Prime Minister, but the carefully derived crystallization of wisdom from a respected cross-section of quasi-expert opinion. It was, in short, a way of getting legislative initiatives into a House which might otherwise prove reluctant to introduce them, and giving them a veneer of respectability to ease their passage.

A similar sort of device had already been successfully tried in expert commissions, appointed to make recommendations on certain aspects of policy regarding black South Africans. In the period 1979 to 1981 a number of Acts were approved by Parliament, giving effect to their proposals. Strongly influenced by the new breed of Afrikaner capitalist, who like his traditional English counterpart favoured a freer labour market and was more sympathetic to black worker grievances both because they did not threaten him directly and because they hampered the efficiency of his operations, the Acts produced a number of important changes.

The most significant was the ending of the ambiguous status of black trade unions and their full legalization. Afrikaner business had come to realize, after the spate of wildcat strikes in the early 1970s, that unions were now a fact of life, and that it was better to recognize them and try to control them than simply to ignore them. In legalizing black unions, then, the Government also tried to draw their fire by laying down time-consuming and complicated conciliation procedures before strikes could be called. In the event, the new unions which sprang up simply ignored these requirements. This was a development of great potential importance, because it allowed a people, hitherto denied any legitimate way of organizing outside of the church, a future means to do so – and in a context geared to confrontation.

Other measures passed at this time included the virtual removal from the statute book of all job reservation, though this was no more than a recognition of the reality that because there were too few whites to fill skilled labour vacancies, blacks had increasingly been promoted into them. The rationale behind influx control was also changed. Under Verwoerdian apartheid, all blacks except a tiny handful who had met stringent requirements had been denied any legal right to be in 'white' South Africa at all. Now the Government said that in future black migration to the cities would be permissible subject to suitable jobs and housing being available. In practical terms, it made little difference but, like all these measures, it signalled obscurely a new viewpoint in the minds of the white authorities.

The political significance of all three measures lay in their implicit recognition of the 'permanency' of black workers in South Africa, the denial of which had been the absolute bedrock of traditional apartheid. The measures were pooh-poohed by Government critics,

but they were clear signs that Mr Botha was intending a fundamental breach with his predecessors' policies. And given the Afrikaner disposition to legalistic purism, it was bound to undermine the
ideological coherence of apartheid, and therefore erode its force in
the minds of its supporters.

Mr Botha, though, intended something much more far-reaching.
Bearing in mind his Namibian experience, his real intention was to
construct a series of alliances with 'moderate' blacks in order to iso-
late and neutralize the more radical elements. In order to do this, he
knew he would have to make some concessions of principle, but
these could be limited so as to leave the dominant position of whites
unaffected. The 1979-81 changes were part of that price, but it was
the much more intractable question of overall political power that
Mr Botha knew he really had to deal with.

Most black political organizations in South Africa have always
wanted a universal non-racial adult franchise to produce a single
legislature within a single, i.e. unitary, South Africa. This would inevitably mean black majority rule. This was total anathema to Mr
Botha. It would mean the end of white political dominance. Mr
Botha believed the blacks were incapable of efficient and fair government, and that this would spell the ruin of the country. At a more
profound, unarticulated level, he could not but be aware that political power for blacks would erode white privilege, and would more
especially lead to a dismantling of the state-protected economic position of many Afrikaners. So he was totally opposed to one person,
one vote. Indeed, one might go further and say that his major political objective was to ensure it never happened.

None the less, some accommodation of black political aspirations
would have to be made. Under orthodox apartheid, these were to be
voiced in the homelands. Mr Botha knew that this was unacceptable
to most blacks, and that the homelands had failed to fulfil the role
envisaged for them. It was quite clear that even as economic entities
they had largely failed. So Mr Botha accepted that alternatives
would have to be found. National Party traditionalists would not
allow him simply to junk them, and some homelands did work after
a fashion. Moreover, the blacks who governed the homelands had
every interest in maintaining their fiefdoms, and in opposing a national democracy which would sweep them out of power. So in constructing a system of alliances, the homeland leaders, together with
their rural constituents, would provide strong basic building blocks.

Mr Botha therefore determined to continue to pay lip-service to the homelands, and even, where possible, continue to promote them.

The real problem was all those blacks – probably about half the black population, or about 12 million – who lived outside the homelands. How could they be accommodated politically? One thing was clear: they had to be prevented from coalescing politically, so the principle was to give them representation on a fragmented basis. Mr Botha's intention was to begin by giving blacks outside the homelands greater democracy at the township level. In 1982, therefore, the Government ended formal white administration of the townships, intending to hand them over to black municipalities formally elected by all registered blacks within their area. Implicit in this scheme was a further recognition of the 'permanence' of blacks in 'white' South Africa, but Mr Botha believed it would allow the Government to claim that blacks were being enfranchized, that it would dissipate a certain amount of political frustration, and that it would probably produce a moderate, conservative local black leadership. Concerned to deliver better amenities to their voters and anxious to preserve the personal rewards of office, they would ally with the Government in restraining political militancy.

This was a start, but Mr Botha knew it would probably not be enough. Some representation for blacks at national policy-making level would also have to be devised. The ideal from his point of view was to have some form of loose federal structure in which white representatives formed a solid block while other race groups were represented in as many fragmented blocks as possible. It was not his intention that such a body should be brought into being for the moment, and even if it was, he saw it as remaining purely consultative for several decades. Whether it might eventually evolve into something more formal, perhaps even with legislative power, was for future leaders to judge. He felt, however, that a few halting steps in this direction would begin to lay the basis for a conservative system of alliances, and would signal to moderate blacks that there was hope after all.

The ultimate intention was to restructure South Africa into eight new federal units. Some would be essentially white (based primarily on white rural areas), some black (based primarily on the homelands), and some mixed (based on the multiracial cities). Delegates would be elected at local and regional levels, and then sent up to the federal umbrella body. In all this, the arithmetic could be juggled so that the whites preserved a dominant, but no longer monopolistic, position at national government level. What was especially significant in the overall scheme was that it allowed for joint black-white participation at different levels of government in certain limited areas – perhaps the aspect of government thinking with the most revolutionary implications.

All this was a long way into the future however. Mr Botha recognized that it was too much to expect the mainstream of Afrikanerdom to go along with these sorts of ideas just yet. No suggestion of what might be afoot was to be allowed out. None the less he began to take some tentative steps in this direction. The best way of deceiving his own people was to talk about economic, rather than political, restructuring. From 1981 onwards elaborate plans were published for eight new 'economic development zones' – zones which could one day provide the basis for a new federal structure. Meanwhile talk of economic development would alarm no one.

As especially interesting sub-plot was the role of two men: Professor Jan Lombard, an economist at Pretoria University, and Chief Gatsha Buthelezi, leader of KwaZulu, the Zulu 'homeland'. Lombard, a close adviser to Mr Botha, was the architect of this federal idea. He had put it forward in a report for private business in 1980, and it was significant that Mr Botha now appointed him to take charge of the economic development programme. Chief Buthelezi, a member of the Zulu royal family, was the leader of the largest black language group, and had long been recognized by the Government as the leader of the Zulu 'homeland', KwaZulu. Despite this compromising position, he had always been an articulate opponent of apartheid, and had consistently refused to agree to 'independence'. None the less he was conciliatory towards whites, and opposed to black radicalism. Any system of alliances would be given added weight by his presence. Lombard's report had actually suggested black-white power-sharing between KwaZulu and 'white' Natal as an experiment in federal living, and Buthelezi would almost certainly have emerged the leader of the new entity, greatly enhancing the area under his control. Though the Government officially distanced itself from this recommendation, it remained on the shelf as a future enticement for bringing the chief into the system of alliances.

In all this process of reform by stealth, Mr Botha had a complex juggling operation to perform. For while allaying white fears, on the one hand, he had also to hold out the carrot of progress on national policy-making to blacks. To try and signal the kind of federalism he had in mind, Mr Botha began to talk airily about a new 'constellation of Southern African states'. The practical effect of this was to formalize and increase regular meetings between the white Government and the homeland leaders (treated by the Government as leaders of independent countries), and Mr Botha sought to bring into this process regular meetings with black councillors from the townships. It remained no more than a series of multilateral talks, but one could see how the Government might believe it could develop into an embryonic form of conservative political alliances.

Meanwhile, one aspect of alliance-building was already public: wooing the Coloureds and Indians. Mr Botha soon discovered that three separate Parliaments would not be acceptable to them. They wanted a single Parliament with a common voters' roll. This, on the other hand, would be unacceptable to whites. So a uniquely South African compromise was devised. There would be one Parliament, but with three racially separate chambers. The Indians and Coloureds would have their own Cabinets which would liaise with government through Parliamentary committees. The post of Prime Minister was to be abolished, and an executive State President with wide-ranging powers was to take his place. This would enable the State President to bypass the white chamber if necessary, and would allow him to bring Coloureds and Indians into his Cabinet.

It looked as though it might win significant Coloured and Indian support. But even this was too radical for more conservative elements in the National Party, representing blue-collar and rural interests. No doubt also aware of the way Mr Botha's general strategy was developing, sixteen members of the National Party broke away in Feburary 1982, to from a new right-wing Conservative Party, loyal to traditional Verwoerdian apartheid, and led by the arch-*verkrampte* Dr Andries Treurnicht (known to the English press as 'Dr No' because of his opposition to reform).

Growing right-wing alarm at the way Government policy was developing could also been seen emerging in this period by, for example, a short-lived, but colourful, small protest movement among Afrikaner housewives in Pretoria. They called themselves the *Kappie-kommando* or bonnet brigade. Incongruously dressed in the boiling Pretoria sunshine in the full regalia of *Voortrekker* women, replete with large bonnets and full-length skirts, all their costumes were black, and their most notable protest involved carrying a coffin to the magnificent Union Buildings – built on a hill overlooking Pretoria by Sir Edwin Luytens's protégé, Sir Herbert Baker, and now the administrative headquarters of the government – to symbolize what they saw as the murder of Afrikaner traditions. The invocation of *Voortrekker* imagery and the use of the term commando, that long-esteemed source of confidence and security to the Boers in their isolation, were particularly significant. And a similar theme surfaced in a more sinister way when a group calling itself the *Wit Kommando*, or White Commando, began fire-bombing the homes or offices of white 'traitors', interestingly, Dr Jan Lombard's office being one of their targets. Neither of these movements had much impact or survived in that guise for very long, but it was a pointer to the way things were developing.

This was not the only problem in trying to pursue reform. The black local authorities, central to the idea of constructing alliances with moderate blacks, were already being condemned by black activists as devices for perpetuating white control. Elections to these bodies in 1983 produced a derisory vote, generally not even amounting to a double-figure percentage turn-out. The Government was undeterred. It could not adopt a more radical policy – the conservative backlash was all too evident. It could not retreat from reform – the risks were too great. It had no alternative but to pursue its chosen strategy.

In November 1983, the new executive State Presidency and Tricameral Parliament were accepted by two-thirds of the white electorate in a national referendum. In September 1984 Mr P. W. Botha became the first such President, and Coloureds and Indians were elected to the new bodies. For the first time in nearly thirty years, non-whites could again vote representatives beyond the doors of the Parliament building in Cape Town, the old Cape Colony Parliament over which a statue of Queen Victoria still stood guard. Exclusively white representation had lasted barely three decades. These changes were also dismissed by many critics as cosmetic. So, in a sense, they were. But this was not the whole truth.

The truth was that the economic changes which had been taking place in South Africa for many decades were producing a situation in which apartheid was no longer viable. The vast expansion of the South African economy, though it had brought great advantages to whites, had also been drawing blacks more and more into the economy. As the demand for skilled labour began to exceed white

131

South Africa's capacity to meet it, so blacks had – in defiance of the law, but in keeping with the iron logic of economics – been graduating slowly upwards into those vacancies. Quite apart from that, the general prosperity of the economy had filtered down through the black community, raising living standards – though they remained well below the whites', improving education and political awareness, and generating new expectations.

In such a situation apartheid had actually outlived its usefulness to many whites, and was becoming increasingly difficult to sustain. The internal tension between a rigid framework and a dynamic economy was beginning to destroy the edifice of apartheid. Of course, only a fool would imagine that the whole construct would come tumbling down at once. The rot would set in slowly, gnawing away at the structure. One or two ramparts would topple over first. Gradually, sections of it would cave in. The broad foundations would remain in place, being slowly riddled by the cancer of decay. Finally – only at the very end, but in one great subsidence – they, and everything still standing with their support, would hurtle to the ground with an enormous crash.

From early in the 1970s, when petty apartheid first began to be abolished, and continuing right through into the mid-1980s, the so-called cosmetic changes in apartheid actually marked the start of the process of inexorable erosion. The legalization of black trade unions, the change in the Pass Laws, the contemplation by the state of new ways of accommodating black political aspirations – none of these amounted to a revolution, but the ramparts were beginning to fall. The bringing in of the Coloureds and Indians to Parliament – incomplete, gerrymandered, distorted as it was – was important, not for what it did for those communities, but because of what it said about the deep and mortal malaise of apartheid. The building still stood: but it was rotting before the world's eyes.

Thus we can look back and say that Verwoerdian apartheid reached full maturity in 1960 and began its long battle against death in 1970. Verwoerd's own demise marked its highpoint – and the start of its decline. By the mid-1980s apartheid was still healthy enough to corrupt an entire nation's life, but just on the horizon, Judgment Day was beckoning.

Although the Government clearly intended these changes as a device to perpetuate white dominance, they showed, in fact, its increasingly defensive position. The initiative no longer lay with the

Government: they were simply responding to events. People in such a situation find it harder and harder to regain the advantage. History provides few examples of their plans turning out as they hope. So it was with the South African Government. Reform had been in the air before Soweto, but change had been vastly accelerated by that landmark event. The lesson had been learnt by South Africa's long-suffering blacks. The danger signals should have been clear to the authorities. From all sides came dire warnings about the effect on blacks if they were actually excluded from the new dispensation. The Coloured and Indian vote for the Tricameral elections was evidence of grave disapproval, with at least two-thirds of both communities boycotting the elections.

The Government ignored the warnings. In terms of *realpolitik* they could do nothing else. But it was not enough. The Tricameral system lit the fuse of a fire which had been long building. In more ways than one, it marked the beginning of the end of white rule.

9

INSURRECTION

If Soweto had a transforming impact on white South Africa, its effect on black South Africa was even more galvanizing. It demonstrated to them that blacks were not impotent. They began to feel a new confidence, or at least a sense that they could contribute to their own destiny. And it also pointed the way forward to an unarmed, impoverished, and completely disenfranchised people: they saw that the answer to their long suffering under apartheid lay in the streets.

It is a supreme irony that the National Party, in successfully destroying the Black Consciousness movement, breathed new life into an enemy even more potent, and one which would take this message to its people – the African National Congress.

As police crack-downs broke up the Black Consciousness organizations in 1976 and 1977, hundreds – possibly thousands – of young activists fled across South Africa's vast, largely unpoliced borders. They took refuge in Swaziland, Lesotho, and most especially Botswana, and the authorities there put them in touch with earlier exiles. The youngsters found two main political groups operating abroad – the African National Congress and the Pan-Africanist Congress. In theory they should have had more in common with the PAC, which had, after all, broken from the ANC precisely because of its ties with whites, a sentiment which should have appealed to those who had grown up in the Black Consciousness tradition. Of the two bodies, however, the ANC was bigger, better organized, and better financed, with a larger worldwide network of diplomatic contacts. Inevitably they had a stronger presence on the ground, and were better placed to fly many of the new arrivals abroad, or to organize transit camps where political ideas were invariably discussed. Links were therefore formed with an organization the

134

youngsters had had little contact with in South Africa, and whose political stance they had previously spurned.

This had been because, in many ways, Black Consciousness as a movement had represented a recasting of the central ideas of the PAC in a modern context. To that extent, it actually constituted a further attempt to implement the organization's strategy after the failure of *Poqo*. This orientation had meant a long eclipse for the ANC within South Africa, and it was noticeable during the Soweto years that people like Winnie Mandela had been the object of great suspicion and distrust on the part of young blacks. For her, and all the ANC, it had been a period in the wilderness. But the destruction of Black Consciousness at the hands of the South African police had produced a mortal crisis of strategy. The movement had failed because its organization had not been robust enough to withstand the attack on it, and this was related to its failure to have built links both with the wider black community and other sympathetic forces in South Africa. In the end, its isolation had been its downfall. The ANC, on the other hand, had always stressed the need to build a strong organization, to win the political support of the entire black community, to weld them into a network of opposition, and to forge links with anyone else who would help. In the political vacuum after the collapse of Black Consciousness, it was the only alternative which made sense.

The failure of Black Consciousness, therefore, represented the failure of the ideas of the PAC. Only the ANC's ideas remained to be tried again. A political coming-together between the Soweto generation and the ANC was therefore logical, and happened. In the first years after Soweto, however, both the ANC and the youngsters were powerless to put this strategy into effect within South Africa itself. But with a large infusion of new blood, and of people with up-to-date local knowledge, the ANC was able, in the interim, to pick up where it had left off in 1964: they resumed the campaign of sabotage.

Considerable numbers of the new refugees were dispersed: to higher educational institutes in the West, to sympathetic Communist capitals in the East. They received money, support and training in sabotage, some of it in those capitals; most of it in training camps in countries like Tanzania. They began to find their way back to South Africa's borders: some went to Lesotho; most to Mozambique, which became the major jumping-off point for infiltration into South Africa.

135

The PAC was by no means dead, however. It also played a part in accommodating some refugees. Swaziland was its main base, but, without perhaps realizing it, the failure of its political ideas implied by the failure of Black Consciousness, left it disoriented. It had no significant guerrilla strategy. Most of its protégés ended up squabbling among themselves, or stirring up trouble for the Swazi authorities. The PAC's continued existence was testimony to the longevity of the emotions which shaped its philosophy, and those feelings remain important today, and will continue to play a significant role in South Africa's future. For the moment, however, it was the PAC's turn to be eclipsed, and it contributed little to the next phase of assaulting white power.

The first significant evidence of the renascent ANC came in 1980 with a most spectacular act of sabotage. Three ANC recruits from the Soweto generation penetrated the state oil-from-coal refineries at Sasolburg in the Orange Free State, one of the most heavily guarded sites in the country. They blew up six oil storage tanks, creating a smokestack 600 feet high, and days later the pall was still drifting across Johannesburg 60 miles away. One man involved was later imprisoned but it left white South Africa in no doubt that it had failed to put the spectre of black nationalism to rest.

Over the next four years there was a dramatic escalation of sabotage. The most important incidents were an attack on the unfinished Koeberg nuclear power station near Cape Town in 1982, which caused severe damage, and a car bomb outside the Air Force headquarters in Pretoria in 1983, which killed 17 people and injured more than 200. This latter attack was the first major offensive against civilians and although the ANC apologized for it, saying it was an accident, it deeply alarmed white South Africans.

It stung the Government into taking tough action. Three days later, South Africa bombed ANC bases in Mozambique (also killing civilians), and stepped up support for guerrillas of the Mozambique Resistance Movement (the MNR), who were successfully destabilizing the Government in Maputo. The devastation unleashed on Mozambique was such that its President, Samora Machel, eventually had no option but to seek a truce with the South Africans. In March 1984 the two Governments signed the Nkomati Accord: South Africa promised to stop supporting the MNR, and Maputo agreed to throw ANC saboteurs out of Mozambique. Though the South Africans reneged on their part of the deal, the Mozambicans did not. The ANC presence in their country was reduced at a stroke to a token diplomatic mission, and thus ended phase one of the reawakened ANC.

By mid-1984, however, this was no longer the bodyblow it might have been. In the few short years since Soweto, developments in black politics within South Africa itself had not only transformed the ANC's prospects, but had assured it the ultimate victory it had been aspiring to for more than seventy years, and which, until only a few years before, had seemed extremely distant, even improbable.

For the young blacks left behind after Soweto, a profound rethink had been necessary. And while they were reassessing their strategy, a new generation of young blacks, who had been only primary school pupils during the watershed years of 1976-7, was growing up. The former were to provide battle-hardened leadership, the latter shock-troops, in the new war which was to begin.

Like their 'comrades' in exile, the youngsters had quickly reached the conclusion that a lack of proper organization had been the central weakness of Soweto. Their ability to do anything about it was limited, not only because of police surveillance, but because they were not in a position to dictate to the black community at large.

Yet the paradox is that that community – conservative by instinct as most communities are, largely apolitical, deeply alarmed by the trauma that 1976-7 had inflicted on it, and anxious at all costs to avoid trouble – began, in a largely unthought-out way and only half consciously, to respond to the barely articulated call.

One must conclude, for there is no other explanation, that, however obscurely, Soweto had made a deep impact on their parents too. Although the older generation had stood apart when the crunch had come, some at least had recognized that whatever their misgivings about the unrest, it had begun to have results. Some, too, had been stung by the fact that while they had never offered resistance to white rule, their children had not only done so, they had been prepared to die for it. In the political argot of the township streets, a process of 'conscientizing' had taken place. It should not be overstated: these sentiments were voiced by only tiny handfuls of parents; only the smallest proportion of older blacks began to think explicitly in these terms. But deep within the urban black community, something profound and fundamental had been stirred. The ripples of the new South Africa which was being born touched all of them. A wholly new dispensation was coming into being. Old

137

rigidities were being broken down for good. They were only dimly aware of it, yet they could not remain immune.

From the late 1970s, and especially in the early 1980s, these developments resulted in an extraordinary burgeoning of what can loosely be described as black community organizations. Church organizations already existed, but most were politically conservative. Some of these started to become more political, or new ones were set up. Social welfare was often their official purpose. In reality, they came increasingly to look after parishioners' 'human rights' – to support and assist those in trouble with the police, for instance. Women's groups sprang up, often spawned by church bodies. 'Consciousness-raising' was a major part of their activities. Following the lead given during the 1976-7 unrest by *ad hoc* groups like the Soweto Committee of Ten, virtually every township evolved its own 'civic association'; large townships like Soweto, which were actually cities in themselves, often had several. They became important forums for articulating all kinds of grievances, from petty local disputes to the wider issue of apartheid. Rent associations, especially concerned with complaints against higher payments, or particular individuals' inability to pay on time, became common. Parents' groups sprang up to express anxiety about their children's education. Young blacks were forming their own new organizations. Younger children joined 'youth' organizations; older children formed 'student' bodies. The cultural and educational courses they organized themselves became potent methods of strengthening their opposition to white supremacy.

Meanwhile, the new black trade unions slowly began to find their feet. It is noteworthy that politicized Coloureds and Indians frequently joined these bodies, and were soon moving into key leadership positions. The unions urged caution on their members. They saw at once that it was more important to recruit and organize than to confront. Consequently, they often avoided industrial conflict, but put a vast effort into signing up new members and into setting up chains of command which penetrated right down to the smallest factory units. From being a largely non-unionized population, black South Africa could count more than 1 million unionists in its ranks within barely five years. Two important confederations were formed, providing co-ordination and further organization at a supra-union level, the Federation of South African Trade Unions (FOSATU) and the Council of Unions of South Africa (CUSA).

This massive organizing phenomenon, embracing substantial elements of the entire urban black population, was not, as we have seen, the work of young blacks. They recognized that it represented the way forward; they encouraged it as much as they were able, but they were not responsible for it. Vast sections of the urban black population, to say nothing of rural blacks, remained outside these new bodies. But their evolution was a development of the greatest moment for South Africa's future and in so far as they had come into being, they stemmed from the deepest instincts of a largely powerless people to find new strength. There was also no coterie of 'agitators' bringing this about: the ANC was almost entirely absent and would not have been able to effect such a huge transformation even if they had been there. Today, indeed, the ANC still remains no more than a shadow in these organizations. But their evolution is very much in line with its own thinking, and, of cardinal importance, despite its absence from their counsels, it has become the major beneficiary of their existence.

The secret of these organizations lay in their having found a new answer to the enduring difficulty of retaining leadership in a society where leadership had always previously been suppressed as soon as it had appeared. These organizations sprawled across large sections of each township; they spread out over the entire country. Their membership was intimately woven into the very fabric of their societies. It overlapped, intermingled, intertwined. It drew into this vast complex network labourers, factory hands, domestic servants, shop assistants, and porters. It forced them to think about their condition. It gave them each little jobs to do. It showed them how other black people organized things. It taught them where to turn when help was needed. Though it embraced a mere fragment of black society, it provided a broadly based engine for political change. And large proportions of its members were effectively being taught the rudiments of leadership, potentially able to take up the baton as successive layers of leaders might be stripped away by the police. Not only did this ensure continuity at the top; it also meant the organizations would not collapse when the assault came.

That moment of truth was not long coming. In 1983 the Government's Tricameral Parliament scheme received its finishing touches. Outraged at the total exclusion of all black people from this new constitutional arrangement, perhaps as many as 600 of these organizations came together in August that year, near Cape Town, to campaign against it. Once again, it was significant that much of the impetus for a nationwide movement came from Indian and Coloured organizations, whose communities would be called upon the following year to vote representatives to the segregated Houses.

The movement called itself the United Democratic Front (UDF). It proclaimed itself non-racial and, indeed, beside black, Coloured, and Indian members, it included even a sprinkling of whites. It repudiated violence. It saw its role entirely as an *ad hoc* campaigning body, not as a new political party. It explicitly recognized the exiled 'liberation movements' as the country's legitimate political leadership. It acknowledged the 1955 Freedom Charter, but did not require supporters to swear loyalty to it.

In all these declarations it was clear that the political ideas of the ANC had struck root. The UDF could not openly support violence for that would not only have meant immediate police action, but it would have deterred most of its members. It could not set itself up as a party, for that, too, would have attracted banning, and would have divided its supporters on details of principle. But non-racialism, recognition of the 'liberation' movements, a muted obeisance to the Freedom Charter, and the very notion of itself as a 'popular front' were powerful echoes of what the ANC had been talking about for thirty years. The deference to the ANC could also be seen in the UDF's election of Nelson Mandela, Walter Sisulu, and Dennis Goldberg – all imprisoned ANC men – as their patrons. The ANC's message and claim to leadership had filtered through the screen of imposed silence, despite everything. And it was for the same reason that the youngsters-in-exile had embraced the ANC: its strategy was the only one that made sense.

None the less, many politically aware blacks could not support the UDF. The differences of view which had split the nationalist movement decades before were still operating, for those differences had sprung from black beliefs about the way reality should be organized, and reality had not changed enough in its fundamentals to produce wholly different responses.

A rival umbrella grouping, the National Forum (NF), had set itself up in June of that year. Based around the Azanian People's Organization (AZAPO), its coming into being reflected the old ANC-PAC cleavage. Like the PAC, the NF was in practice opposed to the participation of whites in the struggle against apartheid. But in view of the effective failure of PAC ideas, a new critique had to be

140

evolved. Under the influence of Black Consciousness men* recently released from prison, the NF grafted onto black exclusivism a new, radical anti-capitalist stance. Their argument was, in short, that in the context of South Africa, apartheid, in one guise or another, was an inevitable instrument of capitalist exploitation. Getting rid of formal apartheid would not end black oppression. The overthrow of capitalism itself was therefore a necessary condition to achieving that. This was in marked contrast to the UDF's more pragmatic line which paid only token lip-service to these economic issues.

The NF, however, was much smaller than the UDF, comprising mainly black intellectuals and students, many of whom were remnants of the Soweto generation, and it had nothing like the UDF's broad network into the wider black community. Consequently, though it was also to be involved in the forthcoming resurgence of black political activity, it played a far less significant role.

The UDF cut its political teeth on the campaign against the Tricameral Parliament, and it was much more successful than many had expected. The large abstention in the Coloured and Indian elections was largely its doing, and followed a massive campaign of leaflets and meetings. But once that was over, the question of where to turn its attention next presented itself. The UDF, in keeping with its strategy of involving ordinary people, put much energy into 'educating' the populace on local grievances, and also began a political attack on black local councillors, whose co-operation with the Government in running the townships was central to the Government's thinking. They were dubbed 'sell-outs' and 'traitors'.

In late August and early September of 1984, the increasing political feeling within the black community which these organizations and campaigns expressed, began to spill over into the streets where youngsters in particular were less prepared to rein in their frustrations. Incidents of rioting and stone-throwing at police vehicles began to proliferate. On 3 September the day on which the new Tricameral Parliament was to come into being – many UDF-affiliated residents' associations launched protests against newly announced rent and bus fare increases. By this stage a national schools' boycott, organized by the UDF body the Congress of South African Students

---

* The choice of the Black Consciousness name, Azania, for South Africa also testified to the ideological continuity between the PAC, Black Consciousness, and the National Forum.

(COSAS), was also gaining wide support. In many different parts of the country, 3 September saw a sudden eruption of anger, which caught white South Africa, at least, unprepared. In townships to the south of Johannesburg – in the heavily industrialized area known as the Vaal Triangle, which includes the politically historic township of Sharpeville – large rent protests by the residents were broken up by the police only after running street battles. In the East Rand area, east of Johannesburg, students began pelting police vehicles with stones and bottles. In Sharpeville, most unusually of all, an enraged mob set upon the deputy mayor and killed him, the first attack of this kind. The rioting and violence was of an intensity and breadth not seen in South Africa since 1977. White South Africa was not sure, for a few hours, what it signified. They thought it would probably all be over by the next day.

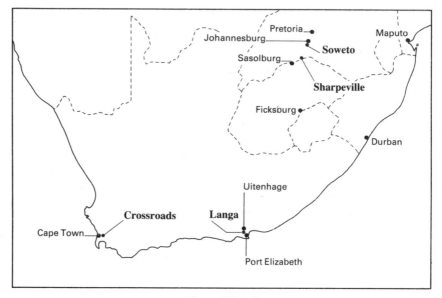

Unrest 1984–6

In fact, the next day brought no let-up. The rioting simply went on, and on, and on. Looking back, it is clear that 3 September marked the beginning of a low-level insurrection which has gripped South Africa ever since, and which, far from diminishing, has been growing steadily. And behind the local issues which were the focus

142

for the various protests, the real cause of the unrest was the anger felt by blacks at their exclusion from the new political system. The Government had not realized how strongly blacks felt about this, and their miscalculation was to cost them very dear.

The next two months saw what had been initially isolated incidents gather force and momentum, till several parts of the country – especially the Vaal Triangle and the East Rand – became engulfed in continuous turmoil. Running battles with the police caused the death toll to soar. Within the first month alone, more than sixty people died. The Government banned all political meetings, but as they could hardly stop funerals, these open-air gatherings quickly turned into political rallies. On 23 October, with the Army called up to back the police, the security forces launched a massive house-to-house search operation in the Vaal Triangle, as much to show their strength as to gather information. For a few days, the Vaal Triangle cooled down, but on 5 November, in a development which was much more alarming for white business, the trade unions called a two-day general strike in the Witwatersrand, the whole area from the West Rand through Johannesburg to the East Rand, and in the Vaal Triangle. This is the mining and industrial heart of South Africa, and the labour stayaway was virtually absolute.

The Government decided to get tougher. The day after the stayaway ended, it arrested all the strike leaders. In a five-day period about 1,000 people, largely UDF activists, were also rounded up and detained. The Government seemed to believe that the UDF was organizing the unrest. In a broad sense, the UDF's political campaigning was indeed responsible for imparting a new sense of purpose in the black community, and was also important in defining objectives. But the youngsters in the streets did not take instructions from the UDF, which was often trying to harness their energies for more mundane political work, rather than see it dissipated.

The arrests, therefore, made little difference to the street violence. And the UDF's organizational strength enabled it to continue with new, unknown leaders so that it was not affected all that much either. And now, from its original core in the Transvaal, the unrest spread to new areas: in early 1985 to the Western and Eastern Cape; later in that year to Natal. All the time a new phenomenon was evident: townships in some of the most benighted, out-of-the-way and backward parts of South Africa – townships which had never been politically active and represented some of the politically weakest parts of the black community – these suddenly began to see the first outbursts of militancy. They included townships in the *platteland*, the country districts, which are bastions of white racism and where blacks have traditionally been silenced by a greater local willingness to use force against them. But now even these areas were affected: townships in the Western and Eastern Orange Free State; the area immediately north of Pretoria; the Eastern Transvaal – they all saw the flare-up of unrest.

One of the most striking features of the unrest was the way its focus kept shifting. Although incidents were taking place all over the country at any given time, they tended to be more heavily concentrated in one region. In the first few months, for example, the major thrust had been in the Vaal Triangle and the East Rand. At the beginning of 1985, it swung to the Western and most especially to the Eastern Cape. After that it moved to Natal, and then back to the Transvaal. In 1976-7 the crowds had learnt that it was impossible to sustain intense unrest over the whole country for long periods. Now it was as if there was an almost subconscious realization that each region should take its turn, for whenever unrest began to flag in one area, it would start up again in another.

This whole insurrectionary upsurge was a phenomenon quite unlike anything modern South Africa had ever seen. Its breadth and depth was quite exceptional. The intensity and the duration was unparalleled. Above all, it unleashed violence of such an horrific and shocking kind that it was, in many respects, without precedent anywhere in the world. But in the South Africa of the mid-1980s it became a matter of daily routine for black township-dwellers all over the country. This is even more spine-chilling when one considers that this was just the beginning of a civil war which still had years to run. There can be no more absolute indictment of apartheid than the spectacle of such ferocious brutality being inflicted by a society on itself.

One kind of violence was the result of confrontation between young black demonstrators and the security forces. Such confrontation became so institutionalized throughout the country that it was literally impossible to keep track of the incidents. A whole way of life grew up around them. They were sparked off in any number of ways. There might be a funeral, or a political meeting, or a school boycott, or a protest march, or even just crowds of youngsters roaming the streets. Under the powers given to the security forces, any

144

gathering where more than a handful of young blacks were present could be deemed illegal. So the security forces would go in to break it up. The usual procedure was for police Land-Rovers, with protective anti-riot metal screens covering them, to head the convoy, with Army Hippos – specially built, tall, ungainly armoured personnel carriers, designed to withstand the force of a landmine exploding under them – bringing up the rear. The vehicles would hurtle forward at speed and head straight for the crowd, who, as the vehicles ploughed through them, would scatter, unleashing simultaneously a bombardment of thrown objects: bricks, stones, bottles, sticks, petrol-bombs, anything that was to hand. In most cases the security forces would lob canisters of tear-gas as they roared by to break the crowds up further. Young blacks quickly learnt to take counter-action though. Water was an effective antidote and so whenever a confrontation was anticipated they would prepare themselves by tying handkerchiefs dipped under a nearby tap around their mouths and noses. Indeed, in many instances, nearby residents would actually put buckets of water outside their front gates to help the young-sters whenever trouble was expected, since taps were hard to find. None the less, the tear-gas was usually effective in stopping the demonstrators from congregating. Of course there were other means of breaking up crowds: when they were smaller, with dogs or *sjamboks*, long whips made from rhinoceros hide; when they were lar-ger or more menacing, with bullets, usually fired from the protected rear of the Hippos.

One of the largest single instances of this kind of violence took place in February 1985, just as the unrest began to surface in the Western Cape. The Government had been fighting for almost a de-cade to clear a squatter camp near Cape Town – Crossroads – and remove its 87,000 residents who were living there illegally under the Pass Laws, either by sending them back to their 'homelands' or to an inhospitable camp they had built for them at a place called Khayelitsha. In a new attempt to do so, eighteen residents were shot dead by the police. Not only did this highlight the cruel policy of forced resettlement, but it reemphasised police willingness to shoot unarmed people if they resisted. Scenes of this confrontation, broad cast by television crews to the far corners of the globe, unleashed a barrage of world criticism on the South African Government. An even worse incident followed soon after. In Langa township near Uitenhage in the Eastern Cape, on the significant date of 21 March –

the twenty-fifth anniversary of the police killings at Sharpeville –
perhaps as many as forty people were shot dead in another confrontation with police as they were making their way to attend the funeral
of people killed in a neighbouring township. This, too, caused a
storm around the Government's head – but the killing went on. In
May 1986 there were reports of at least eighty black people being
killed during a four-day attempt by the security forces to end violent
disturbances in the township of Alexandra, right in the midst of
Johannesburg's fashionable northern suburbs.

But a second kind of violence also characterized the insurrection –
black-on-black violence, or violence between blacks and other non-
white people. The commonest form this took was that of attacks by
young black radicals on 'collaborators': councillors, black policemen, and police informers. It was these acts which gave a special
barbarity to the South African conflict, and engraved its horror on
the world. Stemming from generations of stored-up hatred and bitterness, and unleashed on targets who were surrogates for the real,
but inaccessible, enemy – the whites – they were a literal manifestation of the savage and gruesome wounds inflicted on an entire
people. Denied virtually all avenues to express themselves, the black
mobs vented their profound trauma by the only means still available
to them – the most basic. In townships all over the country, month
in and month out, they took their vengeance. The luckiest victims
were given warnings to quit their posts. The somewhat less fortunate were roughed up or had their homes and belongings fire-
bombed. The least fortunate were dragged kicking and screaming
out of their homes and were encircled by enraged mobs, who then
proceeded to yell abuse at them. When they had been sufficiently
terrorized, they were finally murdered. In the early days of the conflict, they were usually hacked to death with machetes. Soon,
though, petrol was being poured over them, which was then set
alight. Television pictures showed the results: people writhing and
screaming in agony, their whole bodies literally consumed by
flames; charred, and still smouldering corpses, littering the ground
in twisted shapes. Later, the crowds devised a more economical,
peculiarly South African form of execution: the dreaded 'necklace'.
They would fill a tyre with petrol and put it around the victim's
neck. Then, after the denunciations and pleadings had been conducted, the petrol would be ignited. Victims' hair and faces would go up
first, but eventually most of their bodies too. It took longer – but was

just as effective in the end. In 1986, a new refinement of murder was reported: a crowd dug a hole in the ground, turfed a victim in, and proceeded to bury him alive. The security forces dug him out an hour later, but they were too late.

In the panic which inevitably followed from this welter of killing, councillors in widely dispersed parts of South Africa began resigning in droves. It is impossible to count the number of attacks on black police and informers, but, by the beginning of 1986, at least 550 of their homes had been ravaged. They, their families, and their belongings were being systematically evacuated from the townships, to be rehoused in tents in 'white' areas, and destined to remain pariahs in their community for many years.

In August 1985, another variant of violence within the non-white population made its gruesome appearance. A State of Emergency had been declared by the Government in the Southern Transvaal and the Eastern Cape, and as it took effect causing the arrest of thousands and producing a general dampening-down of trouble in those areas, the unrest immediately moved to an area outside the scope of the Emergency, and one previously unaffected by rioting – Natal. There, a prominent UDF civil rights campaigner, Victoria Mxenge, had been murdered by unidentified killers. A meeting called to protest about her death was soon after broken up. Mobs of enraged young blacks then went on the rampage. Since the black townships were located a long way away from the white suburbs, they sought a target nearer home: the Indians, who, though also victimized by apartheid, had carved an economic niche for themselves by operating trading stores for blacks, and had indeed grown rich on the proceeds. In a wave of communal attacks which recalled the events of 1949, young blacks just north of Durban launched an onslaught on them. The Indians fled in panic, leaving their homes and property behind. Fearsome destruction was inflicted: homes, possessions, businesses were ripped apart, hacked to pieces, or fire-bombed. An entire community's world was ravaged. Even the Mahatma Gandhi shrine to the ideals of non-violence was reduced to smouldering rubble. For several days the destruction continued.

Its ending was accomplished in circumstances which saw an ominous new twist to black-on-black violence. Most of the young blacks loosely supported the UDF, and the people who stopped them were blacks from a different organization, Chief Buthelezi's Zulu movement, *Inkatha*.

147

Chief Buthelezi had been a member of the ANC while it had been still legal. After it had been banned, despite his continuing opposition to apartheid, he had taken his place as the state-salaried leader of the designated Zulu homeland, KwaZulu. Refusing, none the less, to accept a sham 'independence', he believed it would provide him with a power-base. As the leader of the largest and traditionally most powerful black grouping – the Zulu – he, perhaps not unreasonably, entertained aspirations to be a future national leader. But talks with the ANC abroad made it plain to him in the late 1970s that they regarded him as a 'sell-out' and had their own ideas about forming a future national leadership. It was clear that there would have to be a contest between them – and Buthelezi was not the man to walk away from a challenge. His *Inkatha* movement, said to be 1 million strong, but which can probably command the support of nearly 4 million inhabitants of KwaZulu, mainly Zulu rural peasants, provided him with a strong, coherent political organization, and indeed, a kind of small army.

Inkatha men were widely believed to have been behind Mrs Mxenge's killing; they were thought to have been responsible for breaking up the subsequent protest meeting. They were certainly unleashed by Chief Buthelezi onto the rampaging UDF youth and were the instrument by which the unrest was stamped out. In this action, many UDF supporters were killed or wounded, and any possibility of future co-operation between *Inkatha* and the politically more radical elements in South Africa thereby finally destroyed. A deadly antagonism was consolidated, which continues to rumble on in sporadic violence between them in Natal even today. This has serious implications for South Africa's future, a question which will be returned to.

A lesser factor, but one that cannot be ignored either, was the emergence of tension between the UDF-oriented youth and those supporting the NF, more particularly between COSAS and AZAPO. Periodically during the insurrection, violence broke out between them, mainly in the Transvaal. On the whole it was not as deep or as large-scale as the clashes with *Inkatha*, but – especially as it continues to surface every now and then – it remains a pointer to future difficulties.

This general picture of violence erupting in many different directions and inflicting death, horror, brutality, and suffering on whole peoples is a grim, but fitting, testimony to apartheid's viciousness. This is the legacy Afrikaner nationalism has bequeathed its country. Such is the orgy of devastation and destruction of life and property and security that apartheid can claim as its achievement. The full scale can be judged from the stark, but eloquent, statistics. From the time the unrest began in September 1984 until April 1986 – a period of 20 months – 1,559 people had died as a result of the disturbances. About half had died in confrontations between blacks and the security forces, and about half had been killed by blacks themselves. And it was clear that this trend was continuing to rise remorselessly. In the last four months of 1984, 149 people died. In 1985 as a whole 879 people died, representing a rate of death twice as high as in 1984. In the first four months of 1986, 531 people died, and this itself represented a doubling of the 1985 rate.

In all of this, despite challenges to its position, the UDF remained unqestionably the major political force. No other political group could demonstrate anything like its wide and deep support. No other group could make any substantial inroads into its hold on the black community. And what this means is that the real beneficiary in South Africa's insurrection has been the body to which the UDF looks for its legitimate leadership – the ANC.

It was evident from early in the insurrection that the ANC would profit the most. Even before the insurrection had begun, the ANC-in-exile could see clearly how things were developing. Since Soweto they had been moving towards a two-pronged strategy: continuing the 'armed struggle', but simultaneously encouraging discontent back home. As events in South Africa unfolded, that part of the strategy became more obviously viable, and in his January 1985 message, broadcast on the ANC's radio service from Addis Ababa, its leader-in-exile Oliver Tambo had spelt it out succinctly: *'Render South Africa Ungovernable'*. It was quite clear, however, that even if its Mozambique bases could be recovered, the ANC's sabotage campaign could never be more than a nuisance to South Africa's rulers. But making the country ungovernable was a threat of a different order. If sustained strongly enough, and long enough, it could transform the position. The young blacks who were generally in the forefront of the unrest hardly needed to be told: they had worked it out for themselves.

But the ANC benefitted in the internal situation, in part because it was preaching a message to which young black South Africa was susceptible, in part because its record against white supremacy was

unimpeachable, but most importantly of all, because its long martyrdom had given it the status of leadership among a people who
could not provide enduring leadership for themselves back home.
Paradoxically, exile, both internal and external, gave the ANC victory: it preserved it intact so that when the moment came, a leaderless people would have no other recourse.

The growth of support for the ANC was evident everywhere. With
political meetings banned, funerals provided the only legitimate
occasion on which politicized people could come together openly. So
funerals quickly became *de facto* political rallies. From the very first
funerals of unrest victims, ANC flags – completely illegal – began to
fly; banners and placards universally invoked its name; ANC songs
were sung and slogans chanted; the names of Nelson Mandela and
Oliver Tambo were openly shouted, and were even used as taunts
against the security forces. Prior to September 1984, men and
women had gone to jail for less. Now, with the security forces mani-
festly unable to control the townships, these names were proclaimed
with impunity.

As internal pressure on the Government to release Mandela
mounted, the outside world, too, began to urge this on them. By the
beginning of 1985, President Botha had felt obliged to make at least
a token gesture in that direction. He had offered to release Mandela
on condition Mandela rejected violence. Mandela made his response known in a public statement read by his daughter Zindzi to a
mass rally in Soweto. 'My father says no' was the brunt of it, but the
mere fact that Mandela was now able to issue his first public statement in twenty-one years with the freedom his new status and the
crowds around his daughter allowed, was a clear indication of the
extent to which the Government's power to command events had
been impaired.

The ANC in exile, though able to exert little direct influence on
this domestic situation, did, however, see opportunities to compensate for the loss of their guerrilla bases in Mozambique by establishing new ones within the country itself. For in the inability of
the security forces to control the townships, and the greater freedom
produced by the disruption of informer networks, they were able to
operate with more freedom. Thus, despite the South African-
Mozambique accord, acts of sabotage continued uninterruptedly. A
rash of landmine attacks towards the end of 1985 along the South
African border with Botswana suggested the ANC were using a new

entry route. But South African military incursions into Botswana prevented that from becoming a major threat. The more important development was the use of the limpet mine by ANC operators. Small, easy to conceal, and easy to operate, the ANC was able to pass them to cells of youngsters – often members of the UDF-affiliated COSAS – within towns and cities, which kept the pressure up, and was probably responsible for the Government's banning COSAS in August 1985.

By the middle of 1985, the Government's capacity to retain the initiative was shown to have failed in another area. For it was clear that their strategy of co-opting moderate blacks into the political system through local councils had broken down irretrievably. The resignations and general terrorization of councillors meant that almost nowhere could they any longer carry out effective local government, let alone organize future elections. Of the thirty-eight major councils in the black areas, only a tiny handful – five at most – were still functioning semi-normally.

In this respect, as in so many others, the Government had been its own worst enemy. The idea of creating a system of co-optable and compliant blacks through democratic local government was not, when conceived in the early 1980s, a demonstrably unworkable one. But when it came to implementing the scheme the Government had not felt able to withstand those voices within its own ranks which argued that if blacks were going to be given more self-government, they would have to pay for it. The increases in rents, municipal utility charges, the public bus and rail fares announced in late 1984 were the result of such thinking. And the black councillors, newly elected on flimsy turn-outs which should have warned the Government of their starting handicaps, had immediately been charged with collecting the increases. Ordinary black citizens who might have given the muncipal council system a chance, were thus at once alienated from and embittered against the councillors. Unhappily for these men and women, it proved in many cases to be quite literally their death warrants.

As the crisis lengthened from months into years, the Government did respond by trying to bring in reforms, but any benefit was immediately undone by actions on other fronts. 1985, for instance, saw the introduction of 99-year property leases for certain categories of urban blacks, leases which allowed them to buy property in the townships and thus underscored the Government's recognition of

151

their permanent status there. The Mixed Marriages Act, outlawing inter-racial marriage, was scrapped, as was Section 16 of the Immorality Act, which had made sex between races illegal. The Newspeak statute, the Prohibition of Political Interference Act, which had banned multiracial political parties, also went. But at the same time as the Government was being propelled into further erosions of apartheid, the police were bludgeoning to death Andries Raditsela, a senior black shop steward in their custody, and imposing (in July 1985) a partial State of Emergency, together with a blanket ban on media coverage of any unrest – measures which had the effect of simply giving the security forces even more power to harass township residents than they already had, and undid any credit the reforms may have won the Government.

This illustrates a key weakness in the Government's reform strategy, a weakness all repressive regimes experience when trying to liberalize. While trying to bring about changes which might be effective in defusing tension, many of its own supporters, brought up in a different tradition, are both reluctant to support policy modifications, and are still preoccupied with considerations which run counter to the new direction. This sets up an internal contradiction. At one level, it renders every initiative suspect in the eyes of those it is intended to woo, because every improvement is offset by reversions to type. It also weakens, not only the Government's strategic coherence, but its grip on its own nominal agencies. It is clear from a number of examples – the conduct of the military intelligence in continuing to support the MNR after the South African-Mozambique Agreement; the resistance by local police to national directives (a phenomenon highlighted by the enquiry into the Langa shootings) – that central Government is finding it increasingly difficult to keep such powerful bodies, used to exercising arbitrary control, in line, and it carries serious implications for the future. Meanwhile, it meant the reforms had no significant effect on the unrest.

But by mid-1985, it was also clear that, despite the system of black councils having broken down, and the Government's loss of control of many townships, especially those in key economic areas like Pretoria, the Witwatersrand, and the Western and Eastern Cape, the unrest still remained confined to black areas. It had not yet begun to spill over into the country's economic life, and for virtually all white South Africans, generally living well away from the black townships, life continued fairly normally.

152

The UDF realized that this was not enough. They had to try and find a way of extending the assault on white power, and breaking out of their own areas. The youth had instinctively tried to do this themselves. In the middle of 1985 there had been isolated instances of mobs trying to move into white suburbs to petrol-bomb houses. They had been beaten back by armed white residents. There had been isolated incidents of whites being caught up in city-centre protests and being beaten, but the police had always been on hand in large enough numbers to stop them. There had been sporadic cases of whites being attacked, either on the fringes of black townships or along roads passing near them. In December 1985 there was a limpet mine blast in a white shopping centre near Durban, which killed five whites. These were all isolated occurrences, however. Blacks were not yet strong enough to take on armed whites and the security forces beyond their own townships, at least not in any systematic way.

In the latter half of 1985, therefore, those UDF leaders who had avoided detention by going into hiding joined forces with those who had moved up to fill the leadership vacuum to try and evolve a further strategy. They decided to try economic muscle. The trade unions were not keen to assist them at that stage. The major union groupings had been trying for several years to unite in one super confederation, and negotiations had reached a delicate phase. They did not want to upset the prospects for success by doing anything which would antagonize potential members or attract police attention. The UDF in the Port Elizabeth-Uitenhage area decided to launch a local boycott of white shops, and within a very few weeks it was having a marked impact on white business. So much so, indeed, that white local councillors, defying national Government, met with some of the UDF leaders, including those in hiding, to try and bring their grievances to an end.

The success of the Port Elizabeth-Uitenhage boycott spawned similar campaigns all over the country. A particularly successful one was held in East London. Even in benighted rural areas like the small Orange Free State town of Ficksburg, the success of the tactic produced the extraordinary spectacle of dyed-in-the wool veteran Nationalists speaking the language of racial conciliation. By the turn of the year, the important urban centres of Pretoria and Johannesburg, and smaller Transvaal towns like Warmbaths, were also affected.

By the middle of 1986, however, the economic boycott's main impact had been to concentrate the minds of some local white councils and business people, and to encourage them to think of reform. It had not yet succeeded in producing any general mobilization against the white economy and undermining it in any fundamental way. The obstacles were too great: unlike street rioting, it needed careful organization and constant management, which was very difficult for people on the run. Blacks had to live. White shops were often the only source of food and household goods, or the alternatives were not able to meet the full demand. In some cases, intimidation or counter-strategems like the security forces stopping supplies to black stores, undermined the effectiveness of the boycott. There was also a very real danger for the UDF in such boycotts: in many places, mobs of youngsters helped to police the campaign by operating impromptu roadblocks. They would frequently force older blacks to undergo searches, and make them drink detergent or pour sugar and flour onto the road if they found evidence of the boycott being violated. This created considerable antagonism among older people, who often have no real alternative except to buy goods at white stores. So the UDF had to wage this campaign with caution, and this too made it less effective than in might oterwise have been.

It is clear that any sustained onslaught on South Africa's economy will always be subject to the weakness that it ultimately affects blacks as well as whites. The degree of organizational sophistication required means also that, in the end, only the black trade unions can effectively mount such a campaign. In November 1985, a large majority of them finally came together in the new Congress of South African Trade Unions (COSATU), which, with half a million members, became one of the largest bodies of organized labour ever seen in South Africa. However, significant elements of the unionized workforce remained outside its ambit, CUSA being a notable absentee. And despite militant political pronouncements at its inaugural meeting, COSATU has had to tread very carefully, weighing political action against the need to consolidate recruitment and organizational structures, pursue traditional goals of better wages and conditions, keep its members rallied and united behind it, and avoid police action against it. All this militates against hasty intervention in the political arena, though it by no means precludes it. The full impact of black union power has not yet been felt, but events will in due course ensure that it is.

154

Ironically enough the greatest damage to South Africa's economy during the entire first two years of the unrest was perpetrated by no less a person than President Botha himself. It was his now notorious 'Rubicon' speech in August 1985 which brought this about. The speech, delivered to the Natal Congress of the National Party, was televised worldwide because it had been much trumpeted by the Government itself as presaging a new programme of radical reforms – 'crossing the Rubicon' of abandoning apartheid. In the event, not only were there no new reforms, but the President also adopted a tough, aggressive attitude towards black militancy. On the eve of the speech President Botha is reported to have encountered considerable resistance to his proposals from members of his Cabinet, who were worried that the party would suffer as a result in forthcoming by-elections to the white Parliament. In yielding to their arguments, the President showed once more that the imperatives of an earlier political dispensation still outweighed those of the new in his own mind.

The world reacted in horror and alarm. The very next day the South African currency, the rand, began to plummet, and within five weeks its value had fallen by about fifty per cent. Within a fortnight, trading in the currency had to be stopped, and its lowered value meant South Africa had to impose a freeze on the repayment of foreign loans which were then outstanding and which could no longer be met. The fall in the value of the currency meant higher import costs for South Africa, and affected the whites especially as they had a greater propensity to buy imported consumer durables and luxury goods. The freeze on debt repayments also created a severe crisis of international confidence in South Africa. The situation was not helped by the arrest of 800 schoolchildren in Soweto and of the Revd Allan Boesak, an internationally distinguished Coloured theologian and UDF activist; the banning of a large march on Pollsmoor Prison, near Cape Town, where Nelson Mandela was now held; and a gold-miners' strike in the Transvaal – all in the midst of this financial crisis. Normally these occurrences would have been passed off as routine, but now they helped to heighten the international perception of imminent catastrophe.

By February 1986 the South African Government had reached agreement with its international creditors on a rescheduling of the debt payment, but the rand had failed to recover its former strength and foreign confidence remained fragile. What this meant was that

South Africa could no longer expect any major infusions of overseas capital investment in the future. Growth would therefore depend on export earnings, particularly through the sale of gold. For a country with a high black birth rate and an unemployment or under-employment figure of as much as twenty-five per cent of the black workforce, this was ominous indeed. It meant the country would almost certainly not be able to generate enough development to make substantial inroads into this problem, and was therefore fuelling further discontent in the future. Meanwhile, white living standards would have to suffer, and the economy would be increasingly forced to try and produce local substitutes for imports. In some ways, this could be beneficial to the local economy, but the stresses and pressures on an economy under-financed and under siege would undoubtedly create a highly vulnerable situation.

And the alarm generated by President Botha's Rubicon speech made it certain that the United States Congress would vote to impose new economic sanctions on South Africa. President Reagan, who wanted to maintain some leverage over Pretoria, pre-empted this by the stratagem of issuing an Executive Order imposing lesser sanctions first. None the less South Africa was worse off than it might otherwise have been.

As it happened, President Botha's tough stance also failed to stem the incipient tide of white reaction. In the by-elections, for the first time ever, the National Party lost a seat to the Herstigte Nasionale Party, the right-wing breakaway party which had been formed in 1969. The seat – Sasolburg – consisted largely of blue-collar workers employed in the huge state Sasol refinery and of rural Afrikaners, the classic constituency threatened by black economic and political advance. By April of the following year, 1986, the Government had anyhow been forced by continuing unrest to yield to moderate black sentiment, scrapping the entire Pass Law system and ending the State of Emergency and the ban on media coverage of disturbances, thus illustrating all too clearly once again the centrifugal forces pulling the Government in self-contradictory directions.

So, two years after the unrest had first started, it continued unabated. Indeed it had intensified, with the average level of death rising steadily. It had unleashed on South Africa some of the most gruesome and horrific scenes in its history: blacks being doused in petrol by other blacks and being burned alive; councillors and informers being hacked to death or being incinerated in their petrol-bombed homes; countless stonings and lootings. Violent confrontation with the police, much of it extremely ugly, had become completely routine. Small children – often as young as seven – were being frequently beaten to a pulp by police *sjamboks*; thousands upon thousands had been detained without trial, many of them also children, and many had been brutally tortured. Hundreds upon hundreds had been killed. It was blood-letting on an epic scale.

In scores of townships an extraordinary situation had come to pass. Anarchic mobs of youngsters, increasingly resisting the control of black political organizations – many of whose leaders were languishing in prison – had effectively driven the security forces out and taken over. They were routinely mounting impromptu road-blocks, subjecting older blacks to searches, lectures, and beatings. The never-ending funerals had become mass political rallies, with the ANC flag flown, and liberation songs and speeches defiantly delivered. The schools were usually empty. These young bloods not only ran amok in the townships, imposing new strains on an already beleaguered populace, they dispensed the power of life and death at whim. Anyone who fell foul of them was killed without question. In political terms, what this amounted to was the effective end of white rule in the townships, and a massive resurgence of support for the ANC. That support was now being expressed openly and with impunity, in a way that had never been possible before and with the white government powerless to stop it.

Beyond the townships, life continued fairly normally in South Africa, with the economy in particular as yet undamaged to any significant extent by the insurrection. But the insurrection had been started, and consolidated, in its home territory. It had reached the point where it was difficult to conceive of it being beaten back. That possibility could not be dismissed, but it seemed on balance unlikely. If so, it provided a launching pad for a wider assault on white power, and for the progressive erosion of white supremacy throughout the land. These questions will be resolved in the future. Quite how they will be resolved – and over what timespan – is what will now be considered.

10
WHITES TODAY

For white South Africans, these are the most difficult years they have ever had to face in their long and turbulent history in South Africa. Past dangers and battles were deeply frightening – but they were clear-cut, and winnable, and held out the promise of great rewards. The perils and challenges now confronting white South Africa are much more disturbing. They are ill-defined and diffuse. More importantly, they cannot be won, at least not in any conventional way, and hold out only the promise of defeat. That moment when a people who have been on top have to come to terms with a diminished state is always profoundly painful, and their conduct is all the more critical because their continued existence, or extinction, as a group turns on it. What faces white South Africans today is nothing less than life or death as a people – and the threat is all the more potent for being obscure.

There are essentially four components to modern white South Africa. There are the English-speakers, who now make up roughly forty per cent of the white population. They tend to be urbanized and well educated, in commerce or the professions, and as befits their secure economic base and their liberal English tradition, their instincts are to seek an accommodation with South Africa's black majority. They are long used, however, to political passivity. Since the independent union was established in 1910, political power in the land has resided with Afrikaners, and the English-speakers have become accustomed to having no power of initiative. Their skills and their adaptability have enabled them to carve out a comfortable niche for themselves under alien rule, and so it will remain. They are onlookers in the great struggle, whose well-being will be only marginally affected at worst.

The remaining sixty per cent of the white population are Afrika-

ners and they share a strong common identity and deep bonds of
history, culture, and family. The new Afrikaner professional and entrepreneurial stratum – probably about a fifth – is finding an increasing identity with English-speakers, though history makes a rift
with their own people and a political fusion with the English very
difficult. For the moment they remain largely within the National
Party which, for good or ill, has come to be the corporate expression
of Afrikaner political aspirations, and retains a powerful call on
their loyalty. None the less, they, like the English, are moving more
and more towards seeking an accommodation with black South
Africans. They believe such an accommodation can be arrived at by
serious negotiation now, from a position which is still relatively
strong, and without aggressive shows of force. They believe there
are sufficient numbers of moderate blacks to build a new co-
operative power structure which will involve an end of white political supremacy, but which will keep revolutionary forces at bay.

The bottom stratum of Afrikanerdom, probably about two-fifths,
consists of those who are still small farmers, or who live in small
rural communities, and those Afrikaners urbanized only a generation or two back who are essentially unskilled, or semi-skilled, or
who perform only perfunctory clerical duties in state employment.
Retention of land, physical security in isolated settlements, and the
protection of state employment are crucial for them, and these imperatives are passionately felt. In large part this stems from the
bitter experience, within living memory, of real and acute poverty
and hardship, given even greater emphasis by the amazing transformation of their lives under apartheid and the enjoyment of a previously unimagined economic security. The spectre of poverty
haunts them still, not only because of its proximity in time, but because, even today, with a deep world recession and economic
stresses in South Africa, many in their midst are relearning the exi-
gencies of inflation on stagnant wage packets or even the horrors of
unemployment, as they queue once more for the soup kitchens
Afrikaner welfare agencies have recently felt obliged to start up
again. They see themselves as Afrikaners who have fought battles
and wars, lost brothers and mothers in an alien land, fought disease,
infestation, ignorance and hardship, not just once, but over and over
again literally for centuries. At long last they have reached the Promised Land – and the prospect of it being denied them as they cross
the threshold seems a cruel and wicked fate, a denial of justice, and a

humiliation of all their long travail in a country which events have allowed them to come to see as their own and from which history now allows no escape.

They believe, and to a large extent they are right, that an accommodation with black people will destroy their security. They know, in their heart of hearts, that those black people have paid an even higher price than they have to allow them that precarious security. They fear, and again they are probably right to fear, that a harsh settling of accounts is all they can look forward to. Life is like that: few people escape scot-free the suffering they impose on others. For them it is a grim prospect – dependence on people they fear, whom they have ill treated, and whom they regard moreover as inferior. To anxiety and humiliation, we must also add betrayal. For if an accommodation with black South Africa is arrived at it is their Afrikaner brethren who will make it. It was those same Afrikaners who led them out of the wilderness. It was they who shaped the Afrikaner identity, who called on them to follow behind, who used them as the infantry, who honed and directed and codified their deep racist feelings into one of the most virulent political systems the world has ever seen, and who sanctified it saying it was right. Those same brothers used them to achieve greatness for themselves, and now, as the hour of reckoning approaches, they will ditch them.

Such is the stuff of human tragedy. These Afrikaners have much to lose and little to gain. They have always been victims, and they do not want to be victims again. Their frontier tradition is one of hard living and brutal experience. Violence is part of the only way of life they have ever known. The simple pieties of their Old Testament Bible have preserved their self-esteem as the brandy bottle and the gun have eased them on their long trek through South Africa's history. These same instruments will strengthen them again. They will resist to the bitter end.

Already they are drawing up the battalions. The army which will stand true to the faith is in place, and preparing for war. It is called the *Afrikaner Weerstandsbeweging* (AWB) and its title speaks clearly of its purpose: the Afrikaner Resistance Movement. Its leader is a fiery and charismatic man whose name could not qualify him more aptly for the role – Eugene Terreblanche, Mr White Earth himself. He likes to appear at outdoor rallies mounted on horseback, just like a true commando. His rallies conform lovingly to the organizational precepts codified for just such a posterity by Adolf Hitler in his own great battle-plan, *Mein Kampf*: hold rallies by night; carry torches; form honour-guards; sing stirring folk hymns; speak loudly and lengthily. These instructions Mr Terreblanche follows faithfully, but as Hitler was to Wagner, Mr Terreblanche cannot quite match their Germanic drama. His is a ramshackle circus. It has its swastika: three linked 7s – but it looks like the Isle of Man logo. They have their black eagle banners: Paul Kruger's fussy little flag. They do their special salute, but you cannot tell whether they are simply waving goodbye. It would, in truth, be rather pathetic, were it not for the ugly reality that lurks beneath, and the storm-troopers that wait in the wings.

But as the reality of modern South Africa changes visibly before their eyes, as they see their brethren making ready to desert them, many on the right fear that being a *bitter-einder* may carry a less happy conclusion than it did in 1902. This may be neither a war nor a peace they can win. They are going to go down with the old Transvaal tricolour flying, but they know the prospect of defeat cannot be wholly dismissed. So they are preparing their retreat.

It is these Afrikaners who are streaming out of the National Party and joining the right-wing conservatives. They have tried to emulate the early Nationalists and build their strength through unity. They have formed an *Afrikaner Volkswag*, the People's Sentinel, as an umbrella group to rally their various political forces, including the AWB. Its leader is Professor Carel Boshoff, a charming, old-world Boer and theologian, who is very good to his servants. He also happens to be – no prizes here – Dr Hendrik Verwoerd's son-in-law. But in their search for a defensible fall-back position against the possibility of a sell-out, his flock are a people in search of an idea. Professor Boshoff has that idea; he thinks visionaries run in the family. His *volk* are not yet sure what they make of his notion, but they have no other, so they will adopt it.

Professor Boshoff's idea, just like Dr Verwoerd's, is beautifully simple, satisfying the desire for continuity and the quest for purity. If all of South Africa cannot be held as a 'white' country – why, simply reduce it. Professor Boshoff believes in a white 'homeland', a sort of European Bantustan. He envisages an area from the middle of the Transvaal to the middle of the Free State, including of course, the Witwatersrand, which will remain a white country, a last preserve for a perfectly white people. All the rest of South Africa can be handed over to the blacks. Then they will be happy, and the whites

161

will have all the wealth. One has only to state the proposition to see its absurdity, but a people in a mess will clutch at straws. So Professor Boshoff's idea is gaining ground – well, support.

They have even formed a body, the *Oranjewerkersvereniging*, or Orange Workers' Union, which has taken upon itself the awe-inspiring task of laying the foundation of this statelet. They have worked out that a tiny hamlet south-east of Johannesburg, Morgenzon, is the epicentre of this territory still-to-be-born. The *Oranjewerkers* descend on it at weekends to start building houses by hand and tilling the fields themselves, for this will be a state without blacks. The local residents think they are quite barmy, and cannot fathom why they do not simply use blacks like everyone else. One or two, who have managed to grasp the full import of this experiment in new living, think it impressive, but too much like hard work.

None the less, partition – for that is actually what this is about – is an option which is just surfacing within the right, and as the pressure mounts, will grow. Already people have stopped thinking of it as a joke. References to such a solution occur more and more frequently in the rhetoric of the right. They disagree widely on precisely how much should be conceded and how much defended, but, in the end, this is where luckless Afrikaners are heading. They have nowhere else to go.

Between the upper and bottom strata of Afrikanerdom remains a third segment, also about two-fifths of the total. Once again, it is worth stressing that the population does not divide very neatly into these elements; rather, it is strung out along a spectrum on which these categories represent rough demarcation lines. This segment is simply the rest. It probably comprises richer farmers, skilled manual workers, the middle and upper echelons of the state sector, including middle managers, supervisors, and clerical staff, middle-range business people, and those employed in the lower and middle ranks of big business and commerce. These Afrikaners are pig in the middle. They are not ideologically coherent. They are, if you will, the floating voters of Afrikanerdom. And like floating voters everywhere, they will decide white South Africa's future.

They retain a deep attachment to the traditional values and ideas of Afrikanerdom. As is true for all their community, relative affluence is a recent phenomenon. Their parents were probably hard-up; their grandparents certainly were. They will still have close family ties with the lower stratum of Afrikaners. Their collective memory, the Afrikaner sense of isolation in the face of black hostility, and a residual sense of injustice at the hands of the British continue to inform their sensibilities. They are not as threatened, however, by black advance. They are reasonably well educated and have skills which blacks are only now being allowed to acquire. These will make them of value to any future South Africa, at least for a few decades. They have been exposed to a more middle-class way of life and to more liberal values, and they have been more suggestible to them than their worse-off co-linguists.

They remain deeply suspicious of change, but the secret of Afrikaner longevity has been reluctant pragmatism. Within the recesses of their communal persona, they know and understand this. When the British fought them, they fought back. When they realized they had been beaten, they came to terms with the British, and wrested triumph from defeat. They are well aware that the realities of South African life are changing, and they know fundamental choices have to be made. Their pragmatism makes them not unwilling to contemplate change, but they do not want to yield to it at once from what they see as now being a relatively weak position. They want a fight first, for they believe the whites are still capable of overwhelming the blacks.

This is what they would most like to do. Fight it out, and then, when the blacks have been cowed sufficiently, reform slowly. Reform so that the whites no longer monopolize power, but remain the dominant political group, with the initiative still, the capacity to dictate the pace of change, and the means to enforce it if necessary.

These are their goals – and they are a long way from abandoning them. None the less, it would not be entirely right to leave it at that. For being pragmatic, a suspicion lurks at the back of their minds that things may not quite turn out as they intend. They want to tough it out, but they are beginning to accept that an overall black political victory with little role for them may not be wholly avoidable. They will do their best to prevent it, but they are beginning to prepare themselves so that if it comes, they will learn to live with it.

One can see from this how the leadership of the National Party, trying still to embrace the bulk of Afrikanerdom, has been forced to settle for a position which is somewhere between the political ideas of the upper and middle strata, and why, concomitantly, they are losing the support of the bottom stratum of Afrikaners to the right-wing Conservative and Herstigte Nasionale parties.

The South African Government today wants to accommodate black South Africans. The more liberal sentiments of the upper stratum have already percolated through to allow changes in the social and economic fields which would have been unthinkable only a year or two previously. It is prepared to make these changes both because they are seen as inevitable and because they are not perceived by the bulk of Afrikanerdom as too threatening. But the real question remains political power. On this the Government is prepared to negotiate, and it will be supported *de facto* by about two-thirds of the white population: the English-speakers, the upper stratum of Afrikaners, and about half the middle stratum. But given the internal complexity of that constituency, it will be a highly ambivalent preparedness to negotiate. It does not want, and politically, must resist, a straightforward surrender to black majority rule. It wants to ease moderate and compliant blacks into the power structure at its own pace, so as to construct that system of alliances which will keep white power concentrated and dominant, and leave blacks fragmented. It does not want to exercise greatly increased force, but it is under severe pressure from within Afrikanerdom to do so. It is still just about holding the line, for the more radical black political demands do not have to be answered yet. But as soon as they do, the Government will not be able to withstand strengthening its hand in the time-honoured way. Middle Afrikanerdom, in short, will set the style, for the Government must retain their support if it is to remain the most significant political organization among the whites. The upper stratum and any potentially co-optable English-speakers would constitute too narrow a base.

It is possible that some of the more enlightened elements within white South Africa might try to go it alone. Big English-speaking business – the huge mining conglomerates like the Anglo-American Corporation, for instance – and to a lesser extent, reflecting their smaller base, Afrikaner big business – the Sanlam insurance giant or the Rembrandt Tobacco Group – feel keenly that the Government's strategy is in real danger of being unable to achieve its own goals. They have an enormous interest to protect, and they want desperately to make a real accommodation now, lest the forces of anarchy undo them. It is for this reason, as an example, that a group of the country's most powerful businessmen met the ANC in Zambia in September 1985, despite wide disapproval in the white community. They may perhaps have hoped to facilitate negotiation with

164

the ANC by the South African Government, but if so they were de-
luding themselves. They carry great clout in South Africa and the
Government needs to listen to what they say. In the final analysis,
however, it will negotiate only if, and when, it wants to. It is more
probable, however, that they simply wanted to put down a marker
of goodwill towards the ANC, and begin the difficult process of finding out whether a *modus vivendi* is possible with them.

They are not the only whites who have begun seeking the ANC
out: English and Afrikaner students have; theologians have; members of the Progressive opposition have; and even some of the more
verligte National Party MPs have indicated a willingness to meet
them. Some commentators have speculated that all these groupings,
with the support of the non-radical majority of Coloureds and Indians, could perhaps coalesce to provide a broadly-based centrist
alliance which could negotiate a settlement of South Africa's conflict
with the ANC. This seems improbable. Not only would the ANC's
terms prove likely, under present conditions, to be unacceptable
even to them, but such a notion presupposes the disentanglement of
these groups from their traditional alliances and a successful ac-
complishment of the complex business of creating a new fusion.
Such realignments are becoming conceivable but they probably require a massive electrolytic charge to bring them into effect. A catalyst of such proportions is some way down the road, and by the time
it is encountered the role for such a centrist grouping will probably
have changed. The bulk of Afrikanerdom must accept, one way or
another, any new dispensation that is worked out, if it is to hold.
And a centrist grouping does not have the power to persuade the
bulk of Afrikanerdom. None the less, the mere fact of such overtures
being made and of such alignments being considered is evidence of
the powerful new subterranean forces at work in white South Africa.

So white South Africa today is a community increasingly coming
to the realization that things are changing, and substantially willing
to countenance reform – within limits. Within it, however, there is a
minority, but a large and significant minority, who are completely
against it. What this will mean for the outcome of the South African
conflict we will examine when we have considered the attitudes of
today's black South Africans.

Before leaving the whites, however, it is worth noting how these
underlying political positions relate to the daily experience of white
South Africans and the changing perceptions they have of themselves.

165

Apartheid was, in many ways, a mad, extraordinary, and impossibly ambitious concept. In evolving, supporting, and implementing it, white South Africa was trying to reconstruct the country in its own image. What they wanted was Europe in Africa – with Africa excluded. This, quite literally, is what apartheid tried to achieve, with Dr Verwoerd's idea that blacks should not be 'South Africans' at all. The apparent success of apartheid, in its early years, was reflected in the way whites thought about their world. In their mind, 'South Africa' was, by definition, a white country. When they spoke of 'South Africa' in the world – in international sport, at the United Nations, or in trade – they thought of that South Africa which was themselves. Blacks were not a part of that country. If they thought about them they concluded they were, well, something else; citizens of 'homeland countries' probably, but certainly not South African. Actually, they did not think much about them at all.

To many outsiders this seemed completely insane. Yet the simple truth is that large numbers of white South Africans still think this way. These are the mental processes which evolve in ordinary people to allow them to do brutal things in their own self-interest. When once you can persuade yourself that South Africa means 'whites' only, then everything that followed under apartheid makes sense.

Yet what is particularly fascinating in modern South Africa is how a people, forced by economic and political reality, to change, are beginning to make the adjustments that the situation requires.

The first prerequisite for a fundamental change of an individual white South African's entire value-system has to be a change of attitude towards black South Africans, or at least, some black South Africans. This is happening. And for those whites who are making the transition there are usually one or two particular experiences which they remember as transforming.

A white woman who managed a small factory found that, because of the shortage of skilled white labour, she could not find a replacement when her white accountant retired. She became increasingly anxious. Then one day a young black woman employed as a secretary told her she had done a course in book-keeping and could she be allowed to try her hand? In desperation her employer agreed. The young black woman turned out to be rather good. At the end of the financial year, her employer asked her to come to her home on a Saturday to complete the books. Having worked all Saturday morning, lunchtime approached. The white woman was in some difficulty. She could hardly send her new book-keeper to eat in the backyard with her maid, but how could she be allowed to eat at a white woman's table? In the end, she decided that the latter was the only honourable course. For the first time in her life, at the age of fifty-five, she found herself eating at the same table with a black woman, and effectively entertaining her in her own home. It was a trivial incident, but it was the beginning of a long process of reorientation. It encapsulates perfectly how a changing economic reality brings changes in social attitudes which in turn bring changes in political attitudes.

The rediscovery does not stop there. A white schoolteacher was invited by her maid to attend her wedding in a 'homeland' an hour's drive from Pretoria. The invitation itself was an indicator of changing ideas among blacks of what was acceptable, and the schoolteacher, under the sway of the same changing sensibilities, felt inclined to accept. A great debate ensued in her home. Her husband and son opposed her going on the grounds that she might get lost and be attacked, or that she might be assaulted at the wedding. Her two daughters thought she ought to go. This was a novel dilemma for a white family. In the end she went, taking her son with her for 'protection', her husband refusing to be party to such an outrageous event. Needless to say, she was not attacked, and met only the greatest kindness and hospitality. For both mother and son, staunch Afrikaners and members of the Dutch Reformed Church who had never had any social contact with blacks before, who had never been to a black home, it proved to be a mental journey which was only just beginning.

The symptoms of such social discovery are everywhere to be seen in South Africa. For many it is no more than black people sitting alongside them on the odd occasions when they have a drink at a five-star hotel. For many, the sight of black people picnicking in formerly 'white' parks apparently serves only to reinforce their prejudices. But the process is inexorable. Even the Dutch Reformed Church, no doubt fuelled by the experience of people like our schoolteacher, has begun *Kontak* groups, in which white women invite black women, often their servants, to take coffee with them in the church hall. They sit awkwardly together, with embarrassed silences and a difficulty of small talk. One cannot but be touched, however, by this birth of a new nation.

167

Of course most of this is still confined to the upper stratum of Afrikaners, but it is no less important for that. Everywhere among whites one encounters a hunger to know what blacks are really thinking; to know what is going on in their minds. Soweto and the current insurrection has suddenly made them realize how ignorant they are, and now it is a matter of great urgency. Visiting foreign journalists, when once they have been subjected to the usual homilies on the 'true' nature of South Africa, wait for the inevitable question: have you talked to the blacks? And then, what are they saying? Most whites have still not broken through the barrier of talking directly to their fellow-citizens, but some have, and the others will slowly follow in their wake.

All this translates into important changes of political attitude. It is common now to find Afrikaners saying that apartheid was a terrible mistake. Dr Verwoerd, architect of modern apartheid and once the darling of his people, is a name almost embarrassingly unclean in many better-off Afrikaner homes. Many whites are now saying they never realized that black South Africans felt the way they clearly do; a variant is to say that blacks never really wanted political rights, but since they have begun to ask for them, it will have to be considered.

Most significantly of all, the concept of 'South Africa' has begun to change. Whereas once it meant 'white', with the Afrikaners believing it meant even more particularly 'Afrikaans', many whites are now beginning to see it in its true meaning: as the home of all South Africa's people. They talk now about no longer being European; they are beginning to accept that they are African. With that acceptance comes the recognition that 'South Africa' is more than themselves. They draw analogies with the United States where a common American identity is not incompatible with the maintenance of, say, an Irish or an Italian or an Hispanic American tradition. So the Afrikaners are beginning to see a broad South Africanism within which they could maintain their special identity – as Afrikaner South Africans. This process, still in its infancy, is profoundly important. For it also implies *accepting* that they themselves are more than Afrikaners. Afrikaner-ness becomes secondary. It involves accepting the surrender of Afrikaner hegemony and an equal place for all other South Africans. But it is comforting, too, for the Afrikaners are beginning to see that their Afrikaner-ness can be preserved within it, and that no one can take it away from them.

168

After more than 300 years, the whites are finally making their home in South Africa. The rebuilding of Europe has failed, and Africa is at last being admitted.

11
BLACKS TODAY

The structure of black society in modern South Africa is extremely complex – and this will cause much future difficulty. It is worth beginning by considering to what extent black South Africans do or do not share a common identity. The South African Government and white racists have long argued that black South Africa has no coherent national identity, and constitutes in reality a series of separate 'tribes', which are virtually 'nations' always potentially at war with each other. This claim provided the rationale for classic apartheid, and continues to provide a convenient rationale for white strategies of divide-and-rule. This alone makes it a question of some importance, but clearly the way black South Africans see their identity also has crucial implications for South Africa's political future.

The concept of South Africa as a nation-state became a reality with the creation of the independent union in 1910. Since that time it has become undeniably entrenched in the minds of white South Africans. But what about black South Africans? There is no question but that the large majority of *urban* blacks also share this concept. Once people have lived in towns for more than a few years, traditional political attachments become greatly weakened in their minds, and constant exposure to the notion of 'South Africa' concomitantly strengthened. It was as long ago as 1912 that a black political organization chose to call itself the *South African* Native National Congress, and the ANC, which it later became, is properly titled the African National Congress of *South Africa*. Even the modern black separatist reference to Azania is nothing other than South Africa by a different name.

But what about *rural* blacks? Even among them, there is a sense of self which goes beyond the immediate locality which they inhabit. Though they tend to live in isolated agrarian communities, disconnected to a considerable extent from everyone except their neighbours, and often barely literate, the idea of South Africa as a whole has also become firmly established in their minds. This is bound to be the case in a country a long way down the road to being a modern industrial and commercial economy, in many respects fully integrated into the advanced Western world.

Unemployment and terrible poverty have been driving people from rural areas to the towns and cities throughout the century. Often the patterns of migration involve movement over hundreds of miles – from the Transkei to Cape Town, for instance. People in the rural areas, therefore, have long seen themselves as linked in some way to a much wider geographic reality. Migrant workers returning home every year bring tales of the cities and gifts from their stores. Most rural black families have relatives who live there. The transistor radio has provided a new way of linking them to this world beyond the fields. The men from Government ministries who come to visit their areas and the white tourists who pass through their domain in gleaming modern cars are living proof of its existence. The recurrence of the term 'South African' on railway carriages, on the broadcasting stations, on the goods in trading stores, and even in visitors' conversations have implanted it firmly in their minds. Many rural blacks find one way or another, at some time in their lives, to visit that wider South Africa, and can never see their homes as disconnected again.

The concept of the nation-state is perhaps still weaker in their minds than among urban blacks, but it is powerful even so. A sense of national identity may be unevenly shared, but shared it is. The South African Government's claim is, to that extent at least, invalid.

None the less, important divisions do exist among black South Africans which though they do not imply a denial of a national identity, are deep and real, and can produce internal tensions. The most basic difference is between the rural and urbanized black populations. Rural people inhabit a world which is overwhelmingly concerned with farming. If they are independent, they grow their own crops and, nowadays to a lesser extent, herd their own cattle. If they are not, they do the same things for white people, working as labourers on white farms. Frequently they do a bit of both. Education and urban culture is penetrating their world, but has not yet destroyed their economic system. It is virtually still a subsistence economy, and they remain, to all intents and purposes, peasants.

171

Urbanized black South Africans, those who live in small towns as well as big, inhabit a quite different world, that of the industrialized West. They work in factories, shops, other service industries, and in white homes. They are paid in wages. They live in congested townships. They buy the same goods – allowing for differences in quality – as whites. They shop in the same stores, with the same clothes, consumer durables, and luxury goods available, even if not affordable. They have their own television stations, even if not many can afford the sets. In short, they are firmly woven into a Western-style economy, with the same consumerist and material values as their white fellow-citizens.

The recent spate of reforms has also succeeded, though as yet to a very limited extent, in fostering the development of a black middle class. Only in the biggest townships, especially Soweto, is such a phenomenon really distinguishable. But there one finds smart new houses, comparable with many white homes, purchased by bond or mortgage. One also finds an incipient entrepreneurial class – shop-owners, small business people, executives in white-owned companies, even the occasional big businessman. The existence of such a group only intensifies Western economic imperatives among urban blacks, holding out as it does the prospect of really achieving material advancement and upward social mobility.

This deep divide between rural and urban blacks has not yet become translated into articulated political differences because of the lack of real political expression for all blacks. But it will prove to be important in the future. Rural blacks will be concerned with questions of land reform and the right to seek employment in towns. Blacks already established in urban areas will be concerned with wage and promotion questions, and with protecting their position from rural migrants who will threaten them by providing cheaper labour. These differences will be magnified by the different cultures of the two groupings. For the moment, however, these tensions remain obscured.

But what about tribalism? Certainly, the South African Government and most whites believe tribal antagonisms are far more important than any others. Precisely because of this, it has become a matter of passion for many opponents of white supremacy to deny their existence. The truth, inevitably, is more complex.

The 'tribe' is, to a considerable extent, a white-imposed idea. Early white anthropologists saw people speaking roughly similar

172

languages in definable areas, and gave them this name. It has suited the South African Government to perpetuate and emphasize this concept. In reality, blacks' affinities were largely to their chieftaincy, or kingdom, which was usually a smaller unit than the white 'tribe'. Since then, white ideology, and especially the installation of white-appointed 'tribal' authorities, has distorted the picture, and certainly some blacks have half-accepted these notions in their own minds, though the chieftaincy remains important. Local attachments – to a chief or to something approaching a 'tribe' – do, therefore, exist. But one must be extremely cautious in interpreting what this means. Their influence is, like the influence of the concept of the nation-state, highly uneven.

Urban blacks – let us say those who have lived continuously for at least a decade in towns or cities – continue to speak their 'tribal' languages, but generally learn a European tongue and other Bantu ones too. They live cheek-by-jowl and are completely intermingled with people from many different areas whose mother tongue may be different from theirs. They are greatly influenced by modern education, by the critical and rational spirit of the cities, and by the common interests and aspirations which all urban-dwellers share. Older, rurally focused loyalties consequently die out, and are now weak at best. So in a city like Soweto, for instance, the thousands of people of Zulu origin who are permanently settled there have little in common with the people of distant KwaZulu except language, and much more in common with their neighbours and fellow-workers, who may be Sotho or Tswana or Xhosa.

But in the rural areas, where about half South Africa's black people – approximately 12 million live, those older identities continue to be important, for there is little mixing with other people, and economic, religious, and social structures continue to reflect tradition. At the political level, the South African Government's 'tribal' authorities help to bolster local sentiments by making individuals dependent on them, and enforcing loyalty or submission.

The intermediate category of migrant workers consists of men recruited in rural areas to work in the cities (usually in mines). They are contracted for eleven months of the year, during which they are housed, usually with members of the same 'tribe', in all-male barracks, either on the mine property or if in townships, quite separately and apart from the permanent township-dwellers. Every year they are obliged to return home for three weeks. Under such con-

173

ditions, they remain a kind of rural black person, transplanted but cocooned in urban areas. Inevitably they, too, retain a sense of rural affiliation, though given a certain unavoidable experience of the broader world, it is somewhat more diluted than among the permanent country-dwellers.

But even among rural blacks and migrant workers, their local identities really only come into play when some stress, usually economic, drives them into a position of competition with other black people. Fighting often surfaces, for instance, on mine compounds. This is not usually because people from different areas simply dislike each other, but is generally sparked off by some dispute over demarcation in a tightly confined space or over access to some privilege, in which membership of the group is the individual's best way of protecting himself. In the rural areas, friction usually only occurs when there is a dispute over land or resources, such as the ferocious fighting which broke out in 1985 on the borders of the Transkei and Natal, when Transkeian Pondos tried to occupy land where Zulus were settled.

Tribalism is a highly suspect notion, then, but it is certainly true that attachments to chiefs, localities or regions which do not correspond very precisely to 'tribes' are still an important factor in South Africa, but almost entirely among rural or semi-rural blacks. Even here, it becomes a source of conflict only under certain special circumstances. White claims about tribalism therefore reflect some reality, but are highly distorted.

In political terms, divisions within the urban black population are actually more significant, since urban people usually take the lead in national politics, and are likely to have a greater influence on South Africa's political future.

The large majority of black people who live in South Africa's towns and cities are concerned, like their white fellow-citizens and urban peoples in modern economies everywhere, with the ordinary day-to-day issues of surviving and trying to improve their standard of living. Of course, in South Africa the question of survival is not as straightforward as it is in the most other countries. A substantial proportion of urban blacks – hundreds of thousands of people – have, until recently, faced a daily battle against the many forces of authority threatening their very presence in these areas. Under the Pass Laws that presence was deemed illegal. That meant they could not legitimately rent accommodation, so they either had to build their own shanties or persuade other blacks who did have the right to be there to take them in. Their every movement was subject to the danger that they might be, and frequently were, stopped by the police, arrested, imprisoned, and then sentenced, sometimes to a fine, sometimes to whipping, sometimes to further jail sentences, or – worst of all – to forced expulsion from urban areas back to their 'homelands'. Those who squatted with legally settled blacks faced the possibility of night police raids; those who had built their own shanties frequently found themselves surrounded by police in the small hours of the morning, rounded up, and made to watch as their poor homes were pulled down and broken up.* They then faced all the usual penalties. Day after day, month after month, many of them fought an ongoing struggle against this curious authority. They would build their homes or squat with others; they would have their homes broken down or be arrested; when they were able to they would return and start all over again; after a while – days, weeks, months, or years later – they would be rearrested. The cycle would go on. During the breathing spaces they would eke out a living as best they could. Settled blacks were not unaffected by this process either. They were caught up in police raids or stop-and-search operations as a matter of routine; when they had given help or support to 'illegals' they, too, were arrested.

In April 1986 the South African Government announced the scrapping of the Pass Laws and their intention to introduce a new system of 'orderly urbanization'. This is intended to allow a freer movement of people to the cities, and their right to build shanties on state-provided squatter sites. What additional restrictions might flow from the non-availability of such sites or of jobs, what other limits might also be imposed, is not yet clear, and will not become clear for several years. What we can say is that great insecurity will continue to haunt millions of South Africans for some time to come. Not only will the legal position remain ambiguous, but a police force, accustomed to decades of harassing people, will need a considerable time to become used to a new political reality.

Security, then, is – and will remain – the first concern for many urban blacks. Finding a job is the next concern. Given the recent depressed condition of the South African economy and a high birth

* Crossroads, near Cape Town, which has figured prominently in the recent unrest, was particularly affected by this kind of daily battle with the police.

rate, unemployment, which has long been a major reality of urban black South African life, can only get worse. Those who are in jobs have their own problems: meeting the rent or mortgage payments; transport costs; the price of food; the cost of all household items. Given a level of inflation which has been stuck above fifteen per cent for several years, and a lower proportionate increase in earnings, themselves a fraction of white earnings, simply making ends meet, even for better-off urban blacks, is an appalling struggle. Ordinary people, in all societies and almost always, are preoccupied with similar material needs. It follows that they are not terribly bothered about abstract political ideas. They simply want to get on with their lives. For urban black South Africans, in whose midst a brutal insurrection has been raging for two years, these events have caused great additional hardship.

One source has been the security forces. Curfews have been imposed, restricting their movement; the police and army presence has been enormously intensified, with a consequent increase in arrests, searches, and general harassment; their neighbours and children have been taken away, shot, wounded or killed, and terrifying pitched battles have been played out around their homes. But another source has been their own children. It is the young men and women of the townships who have been making the insurrection. When they do go to school, their parents wait anxiously to hear whether classroom political meetings or demonstrations have sparked off another confrontation with the police; when they do not go to school, which in many places, and for long periods, has been the case, confrontations with the police are virtually inevitable. For a downtrodden people, who long desperately for their children to escape poverty and ignorance, the disruption of education is a terrible disappointment. In addition their children's lecturing, their threats, their boycott calls and roadblocks, the attacks on surrounding homes, the petrol-bombings, the physical attacks, and in many cases mutilation or even murder, have made daily life even more difficult. Gangsters and hoodlums proliferate. In short, they have lost control of their children and what little security they might have had.

They have few illusions about what 'liberation' might mean. They already have some experience of black authority and they will tell you quite frankly that black police are often far more brutal than their white counterparts. They tell you, in a great outporing of resentment, that black councillors or black ticket sellers at the railway station or many of the other forms of black petty officialdom are almost always corrupt, and have to be bribed in order to give you what is actually due as of right. They know instinctively that in highly impoverished and unequal societies, graft is inevitable as one of the few routes available for material advancement. They have been given hints of what a politicized black leadership might mean for ordinary people: humiliation, intimidation, and death.

To make life worse, reality is even more complicated than that. For, in a way which is not hard to understand, they are also proud of their children. They know only too well the grinding routine humiliations of apartheid. Black mothers and fathers are proud of their children because they have refused to tolerate it any longer. They have shown courage – even a willingness to die. More importantly, the children's war is working. In the last two or three years black South Africans have seen more changes than in all the rest of their lives. Measure after measure has been precipitately swept from the statute book. The Pass Laws have gone. Winnie Mandela stays defiantly in Soweto and talks openly about the ANC. The State President bends over backwards talking about negotiation and the need to accommodate black aspirations. Other Afrikaners have begun 'talking nicely about the kaffirs'. True, it has not yet produced any fundamental change in their lives, but they know it implies something profound and far-reaching. Despite everything, they feel that perhaps the children's way is the only way.

It is this which has prevented them so far from counteracting against the mobs. There have been isolated acts of resistance. Taxi-drivers in Soweto, their trade occasionally threatened by youthful militants, have been known to chase them off in packs. Individual black parents have refused to support boycotts or stayaway-from-work calls. Occasionally they have marched their children to school in an attempt to force them to attend classes. To date, however, these have been only pinpricks against the insurrection.

Nonetheless this real ambivalence in the attitude of older urban blacks towards the unrest could have a marked influence on the course of events. It is significant, for example, that Soweto, the township which was at the heart of the 1976-7 disturbances has been unexpectedly muted in the recent wave of conflict. This is partly because, as in effect the largest city in the whole of South Africa, it embraces people of many different backgrounds and political positions. It therefore lacks homogeneity, and the UDF in particular – as probably the most important political organizing force among urban blacks – has found it relatively unfertile territory for mobilization, recruitment, and political radicalism. Heterogeneity, though, cannot be the sole explanation. After all, it did not prevent Soweto being the seedbed of militancy in the earlier phase of protest. No, the real reason is that, after the 1976 troubles, the Government and especially big business realized that Soweto, sitting at the core of the industrial and commercial heartland of South Africa had to be pacified at all costs, if the whole economy was not to be brought down in an explosion of black frustration. The Government did its part by introducing general reforms, like allowing blacks to own property in townships and lifting restrictions on the growth of black business. These benefitted Soweto more than other areas, it being the home of the most urbanized and affluent blacks. They also directed specific infrastructural investment at Soweto, like the building of a new civic centre and a teacher training college, and a further push towards electrification. Big business, however, came in behind the Government and injected a massive dose of capital. Led by the Urban Foundation, a trust set up by big white companies to promote improvements in townships, it was the business community who were primarily responsible for the huge new house-building programme and for making loans available to blacks to buy them. Much effort went into building smart new banks and offices, and in putting capital into burgeoning black chain-stores, which would not only improve food and household supplies for Soweto's inhabitants, but would make luxury consumer durables more readily available to them too. This thrust has worked, for Soweto does now have a small but identifiable black middle class which has been brought into being in less than a decade. It is the existence of precisely such a population that has acted as a brake on radicalism. From the Government's point of view this is a two-edged sword: as the best-educated and most sophisticated element in the black population, if their aspirations were frustrated by economic recession or political repression, they could turn out to be the most implacable and dangerous adversaries. But for the moment, parents whose standard of living has improved markedly, whose prospects are now better than they ever have been, and whose financial commitments make it imperative to stay at work and not have their daily lives disrupted, have proved to be more resistant to strike and boycott calls. They exert a more restraining influence on their children's activities, than parents who have little more than nothing to lose.

There have already been hints that general counteraction among older blacks may be developing. Early in 1986, in the endemically troubled Johannesburg township of Alexandra, black 'vigilantes' apparently appeared in the night and attacked radical, mainly UDF, youngsters. Fighting between them broke out. The identity of these assailants was never satisfactorily explained, but the township-dwellers believed they were undercover black policeman or police informers. Soon afterwards, in May 1986, a similar phenomenon made itself felt in Crossroads. This was a development of a different order, though. There, literally thousands of *witdoeke*, or white handkerchiefs, as they were called – a name derived from the attackers' practice of tying these symbols around their sleeves – set into radical youngsters, heavily entrenched in the township, with ferocious force. In three days of localized civil war, the two factions between them managed to do what the Government had failed to achieve in a decade of trying: they laid waste to the entire settlement. The *witdoeke* attacked with sticks, clubs, fists, and guns. The 'comrades' fought back with similar weapons. As huge, massed battalions opposed each other, charging through the camp, at least 30,000 black residents fled in terror. At the end of the fighting, Crossroads looked as though it had been devastated by a nuclear holocaust. Hardly a shack had not been set on fire; few other buildings remained standing. The radical youngsters regrouped in the area known as KTC* and, a few weeks later, in early June, with the winter rain and cold already sweeping across the flats from the South Atlantic, another, and successful, attempt was made by the *witdoeke* to smash them. The one remaining Red Cross charity clinic, which had been fighting against all the odds to help the tens of thousands of homeless people, was razed to the ground. Once again, the identity of the attackers remained shadowy. The press had at first labelled them 'fathers'. Since they were generally older men than the 'comrades' it was believed they were conservatively inclined older residents who had grown sick of the radical disturbances. Eye-witnesses, however, swore they had been disgorged from security force vehicles. Certainly they appeared to enjoy a friendly relationship with the police and army, who made only perfunctory attempts to

---

* The name of a local trading store.

stop them. Although it is not clear whether this marked the start of a true backlash from within the older black population, it certainly underscored the dangers for the insurrection.

The UDF leadership have, since early on, been only too aware of it. And it poses real difficulties for them in trying to achieve their political objective, which is now to achieve the transfer of power. For them it is no longer simply a question of whittling away economic and social apartheid – that process is already considerably advanced, at least at a statutory level, and will, from now onwards, simply have to work itself through into the reality of daily practice. There is some room for further advance in these areas. The laws which divide the country into 'black' and 'white' zones remain in force. Since the Pass Laws have been abolished and black movement from rural to urban areas will, in future, be subject to less control (whether explicitly in law or by virtue of the changing political reality), the main effect will be to perpetuate segregated residential areas and education. This, even for reformist whites, remains highly important. In psychological and social terms, these barriers represent the last personal protection from blacks, and their removal would signal the start of a truly multiracial society. As the whites are not yet at the point where they believe a surrender of that magnitude is necessary, they are likely to resist the abolition of residential and educational segregation very strongly. Even so, voices are already being heard, some of them within the National Party leadership itself, murmuring about the possibility of precisely this. To that extent it no longer represents the most major challenge for black political organizations like the UDF.

So their real objective now is to achieve the transfer of political power. Of course this has always been on the agenda of all black political movements. But when the UDF began in 1983, they did not believe it could be achieved at once. They deliberately set their sights on limited, more immediate goals, like ensuring that the Coloured and Indian elections to the Tricameral Parliament were largely a failure. Since then events have moved to take the initiative out of their hands and to produce a situation in which many other specific targets have been achieved by a knock-on effect. So the UDF has been encouraged to think the final goal of political power may be in sight.

At a deep political level, it is perfectly rational for them to pursue this goal. Political power matters more than anything else, because

what it ultimately confers is the ability to *enforce* desired arrangements in every walk of life. Until political power legitimizes – that is,
gives general moral sanction to – and gives access to, the use of
coercion through the armed forces, all arrangements, however re-
forming and desirable, remain precarious, able to be resisted by
those who wish to resist them and susceptible to being distorted or
even withdrawn. Let us take jobs, for example. South Africa cannot
generate, within the next decade at least, sufficient new jobs to soak
up black unemployment. Blacks want jobs – and as soon as possible.
They would also like, if possible, jobs which bring security, the prospect of improvements in their or their children's standard of living,
and patronage. Just as the Afrikaners sought political power and
used it to winkle the English out of state employment – the major
immediate source of such jobs – so black South Africans will want to
dislodge Afrikaners from state employment to occupy these jobs
themselves and this cannot happen without control of the state itself.
If that is too extreme an example, let us take the case of education.
No matter how much the state promises to improve black education
– and it has already been improved – it will always set aside the first
tranche of whatever resources are available for education to ensure
that a basic minimum in white education, to which its white constituents have become accustomed, is maintained. It must do this
for it would lose its power-base if it did not. Black education will
therefore always be given whatever is left over. Only black control of
the state can ensure that this is changed fundamentally. This truism
of power applies in every field. Hence, whatever the moral and phil-
osophic arguments in favour of majority rule – and they are overwhelming – political reality also operates under the surface always
to impel an aggrieved majority towards that objective.

But if political power is now on the black agenda, the means of
securing it have still to be identified and consolidated. Control of the
townships is far from being control of the state. White power has still
to be assaulted in the economy, in white suburbs and cities, and in
the armed forces. The UDF is now trying to lay the basis for that
more protracted and difficult fight. And this is where retaining the
support, or at least the passive consent, of the broad black population is so vital. They recognize that without wider mobilization, they
cannot succeed.

One element of their strategy is to canvass and recruit in the rural
areas, which they regard as something of an Achilles' heel for

181

apartheid. In evolving such a strategy, they are following in the successful tradition of Maoism, which sought to recruit the peasantry and 'encircle the cities'. South Africa's rural areas are vast, difficult to police, lie in a broad belt around the 'white' areas, especially the cities, and provide transit areas for activists on the run. Moreover, the 'governments' of the rural areas – essentially the homelands – are profoundly unpopular among many of their subjects. Their regimes are to a very large extent tyrannical, inefficient, corrupt, and violently repressive. Their very inefficiency gives scope for manoeuvre, while their unpopularity makes them fertile breeding-grounds for opposition movements. It is, however, a tall order for the UDF to recruit widely in these areas. Their police forces, though inefficient, are deadly. The people are even more uninterested in politics than their urban relatives. There is a long-instilled passivity, and substantial unfamiliarity with urban political attitudes. Despite this, it is worth noting that in the homeland of Bophuthatswana in 1985, student demonstrators succeeded in outwitting the local police and staging a demonstration when President Botha came on an official visit. The 'university colleges' in the homelands remain hotbeds of student activism, despite every attempt to crush them. And a number of key UDF figures from the Eastern Cape have not only succeeded in eluding police in the Ciskei homeland, but have been able to use it as a place of refuge. None the less, the UDF will find serious recruiting in these areas an uphill struggle.

In one unstated respect, however, they may be more successful. The ANC, while giving moral support to the internal political movement, can still contribute to that domestic struggle mainly by keeping up the campaign of sabotage. With its access routes through Mozambique still shut off, entry from Angola through Namibia, or through Botswana, are the only real options, and these require later passage through homelands. The UDF, even if it can establish only small pockets of rural support, could provide ANC operators with hiding-places and supplies, and in the longer-run, this could lead to a marked escalation of ANC activity.

It is the urban areas, however, that the UDF still sees as its main arena and given the unrest there and the fact that the vital organs of the South African economy are located there, this is inevitable. In trying to broaden its base in the towns and cities, the UDF has set about forming 'street committees' in the townships – the classic weapon of semi-underground insurrectionary movements. A small number of UDF activists will be charged in a local area with establishing a network of contacts and supporters. The aim is to ensure control. The UDF must keep itself well informed on every development and on each person's political affiliations and movements. It must be able to bring people onto the streets or turn them out at political rallies, like funerals. It must be able to ensure that they stay at home when strikes or boycotts are called. It must exert its authority by showing itself to be omnipresent and woven into the very fabric of everyday life.

This, too, is a tall order. The UDF at present has good organization in the Western and Eastern Cape, and in isolated pockets of the Witwatersrand, mainly on the East Rand and in the Vaal Triangle. Significantly, its presence in Soweto is weak. In Natal its presence is better established, but is subject to constant harassment from *Inkatha*, which prevents it from coalescing.

Because of the danger of a conservative black backlash, the extent to which the UDF succeeds in creating a wider network of urban support will ultimately depend largely on how it manages the inherent tension between young radicals on the one hand and their parents' generation on the other. And its attempts to do so already have shown how difficult this will be.

In national meetings at the end of 1985 and the beginning of 1986, parents voiced strong concern over the schools' boycott, and the UDF had to try and achieve a compromise. The youngsters agreed to end the schools' boycott, the quid pro quo being that closer links with the trade unions would be developed to try and foster a general strike or a series of local general strikes. Neither the ending of the schools' boycott nor the achievement of a general strike was, in fact, achieved. This incident provides clear evidence of the dangers the UDF faces, and its weaknesses. It shows that parental concern at the effects of the unrest is becoming irresistible – but it shows, too, that the UDF cannot impose its discipline on the young radicals, nor command unions to take action they are not ready for. One has to bear in mind that the UDF was already beginning to lose control of the youngsters as a result of the arrests of its entire national leadership in the course of 1984 and 1985. A new leadership did come up from the ranks and take its place, but they were less experienced and because the State of Emergency forced them to keep a low profile, operating in great secrecy and from hiding, it considerably reduced their control. Having spent months on the streets, following their

183

own instincts and becoming progressively embittered against the security forces, but more and more confident of their ability to strike within the black community at will, the youngsters are bound to consider themselves independent of the UDF leadership – and extremely unwilling to bow to its pleas for moderation. At the same time, it has given free rein to many apolitical, but thuggish, youngsters who pose as political radicals and use it as a guise to extract money and goods from ordinary citizens, or to settle old scores.

In trying to check all these youthful elements, however, the UDF cannot afford to dissociate itself from them: they are the shock-troops of the insurrection, the cutting edge that gives it its leverage over the state, and the motor force behind the reforms already achieved. The UDF not only has to tolerate youthful protest, it positively needs it. The great trick is to harness it to the most purposeful ends. If they fail in this, they will face a terrible difficulty. The parents' generation are likely to become progressively more alienated from the young radicals. Not only will they start reacting against them and refusing to heed calls on their political support, they will be inclined more and more to turn a blind eye to any repressive steps the Government may take against the youngsters. This will enable the Government to pick them off more easily, and thus draw the teeth of the insurrection. It would be 1977 all over again. Putting it simply, the youth are in grave danger of becoming isolated from the rest of their community. That would not only leave them vulnerable to being destroyed by the security forces, but it would be an enormous setback to the insurrection.

To try and broaden its control, the UDF has spawned 'people's courts' in townships all over the country. Run by young activists, they dispense summary justice. Their nature varies greatly from area to area. In some instances they act to try and check youthful excesses, and concern themselves with stopping gangsterism and lawlessness. In other areas, they are simply attempts to legitimize attacks on 'collaborators'. Their very unco-ordinated character shows how difficult it is for an amorphous and largely underground leadership to impose its authority in the increasingly anarchic conditions of a country in the throes of insurrection, but they do at least serve the purpose of demonstrating to the whites their own impotence to influence black life.

But the UDF's problems are not simply those of uniting the divergence of the youth and older blacks, or of widening its support. They face challenges to their authority from other important directions.

The conservative instincts of a large body of the urban black population have failed to find expression up till now, partly because the general lack of political expression for all blacks has particularly inhibited organization among such people, and partly because incipient vehicles of expression – for example, black muncipal councils – never had a chance to get off the ground. The homeland leadership currently provides the only political alternative for mobilizing their opinion, but is both too divorced from urban life and too compromised to play this role. But a potential alternative is conservative black churches like the Church of Zion, a movement several-million strong, which, by fusing a Pentecostalist Christianity with strains of traditional African animism, appeals to large numbers of rural blacks and to those elements of the urban population retaining some of their rural traditions, usually those who are less well-educated and employed in relatively menial jobs.

The South African President, in conceptualizing a system of alliances with compliant blacks, has long seen groups like this as potential allies. In 1985, for instance, he took the unprecedented step of attending a huge Church of Zion rally in the Northern Transvaal to address the congregation, reported by the state media to number 2 million. His address was extensively televised. In it he asked for their support, speaking of mistakes that had been made but seeking reconciliation, and appealing to their instincts by condemning lawlessness in the townships. He was given a tumultuous reception.

It is most improbable that conservative, but non-political, movements like this would ever become explicitly involved in trying to direct their congregations' political actions. But by their pronouncements on the condition of life and about behaviour in the material world, they do exert some influence against recruitment into political causes and political activism in general. They are not, therefore, an active challenge to the UDF, but it has constantly to struggle against their moral influence.

A challenge of a much more direct kind comes from that deep-seated South African tradition of black exclusivism, now merged with radical anti-capitalism in the National Forum, and especially its most vital member organization, AZAPO. Though much more narrowly based than the UDF, both geographically and in terms of membership, the NF does have active organizations in the Western Cape and in some of the townships of Pretoria and Johannesburg, and their periodic clashes with the UDF show they remain a potent force. The insurrection, with its promise of a successful onslaught on township authorities, has tended latterly to bring them somewhat closer together, but tension remains.

The real importance of this division lies in the future. For if radical youngsters become disillusioned with UDF pragmatism and 'moderation', the NF might provide an alternative home, and this could drain support from the UDF and lead to intensified conflict.

Perhaps the most significant challenge to the UDF, though, comes from Chief Gatsha Buthelezi and his *Inkatha* organization. Since Chief Buthelezi is also widely admired in the West and considered in some circles as a candidate for national leadership, it is worth examining his role in South African politics in some detail.

It has to be said that Chief Buthelezi explicitly denies that he entertains aspirations to national leadership, but he does head the largest language group, he does have a strong regional base, he is an impressive and ambitious man, and he has courted political alliances and external recognition in a way that is not consistent with the pursuit of purely localized interests. All his actions suggest an intention to consolidate his power as much as he can and to adopt a wait-and-see approach. It seems highly likely that if he saw an opportunity for national leadership, he would jump at it.

He has, for instance, created and consolidated his essentially Zulu quasi-cultural organization *Inkatha*. He was also the moving force behind the creation of the South African Black Alliance in the early 1980s, which consisted of a coalition between *Inkatha*, and Coloured, Indian, and Swazi-speaking political parties. The Alliance foundered, however, when the Coloureds withdrew over the its acceptance of the 1983 Constitution setting up the Tricameral Parliament. In 1985, he also helped to establish a Convention Alliance, bringing together a multiracial collection of individuals favouring negotiation over South Africa's future, which has not, however, figured much since.

Chief Buthelezi publicly favours majority rule within a unitary South Africa as a long-term goal, but is prepared to accept black-white power-sharing, if necessary in some federal system, for an interim period of unspecified duration. He opposes the use of violence for political ends, and is also strongly opposed to the application of economic sanctions by foreign countries against South Africa on the grounds that it would harm black South Africans.

186

These positions make him an attractive potential ally for both the South African Government and Western governments. The South African Government would dearly like to bring him into a system of alliances which, given the numbers he commands, would add considerable weight. Negotiations between them have limped along on and off, but Chief Buthelezi demands the release of political prisoners, the legalization of all black political parties (which would include the ANC), and a clear statement of intent from the South African Government before he will enter into any public arrangement with them. For the moment, the South African Government is ambiguous about these requirements and any such deal seems uncertain at present.

Meanwhile, Chief Buthelezi is pursuing the possibility of a regional federation between KwaZulu and Natal (which would actually reconstitute the old pre-apartheid Natal). After the Lombard report proposing such an idea had been given a cool reception by the Government in 1980, Chief Buthelezi appointed his own commission, the Buthelezi Commission, which then proposed the same scheme. It too was cold-shouldered, but the Chief has sensed that after the shock of the recent insurrection and the accompanying violence in Natal, white people there – predominantly English-speaking and traditionally mildly liberal – might be amenable to such overtures. He is therefore talking to the major white interest groups in Natal to explore the possibility of a *de facto* experiment. The Government would favour such a scheme. It has very little support in Natal so it need not worry about losing votes there; it would like to see how such a pilot project worked out; and it might encourage the Chief to deal with them publicly at a national level. But because the Government fears the response of their electorate outside Natal, they would not openly endorse such an arrangement – they would merely not stand in its way. From the point of view of Chief Buthelezi, who would almost certainly emerge as the leading figure in KwaZulu-Natal, it would broaden his base and give him an outstanding opportunity of wooing white moderate opinion elsewhere. Such a federation is therefore very likely within a year or two.

One can see from this that Chief Buthelezi's political *modus operandi* and his goals are diametrically opposed to the ANC's. As his position on, for instance, the 1983 Constitution and sanctions (which the ANC favour) has become clear, the antagonism between him and the ANC-oriented UDF has sharpened. This has been intensified by the UDF's limited success in recruiting in the townships around Durban, which the Chief regards as part of his fiefdom. Hence, the continuing violence between them in Natal. In mid-1986 Chief Buthelezi also created a 'moderate' trade union movement in Natal to counter the growing influence of UDF-linked unions there, though given its local flavour and lack of links with more powerful national groupings, it is unlikely seriously to rival the established trade union groupings.

Whether the Chief could ever expand from his KwaZulu-Natal base to command broad support beyond it, is also doubtful. Polls of black political opinion in South Africa are rare and unreliable. The most trustworthy polls suggest, however, that outside KwaZulu he enjoys very little popular support. Indeed, they have frequently shown him as having percentage support below double figures and consistently trailing behind even such white liberals as the PFP MP, Helen Suzman. Even in Durban, an overwhelmingly Zulu city, there appears to be little support for him. His power-base seems then to be essentially among rural Zulus, which would also include Zulu migrant workers as far afield as Soweto. In straightforward popularity terms this is too narrow a base to constitute a spring-board for national leadership, especially given the profound hos-tility such a bid would provoke, both from ordinary blacks of other language groups and from his political opponents.

None the less, the potential may be there for a conjunction of white, Coloured, and Indian interest groups, urban conservative blacks, other homeland leaders, and the Chief – and this would con-stitute a powerful check to the UDF and the ANC. In fact, it follows from this that, despite his public support for majority rule, Chief Buthelezi's best hope for national leadership lies in preventing straightforward majoritarianism, and in trying to arrange precisely such a coalition. With these powerful interest groups conspiring to prevent a simple transfer of power, the UDF will find achieving that goal more difficult. And even if that transfer does take not place, Buthelezi at the helm of KwaZulu alone or KwaZulu-Natal will al-ways remain a major regional force deeply antagonistic to them.

So, South Africa's blacks today share a common sense of national identity, but remain deeply divided. The major division is between rural and urban blacks, and within the rural population especially, local attachments constantly threaten to split them. Within the urban population there is a widening gap between ordinary non-political people and the young radicals, with the UDF trying to expand its base by bridging both. Its position is challenged by conservative churches, by the NF, and by the regional figure of Chief Buthelezi.

Before we go on to consider what this might mean for South Africa's future, however, it is important to recognize some critical changes of mood among South Africa's black citizens. The insurrection of the last two years has succeeded in bringing about one fundamental change, among both the UDF and the radicals, and their opponents. This would remain true even if, by collapsing tomorrow, it never accomplished anything else. That achievement has been to transform the way black South Africans see themselves in their country.

They have begun to feel, in varying degrees, that a new reality has come into being in their land. The sense that the *ancien régime* is crumbling is all-pervasive, and to the extent that Afrikaner politicians have committed themselves publicly to abolishing a vast array of apartheid measures, it is also true. Given the population dispositions in South Africa, the growing acceptance of reform within the white community, and the increasing sophistication of the black population, all of it reinforced by the realities of South Africa's advanced economy, the erosion of apartheid is also beginning to look to many blacks as though it is irreversible. They stand today between two worlds. The old order is disappearing, but the new order is not yet fully formed. It is a period of great uncertainty for black South Africans. Many, who have spent their lives in a world of rigid segregation and with black people's roles strongly defined, highly limited, and vigorously enforced, the process of relatively sudden transition is deeply alarming, a disquiet in no way assuaged by the brutal violence precipitating it. The destruction of old certainties is always threatening, even for those who may profit by it. Yet, despite misgivings, black people in South Africa today can see that, for the first time in living memory, a dynamic is at work in their society which is tilting the balance of power in their direction. Among many blacks, consequently, a new confidence is evident. They may not believe 'liberation' is around the corner, but even in the lowest echelons of daily life a new assertiveness, and a more active sense of resistance against injustice, is clearly detectable.

At a political level, black South Africa is not sure what to think

189

about the future. Some – many – believe the day of 'liberation', or at least black rule, is in sight. Others feel it is still far distant. Many welcome unreservedly the prospect of changing the prevailing order; others, though grateful for any improvement, are deeply fearful of what may happen.

A new confidence, the whiff of victory, but great uncertainty about where they are going and what will emerge: that is the condition of black South Africa today.

Only one certainty unites them, and unites them with their white fellow-citizens: South Africa will never be the same again. Verwoerdian apartheid is dead. Their long and total subjugation is over. But what will replace it? It is to this question we must finally turn.

12
THE FUTURE

The question of South Africa's future understandably provokes enormous interest and debate. For South Africans, the past is past, but their future is being shaped even now. Their every action contributes to it, but uncertainty about its outcome makes choice agonizing. Foreign governments and millions throughout the world also have their limited part to play, but wonder how best to do it. So let us try to clarify the issues.

South Africa's insurrection began as a confused expression of black outrage, without clear objectives. As the weeks of turmoil have lengthened into years, the insurrection has started to become a civil war, and the issue is becoming increasingly defined. It is now a struggle for political power. The question is whether the white minority or the black majority shall rule. Those organizations – the UDF and the ANC – which are most potent in the conflict are forcing this issue to the fore, and in doing so they are merely articulating the changing reality of a deeply divided society. The black majority must win, and for the same reason that has always asserted itself in South African history: economics.

Apartheid, despite the heavy toll in human suffering and the bloody carnage of its demise, has succeeded. It protected the Afrikaners long enough for the majority of them to lift themselves up out of poverty and to establish an independent economic base which will endure. But there has been a hidden cost. The great burgeoning of the economy required a huge pool of black labour and has, in effect, given black South Africa the leverage it needed to end white supremacy. There can be no going back. They are now so inextricably interwoven into the economy that the only sure way of stemming their advance would be to destroy that economy, and start all over again. Some whites – those Afrikaners whose comparative position

191

must decline – would like to do that. Even now they speak of going back to the land and building a new economy without blacks. But they are a minority. The vast majority are coming to see they are now economically robust enough to have a good chance of retaining their position without political control. In this, it seems, they have learnt more from their English compatriots, who lost political control to them decades ago, than simply how to be good capitalists.

But going on can only imply a shifting balance of racial power. For if the economy cannot function without black South Africa, the education, skills, and expectations it has given them means it can no longer keep them in subjection. And as they seek to translate their material aspirations into reality, it follows they must begin to dismantle the vast gulf between their living standards and those of the whites.

So political power becomes the central issue. For, in order to bring about a truly substantial and systematic redistribution of wealth, some whites – not necessarily the majority but certainly a large minority – will have to undergo a decline. They will no longer be able to maintain the gap between themselves and rising blacks, and in many cases, their actual living standards will have to fall, too, for periodic slowdowns in growth will produce a new, much more intense squeeze on resources, and a much more powerfully charged contest between the whites who have and the blacks who want to have. There will thus be strong imperatives for whites to try and regulate black advance and, when necessary, put a brake on it altogether. Political power, with its conferring ability to shape society and enforce that design, is thus the lever that whites are trying to hold on to – and which blacks need to win control of to achieve their aspirations. That is why the spectre of black political control which has long stalked the white landscape, is now being brought to life.

Yet the black men and women weighed down by the mundane burdens of township life do not necessarily see political power as the issue. In fact, on the surface, only a minority do. But as their desire for a better life creates an irresistible groundswell of frustration, their leaders translate the issue for them. Because only political control by black people can resolve the fundamental mismatch between black and white, and allow black South Africa to restructure the country in their own image, black people are being, and will increasingly be, sucked up into the inexorable struggle to rule the country.

The whites, of course, will resist, and delay the transfer of power as long as they can. They will be forced to make more concessions to the blacks, but will try to limit them in other ways. They will yield here and there, but dig their heels in somewhere else. They will keep taking tough measures to try and retain some control. Every reform will therefore be offset Every act of apparent magnanimity will be suspect. Blacks will find change comes, and yet the long-awaited transformation of their lives remains curiously elusive. So the pushing and shoving, the yielding and the resistance will lock black and white together in a gory tussle into the future. Slowly reality will buckle under the pressure; and suddenly it will snap. White South Africa will discover one morning that power has imperceptibly slipped through their fingers. Black South Africa will be masters of the house.

Many people, black and white, inside and outside South Africa, deny this. They believe there now is a deadlock, with the blacks able to challenge white supremacy, but not dislodge it, and the whites no longer able to rule absolutely, but still capable of stopping the blacks from taking power. The implication of this is that the bloody struggle will go on and on without resolution, neither side able to clinch a decisive victory.

This is a misreading of the situation. For the moment it only *looks* that way. Behind the facade the pendulum is swinging inexorably away from the whites.

Ever since petty apartheid began to ease in the early 1970s, white South Africa has been conceding ground. The pace of reform was very slow for nearly a decade, then it quickened rapidly – and is now turning into headlong flight, as measure after apartheid measure gets hastily flung out. Black South Africa, for its part, has been seeking reform through all this time. At first it was tentative, then bold but beaten back, then renewed with enormously strengthened force, and it has not been beaten back even yet.

White South Africans did not *want* to reform. They were a people who cheerfully, with brusque assurance and an overweening sense of moral rectitude, constructed a system of racial segregation lambasted by the world and virtually unparalleled in modern times. They did this not centuries or even generations ago, but within the last forty years. What has made them change? They have not undergone a blinding conversion; they have not mysteriously become different people. But reality has intruded. Their dream has been shattered by the collision of hopes with needs. Hopes must go, for needs remain needs. They have been forced to divest themselves of apartheid. They have not done it willingly; had there been any alternative, they would have clung to it. Every concession made is evidence of their weakness and not their strength. The gathering speed of reform is thus the measure of their accelerating incapacity, and, by the same token, of growing black strength. There *is* a balance of power, but it is not in alignment. It is shifting unstoppably. At root, behind these political processes, economic reality has trapped the whites. The paradox is that their continued prosperity *requires* black advance, even though it is political anathema to them.

The human capacity to wish away what one does not want is much in evidence in the current debate about South Africa's future. White South Africans who concede the inevitability of change, and their supporters abroad, cling to two arguments to persuade themselves that that change will not necessarily bring black government. Power-sharing between the races, they say, with a guaranteed share for whites, will stop the rot. And if all else fails, the continued armed might of white South Africa will prevent a straight transfer of power.

It is difficult to see how power-sharing can now be brought about. The Government's record to date in trying to strike a deal with potential black allies illustrates the problem. At the time when the President's Council was created, in 1980-1, the Government explored the possibility of setting up a parallel – but of course separate – council of black citizens to represent black opinion on a purely consultative basis. By that stage blacks were already beyond the point of accepting consultative rights only. The Government found no takers, and the idea was quietly dropped. They then hoped that the upgrading of black community councils into fully fledged local authorities in 1982 would produce an army of democratically endorsed co-operative urban blacks with whom serious negotiations about national politics could begin. The poor electoral response, however, was a reflection of the distrust with which these bodies were already regarded, and the councillors elected, highly conscious of it, warned the Government they could not play that role. 'Real' black leaders would have to be found. A Cabinet Committee trying to find credible black leaders became a permanent fixture on the political landscape, taking soundings of the least hostile blacks, desperately trying to find the way to bring the hoped-for alliance into being. It could not find suitable partners either, and any remaining hopes attached to the councillors were extinguished by the destruction of the entire system in the insurrection which began in 1984. By 1986 the Government had set up a National Statutory Council for urban blacks, charged with the same mission. Still no success.

The constant problem has been that what the whites are prepared to concede is always outpaced by the growth in black expectations. Those blacks to whom the Government spoke kept telling it that certain minimum conditions would need to be fulfilled before they could enter into any public liaison. Political prisoners would have to be released, and free black political campaigning allowed, including the legalization of the ANC. They adopted this stance because they knew that black opinion would regard anything less as totally unacceptable, and it would be political suicide for them. The Government would not accept these terms. Legalizing political parties like the ANC, committed as it is to majority rule, would carry the gravest danger for a system of alliances explicitly conceived to prevent that very thing from coming about.

But once events have driven the Government to the point where it has met these conditions, power-sharing might just be possible. Blacks like the 'homeland' leaders, conservative urban groups like the middle class from which councillors were drawn, and Chief Buthelezi all have an interest in preventing majority rule if, as the evidence suggests, it will mean ANC rule. If they are able to claim they have extracted real concessions, they may feel more confident about throwing in their lot with the whites in a bid to stop the ANC.

On paper such a power-sharing arrangement, backed up by the might of the security forces, might look impressive enough. But could it stem the tide of majority rule? The problem for the white authorities is the urban blacks, for they are the most crucial to the economy, the most sophisticated section of the black population, and the most troublesome. To put an end to the conflict now raging, it has to pacify them. The notable feature of any series of alliances the Government could conceivably construct is that its power would lie – in so far as it lay anywhere – almost entirely in rural areas. This is certainly true of the homeland leaders, and it is also true of Chief Buthelezi. The simple truth is that there is not a single urban black township outside Natal, and not that many in it, that he could deliver to the Government. Individual urban blacks, even councillors or former councillors, would not represent anyone except themselves. So a power-sharing deal of this kind would lack what it needs most: the support of urban blacks.

They would not trust it. Every experience they have ever had of the South African Government has shown them that it never means quite what it says. They understand only too well what the Government's game now is: divide and rule. They would see power-sharing for what it really was – a further attempt by whites to keep control. If anything, it would intensify their hostility. Moreover, it would represent a compromise of the most fundamental objective which drives them forward: to create a South Africa which is non-racist. Power-sharing between the races, by its very definition, would be built on racial distinctions. It would perpetuate racial categorization. It would confer on whites as a matter of right, by virtue of the colour of their skin alone, an automatic share of government. Nothing could be more hostile to the very spirit which fuels the insurrection. The insurrection is precisely about ending a world in which white privilege is assured through race alone.

The unrest would go on. Power-sharing, in short, would change nothing. It would simply be a milestone, a marker, along the road to black rule. And because the reality of this is sinking in everywhere, even the Government's potential allies will think twice. It emerged from the Commonwealth Eminent Persons Group – a 'peace mission' which explored the possibility of a negotiated settlement of the conflict in May 1986 – that Chief Buthelezi was moving to a position where he saw no option but to heal the rift with the ANC, and throw in his weight with them. If this is indeed the way his mind is working, power-sharing is even less likely than it was before.

There are other people of goodwill – South African businessmen and church leaders, journalists, foreign politicians – who do not speak of power-sharing *per se* but of a 'negotiated settlement' between the white authorities and the ANC. The idea that the ANC, after nearly seventy years of struggle, with the finishing line in sight, would even consider seriously some kind of deal with the South African Government which fell short of majority rule is preposterous, if only because they would thereby throw away the support they have built up among black South Africans. The ANC is, of course, interested in being legalized in South Africa. It would like to able to hold meetings and recruit openly. It may, at some point, be willing to pledge an act of good faith – like a temporary abandonment of sabotage – if it judged the rewards would be good enough. But it will not make a political deal.

So the prospect of white South Africa now finding an enduring political settlement which prevents majority rule is virtually non-existent. In that case, only the armed might of white South Africa – its police and armed forces – can be their last defence. And surely the whites are too powerful to be forced to capitulate?

If the UDF fails to stop the youngsters becoming alienated from the rest of the black community, the security forces will certainly be better placed to arrest and detain rioters, and though they will not be able to stop some unrest continuing, they may be able temporarily to dampen it down significantly. This would give the white authorities the breathing space they need to begin to reestablish control in the townships, and hearten the white population, strengthening their resolve not to compromise on the basic political issues. In this situation, the parents' generation would also be more resistant to UDF attempts to mobilize them for political and economic action. It will make the UDF's strategy harder to implement, and take longer, but it will not fundamentally alter the picture.

The very marked politicization of black South Africa over the last five years cannot be undone; it can only grow. Weaknesses can emerge; obstacles can be placed in its way. But the dynamic can only be slowed down; it cannot be reversed. Sooner or later, the insurrection will extend itself. Even if the security forces regain some control over the townships, the 1984 insurrection will eventually reassert itself. Once the townships are in chaos again, the push beyond them will resume.

The most significant area of activity will undoubtedly be the economy. It is inevitable that black muscle will begin to make a severe impact, especially given the growing strength of the trade unions, their increasingly political edge, and the weakness of the South African economy as it faces huge demographic pressures, the lack of foreign confidence, and ever mounting sanctions. Already even the very limited boycotts of white businesses have taken a heavy toll, both of white small businesses and of big enterprises like Pick 'N Pay, the huge white-owned supermarket chain which supplies many urban blacks with food and household goods. What we have seen so far is only a pinprick. There will be other and more penetrating boycotts. Some will fail; some will succeed. Each boycott that does succeed, even if limited, will add to the increasing instability of white revenue, and make business harder and more hazardous. Strikes are bound to escalate, as workers demand higher wages and better conditions. The last two decades have seen a steady growth of

197

industrial disharmony, and as black workers push for an ever greater redistribution of wealth in straitened circumstances, the disharmony can only continue to grow. Even the powerful mining houses,
with the ability to sack tens of thousands of workers at will, have not
been unaffected by this process. They have been hit by strike after
strike. So far they have been able to outmanoeuvre the miners' unions, chiefly the National Union of Mineworkers. But with each unsuccessful strike, the union leadership has become more embittered,
more resentful – and more experienced. More sober calculations
will be made in future. More cohesion will be sought before strikes
are called, and more vulnerable targets will be picked. This will be
true throughout the economy.

Life will become increasingly dangerous and uncomfortable for
white South Africans. Not only will their standard of living be affected, but the last two years have seen the first isolated attacks on
white homes and white civilians. Bombing attacks have continued
on a sporadic scale. But as time passes, young blacks will grow more
militant and more prepared to take risks. The last two years of the
township insurrection has inured them to the prospect of arrest, tor-
ture, wounding and death. Young blacks who speak universally now
in a matter-of-fact way of being resigned to dying are a terrible portent for whites. Once an entire generation of young black people becomes used to death all around them, once indeed to suffer and die
becomes a matter less of fear than of honour, it no longer matters
where or how you do so. The security forces can keep young blacks
out of white cities and residential areas at the moment because they
are still holding the line at the exits from the black townships, in
itself already a retreat from holding the line in the streets of the
townships. As more and more young blacks prepare to take on the
security forces – and with an ever-rising birth rate the reserve army
of rioters grows constantly larger – as the assaults on police and
army power become more widespread and more unpredictable, the
white authorities will not be able to hold on even at the edge of the
townships. White recruitment into the Army and police can only be
marginally increased, and the possibility of enlisting unemployed
blacks is substantially neutralized by the increasing difficulty of getting information in a situation where black informers can no longer
operate with impunity. So the capacity of the security forces to extend control is being slowly outweighed by the increasing size and
aggression of rioting mobs. Sooner or later, some at least of those

mobs will start slipping through the net into white areas. For whites, sporadic disruption of daily life, physical attacks, ransackings, petrol-bombings, and murder is only a matter of time.

Nor will the ANC remain dormant. With a full-scale guerrilla war in Namibia and a deepening, widely dispersed domestic insurrection, the security forces will be increasingly stretched and will find it more and more difficult to seal South Africa's borders. Growing numbers of ANC saboteurs will be able to slip into the country. It was noticeable towards the end of 1985 and the beginning of 1986 that the first landmines on outlying border farms started exploding – and this was only the beginning of the process. Among the enormous numbers of young urban blacks no longer attending school, highly politicized, battle-hardened in the streets, and enmeshed in a network of semi-clandestine organizations, the ANC will find that growing recruitment and training for acts of sabotage will be possible, and it will become easier to find and hide supplies. Indeed, during the first two years of the insurrection, not only was there a marked increase in limpet mine attacks in urban areas, but landmines, hand grenades, rocket launchers, and hand guns began to make their appearance in urban black areas, a situation never previously seen in a country so tightly policed. Of course these were very isolated occurrences, but they will become commoner. Major acts of sabotage will increase, and with an increasing radicalization of some sections of white youth, white ANC sympathizers will also play an important part. Several important acts of sabotage have already proved to be the work of whites, and because they are less highly policed and have freer access to sensitive white areas, it is a reasonable assumption that they will continue to be involved in ANC activities.

White South Africa will also come under intensified international pressure as the domestic situation continues to deteriorate. Friendly and hostile governments alike will step up their calls for political change. Sanctions will become more widespread. Most importantly, as foreign bankers see the South African economy becoming more destabilized, they will be falling over themselves to squeeze South Africa into faster repayments of outstanding loans. This financing will have to come out of the country's export earnings, making it harder to import and further damaging growth and living standards.

So South Africa's ruling tribe has little to look forward to except a vast and steady escalation of trouble on all fronts. Armed might has its uses, but it is not quite the right weapon in this situation. It is useful in fighting conventional wars. It is useful in putting down isolated rebellions, or dragooning unresisting citizens into doing things they do not want to do. But what is happening in South Africa is that isolated rebellions have become a general insurrection, and that vast numbers of ordinary citizens are becoming prepared to defy the gun on a systematic and ever-increasing scale. It is quite true that the South African Government, despite what its critics say, has been reluctant to use the full fire-power available to it in dealing with domestic unrest.* This is not from moral distaste, but simply from fear of fuelling worse opposition. There will come a point when, in desperation, they will start using much heavier force. The South African security forces have the capacity to round up tens of thousands, and to destroy homes, to kill not hundreds, but many thousands. As the situation gets worse, the pressure from their increasingly panicked white constituents will force them to move in this direction. But blacks are beyond the stage of being cowed. No amount of force will restore stability, if only because as soon as it diminishes, the trouble will break out again. The trial of strength can continue for many years, but as long as the fundamental issue remains unresolved, repression will not stop the conflict getting worse.

South Africa's Government is finding power slipping out of its hands because its people are no longer prepared to be governed by it – and are prepared to defy it, whatever the consequences. There is no escape for a government that cannot govern: whether it accepts it or not, it ceases to be a government.

The next few years in South Africa will see the working through of this proposition. The Government of the country, and its white supporters, do not yet accept it. Might has always been right in the past, and they have not yet exerted their might to its full. Until they do, until they have tested it to its limits and discovered that the traditional equation no longer holds, there cannot, and will not, be peace in South Africa. It is for this reason that, as night follows day, we shall witness a long blood-letting in South Africa, and one that will get worse and worse.

But the end will come. Too many white South Africans have lost

* This includes the imposition of a national state of emergency in June 1986, which still tapped only a fraction of the forces available to the Government.

faith in the moral legitimacy of apartheid. Too many know it is inde-
fensible to go on without an end in sight. Too many blacks are prepared to continue resisting for as long as it takes. Too many have
come to believe that victory is possible. Eventually, as the country
sinks further and further into violence, anarchy, and chaos, as white
South Africa finds its life becoming more and more uncomfortable,
it will reach a point when the alternative is more attractive – and
inevitable. Then they will sit down with the ANC, and the new
South Africa, already struggling to be born in the dust of the townships, will be delivered into the hands of its black rulers.

Only a fool would suppose that this process will be quick. It will
take years, many years. But one can sketch out some of its phases.
First, the insurrection will spread. Eventually, the South African
Government will feel obliged to yield some measure of political freedom to black South Africans as a way of getting some form of power-
sharing. Power-sharing may be engineered, but if it is, will fail to
resolve the issue. Under these new conditions, though, opposition
black groupings will be able to recruit, canvass, organize – and step
up their opposition. More and more force will be used. At some
point it is conceivable that elements of white conscripts into the
Army will refuse to carry on putting down the rebellion.*

Emigration, already reaching record levels, will accelerate. White
vigilantes, feeling that the Government is no longer entirely theirs
and that the security forces are unable or unwilling to defend them,
will take their guns and add to the violence. On and on it will go till
finally the Afrikaner establishment says enough is enough. We have
been beaten, and now we must talk. Then the surrender document
will be signed.

It will not end there. Many Afrikaners will lose out in the new
South Africa, and they will not, at first, accept it. They will follow in
the long-hallowed Afrikaner tradition of the *bitter-einder*. But with
the bulk of white South Africa and particularly the bulk of Afrikanerdom accepting the new regime and finding, much to their surprise,
that the world has not come to an end, the *bitter-einders* will not have a
solid enough base to sustain resistance. They will be undone in the
end by the fact that the bulk of their white compatriots have thrown

---

* It was noticeable that the number of young whites failing to report for conscription in 1985 and 1986 was substantially up on previous years, and an 'End Conscription' campaign has been gaining ground, mainly among English-speaking
whites.

their lot in, for better or worse, with South Africa's new future. Gradually they will be mopped up. Eventually, black rule will be consolidated.

As South Africa's long agony opens up before our eyes, and as new forces keep bursting onto the scene – black vigilantes and white right-wingery, for example – the conflict appears constantly to be tugged in new directions, and this raises in many people's minds the possibility that South Africa may disintegrate, and sink into a never-ending series of many-sided smaller wars as in, say, the Lebanon. Potentially revolutionary situations are always frightening and allow hitherto unimaginable possibilities to take shape in our thinking. But we should not panic. The concept of South Africa as everyone's state is firmly embedded in both black and white minds, and this attachment will hold. It has a reality in economic and geographic unity which will also underpin that feeling. The bulk of Afrikanerdom and the bulk of black South Africa will want to settle with each other in the end. That will draw the country together again, and the centrifugal forces now threatening to pull the country apart will be reversed. The dissident elements will be diffused and slowly brought to an end. The country will remain unified – and its new government will be the ANC.

Of urban black political organizations, there are only two groupings: the UDF and the NF. The NF is simply too small, too narrowly based, and ideologically too exclusivist and radical to be capable of mobilizing large sections of the population behind it. The UDF, on the other hand, is already a vast coalition of many different elements in the urban population, by no means all of them black. Not only is it broadly based, extending beyond colour, region, religion, and ideology, it is well consolidated, and has shown itself to be the major political force operating among black South Africans today. It has also shown itself able to survive protracted assaults by the security forces. Its links with the other important force in black life – the trade unions – are already forged and powerful. Its general political stance is sufficiently geared to the material concerns of ordinary black citizens to provide a point of identity, but not so ideologically rigid as to frighten them off. Indeed, its very lack of an explicit political programme and its claim to defer to the exiled political leadership, makes it less threatening to the bulk of ordinary blacks. On the other hand, it does have a political profile of not compromising with racism, and this apparent integrity can only win it more support as

202

time passes. The UDF is, therefore, beyond question, the only force capable of harnessing large numbers of black people, challenging the Government, and surviving.

But the UDF, while not explicitly repudiating the PAC, clearly sees the ANC as being the real political leadership of black South Africa. In throwing their weight behind the ANC they are, of course, doing no more than reflecting a growing sentiment within South Africa's black population. Virtually every single poll of black opinion in the last decade has shown Mandela unambiguously the front-runner for preferred leader. Most polls have shown him as being way ahead of all other candidates, sometimes being the preference of more than fifty per cent of respondents. Given the illegal status of the ANC, this probably underestimates his actual popularity. The mere fact of the omnipresence of ANC symbols in black townships is testimony to its support: they cannot reflect the existence of only small groups of agitators, but must grow out of the very community in which they are to be found. There are no such symbols for homeland leaders, Chief Buthelezi, black councillors, or even, except in very isolated instances, for the PAC.

The ANC's hold grows out of the simple fact that is the only uncompromisingly anti-apartheid force which appears to have any potential for bringing white supremacy to an end. It brought black nationalism into being, and it has survived longer than any other black political organization. It has been a consistent voice throughout all the twists and turns of the twentieth century. It has never compromised. It has always preached the philosophy and strategy which now looks like working. It has a small core of activists operating within the country, and a vast network of semi-legal organizations in the UDF, which it will inherit when the time comes. The people of South Africa know it has a vast network abroad, with leaders respected and admired throughout the world, and an even more potent leadership symbol ready and waiting in Pollsmoor Prison. It is the only external force which has made its presence felt in South Africa in the last decade. It even receives white South African delegations as it sits across the border in Zambia. Every denunciation of it by the South African Government adds to its credibility. It is the bogey of white South Africa. It *looks* like a potent force and a government-in-waiting – and there is no other candidate.

So the ANC will be the victors.

But how long will it take to reach the transfer of power? We are looking at a time-scale of five to fifteen years, and the best guess is that it will probably take about seven.

Sketching it out crudely, we must suppose that, under the assumptions most favourable for the ANC, it will take at least two or three more years for economic and security conditions to start affecting ordinary white citizens in a marked way. It will then take at least two years of slogging it out before the bulk of the white community is prepared to contemplate majority rule. That gives us a rough five-year scenario. There was a time when this would have seemed an impossibly unrealistic time-scale, but events in South Africa have developed a momentum and are moving very quickly. In just two years, for example, we have seen a township rebellion become endemic, Mrs Mandela's open defiance and effective overturning of her banning order go unpunished, and the vast panoply of apartheid laws swept away till only two or three fundamentals remain.

Yet the South African Government is enormously resourceful and sophisticated, and has several cards left in its admittedly weakened hand. None the less, it must be highly improbable that the war of attrition can last more than ten, or at the absolute outside, fifteen years. The degree of political agitation within the black community is now so high and generalized that it beggars common sense to believe they will tolerate the present situation or any realistic modification of it that long. White morale is already so low, and the psychological preparation for defeat so advanced that it is difficult to imagine, especially with a rapidly declining economic and security situation, that the majority will be able to hold out that long, even allowing for strong right-wing resistance.

So, at some time within this time range – and five to seven years seems about right – the ANC is likely to become the first black government ever to rule over the entire territory of South Africa. Certainly, by the turn of the century, South Africa will no longer be a white-ruled country.

But what level of violence will accompany this all-out struggle? The Commonwealth Eminent Persons spoke of 'millions' and a blood-letting unequalled since the Second World War. This is right off the mark. In two years of unparalleled upheaval, the death toll has not exceeded 2,000. This is not going to be a conventional civil war with standing armies fighting pitched battles, and in insurrections the casualty figures are always much lower than in staged military confrontations. None the less, the death rate will be phenomenally high compared with, say, Northern Ireland. We are talking about many thousands dying, perhaps as many as several tens of thousands. Considering that that will eventuate from a struggle by a largely unarmed people, it gives a measure of the brutality white South Africa is prepared to contemplate in a vain bid to ensure its maintenance of power.

In the light of South Africa's future, it is worth considering the stance of foreign governments towards the current conflict, for not only does this issue significantly affect South Africa, it bedevils much international political life.

The question of whether or not economic sanctions against South Africa should be intensified will continue to dominate much debate in international relations. The ANC, the PAC, and the bulk of politically active black South Africans, including respected figures like Desmond Tutu, will constantly press for escalation. But the two Governments whose economic and political influence is greatest in South Africa – the United States and Britain – will keep resisting, despite having already agreed to some measures. They will still argue that further sanctions will harm black South Africans more than any good they do, that they will strengthen white defiance and make them more intransigent, and that by maintaining some links with the South African Government, they retain leverage which could be used to encourage reform. Above all, they will constantly argue that sanctions are not effective.

There will be a lot of humbug in this. All the leverage they have had has not produced fundamental reform, for fundamental reform cannot be achieved by persuasion but only by force. The argument about effectiveness is a wilful misconstruing of what kind of effectiveness black South Africans mean. They are talking about *political* effectiveness. The demoralization of white South Africa is an unpleasant but necessary precondition for resolving South Africa's conflict. The longer they resist, the more protracted and bloody the struggle will be; the sooner they concede, the better for all. The more sanctions are applied, the more white South Africa's isolation will be brought home to them, the harder it will be to keep on fighting, the faster hope will be eroded. The more sanctions, the more lives will be saved.

The United States and Britain's real objection stems from their considerable investments there and their lucrative trade with South Africa. The British Government, in particular, with perhaps

120,000 UK jobs tied up in that trade, is not keen to add to the unemployment register with another general election looming.

There is another aspect to it, however. Neither the United States nor Britain is keen to do anything which assists the ANC. They see it as a terrorist organization, with a strong Communist element, a quasi-marxist philosophy, and long-established links with the Soviet Union. They are also aware that it is committed to nationalization of substantial sections of the South African economy, which they believe would be harmful to American and British interests in South Africa. They have accordingly tended to cold-shoulder the organization, and will continue to adopt a lukewarm attitude to it.* They keep hoping for power-sharing and they like the look of Chief Buthelezi – pro-capitalist, anti-sanctions, and generally 'moderate'. Both President Reagan and Mrs Thatcher have received the Chief at their official residences, and much unofficial contact goes on with him in South Africa itself. When they speak of encouraging the South African Government down the road of reform, they keep hoping something less than majority rule will emerge and that the Chief can be winkled into a dominant position.

Here, once again, we see the triumph of hope over experience. Both countries unofficially backed Joshua Nkomo in neighbouring Zimbabwe during the Rhodesian civil war, and hoped to see him installed as leader after independence. Mr Nkomo, however, led a minority party, and it was clear to anyone who studied the country that Robert Mugabe's ZANU party, based on a larger grouping would win. The result was a strained relationship with the independent Zimbabwe Government, which has still not fully healed.

American and British policy is leading them to repeat their mistake in South Africa. Power-sharing, as we have seen, cannot offer any real solution to South Africa's problem, and may indeed intensify black opposition. Chief Buthelezi, impressive though he is, has too narrow a base of support and is too widely hated to be a good political investment for the West. By their reluctance to pursue sanctions against South Africa, the United States and Britain are already seen as collaborators with the South African Government by a whole generation of black South Africans. Mrs Mandela has spoken of them as accomplices to murder. It has become commonplace at funerals of unrest victims to see placards denouncing the

_____
* This will remain true, despite limited contacts with the ANC since June 1986.

206

United States and Britain, and for ritual condemnations of them from the platform. A wave of anti-Westernism is sweeping young black South Africans, and this could prove very damaging to American and British long-term interests in the country. This feeling can only be strengthened by support for Chief Buthelezi who is seen as almost part of the enemy.

Western policy-makers should acknowledge the course that events will take, and come to terms with it while they have time to do so. They should support the ANC, and strive to build closer links with it now. They will find that their fears are considerably misplaced. The ANC does have an important element within its hierarchy who are Communists. They are, however, both a minority element, and pragmatic. The ANC is a classic African nationalist party, whose lip-service to marxism is both small and much exaggerated. It does have connections with the Soviet Union, but welcomes the closest possible links it can forge with the West. It is committed to some nationalization, but the precise degree is very much subject to negotiation, and the ANC has made it clear it does not foresee a wholesale programme of driving foreigners out. On the contrary, the ANC leadership is acutely aware of the grave problems South Africa will face in the future, and recognizes they will need all the support and help they can get. The American and British Governments would find them surprisingly amenable. But continued coolness will drive the ANC into a position where their supporters will demand action against Western 'collaborators' in the future. So it is better for the United States and Britain to face up to unpalatable realities now.

The day the ANC becomes the governing power will mark a great turning point in South Africa's history. In time the political complexion of the country will begin to reflect the changed economic reality, as black South Africans accede to positions of power and responsibility, and racial segregation, already eroding in principle, begins to disappear ever more quickly in practice. South Africa will become what it has fundamentally always been: a truly multiracial society. Sadly, however, miracles do not happen, and though South Africa will become profoundly changed, problems, difficulties, and conflict will not be magically wished away.

The ANC leadership, in their pronouncements and thinking to date, have given good grounds for believing that when they come to power they will not wish to engage in a great vendetta against white

South Africans. Their philosophy, in theory and certainly in practice, is one of non-racism. They accept the place of whites in South Africa, and they will be at pains to come to an accommodation with that minority. Apart from anything else, they know they will desperately need the skill and economic contribution of white South Africa. Some political scores will have to be settled in order to satisfy their own supporters. Some random street vengeance cannot be prevented. The ANC will take a share in some major mining companies, and will have to nationalize some farm land in order to put through an expected programme of land reform. Afrikaners at the lower echelons of state employment will lose their jobs and will have to find a way of making a living in direct competition with blacks. Most other white South Africans will discover to their surprise that life does not change all that much.

Instead, ironically, black South Africa will bear the brunt of political change. The ANC has not, for many decades, been able to recruit and organize freely in South Africa. It has not, therefore, been able to build up its support in a systematic and coherent way. It will be the beneficiary of the fight against apartheid because it has become the symbol and focus of opposition to white supremacy. But once white supremacy has ended, the rallying point will have gone. Since it has been unable to proselytize, the basis of its current political support will begin to disappear.

There is no natural majority in South Africa which the ANC can harness as its political base. Colour is not such a base. Apart from opposition to white supremacy, there is a low level of ideological or explicit political thinking in South Africa, a function of the long repression of black political life. And among those who are politically aware, the ANC has no monopoly of support. The PAC/NF strain of thinking is also potent. Conservative sentiment will find a vehicle for expression. Many young radicals will violently resist its authority. At a political level, therefore, its position will not go unchallenged.

Similarly, there is no 'tribal' or regional majority. As we have seen, there are important divides between rural and urban blacks. Urban blacks share some points of identity but the potential for internal conflict is considerable – for example, the employed versus the unemployed, the unionized versus the non-unionized, middle-class aspirants versus squatters. Holding a sophisticated modern industrialized economy together in a country as heterogeneous as South Africa and satisfying the disparate aspirations of its diverse peoples will be a task of great complexity, requiring great skill and resourcefulness. In such a situation, the PAC, Chief Buthelezi, those who were formerly active in white-created power structures – former councillors or homeland leaders – and groups yet to emerge could become the beneficiaries, at least to some extent, of popular discontent. The scope for interminable power struggles is considerable.

The ANC will, of course, be in a position of great strength, given its control over government and the armed forces. But it will only avert further bloodshed if it can run and manage this highly advanced society efficiently and fairly. It needs, even now, to be thinking carefully about the enormous tasks that will be facing it, and above all, to be gaining the knowledge, expertise, and experience of leadership it has so long been denied. Meticulous and scrupulous preparation is needed. As the confrontation in South Africa grows ever-pressing and the need to win the immediate battle looms all-encompassingly, it is very difficult indeed for them to set aside the time and manpower and resources to do this. They may find it impossible, but their future burdens will then be all that much greater.

These are some of the difficulties that lie beyond, in the new South Africa that is being born. For us as onlookers, however, the next few years will be dominated by the distressing travail of its birth, which we shall see enacted daily on our television screens. It will seem a gruesome, but mercifully distant, saga of little direct relevance to us. That may be so, but this book has tried to suggest that racism is a potential which exists in all people in all societies, and that whether it remains a shackled force or becomes a dominant organizing principle depends on material, and especially economic, conditions. Human affairs can never, of course, be so engineered that circumstances favourable to racism are always prevented. But the full horror of South Africa may yet yield something of value even for us if it shows the world the dangers in the easy temptations of self-interest and hatred.

Now, as we await the resolution of South Africa's drawn-out agony, we end where we began. The certainty of what is coming to pass enables us to look back on the country's history and see a new shape to it. From the mid-seventeenth century, a long blood-letting in South Africa has ensued from the contest for access to, and control of, limited economic resources. In that struggle, the white settlers won out first over the Khoisan and in doing so, destroyed the basis of their continued survival as a distinct people. Then they took on both the British Empire and the Bantu-speaking black peoples of South Africa, to establish an hegemony over the entire territory. They effectively drove out the British Empire. They successfully subjugated the black peoples of South Africa, and set about institutionalizing and securing their control over them and the country's economic resources. But unlike the Khoisan, these black people were strong enough and robust enough to withstand the onslaught on them and their identity. They found a way of surviving as a distinct people. At first they eked out an existence at subsistence level, and then as the country developed, they became an important part of the economy. By having stayed alive, by having reproduced themselves and kept a strong foothold in the country, they ensured that the contest for supremacy would be renewed. Today we have reached the point where that contest is being staged in a new form, and we can see already that, after three turbulent centuries in South Africa, the Afrikaners' dominance is drawing to a bloody end. Black South Africa has finally won.

It is a story of the greatest drama, made all the more affecting by the protracted impotence and stoical daily suffering of those most wretched of the earth who, only a few years ago, could never have imagined the victory they are about to achieve. It does not fall to all peoples, indeed perhaps to only a few, to come to triumph from defeat. The Khoisan of South Africa, the Indians of North America, the Aboriginals of Australia, the Maoris of New Zealand, the Indians of most of Latin America – they have lost either their existence as a distinct people or the possibility of reconquering their lands. There is no recompense for the dead generations of black South Africans, but the living at least have the consolation of knowing that every drop of sweat, every moment of the unrelenting grind of humiliation and hardship, and the centuries of death and decimation have not gone unrewarded. They have lived to fight another day, and they have truly earned a famous victory.

The green, gold, and black flag of the African National Congress will replace the flags of the Boer Republics and the Union Jack which, composed together in the modern white flag, will have flown over the seat of government for virtually all of this century. Whether Nelson Mandela will live to see that day is in the lap of the gods, but his long silence on a small fortress at the tip of the continent will ensure his followers victory, and his own place in world history.

In terms of survival, however, both the Afrikaners and the blacks are victors. Neither can be destroyed by the other. The Afrikaners too have earned their future. Now, fairer and more equitable terms will have to be established for their life together. History has decreed their marriage, and they will live side by side as equals. The Afrikaners will see it as small consolation, and, since the notion of intrinsic evil is foolish, let us feel sympathy for them in their moment of decline. For them, this future represents a failure of what they believe to be good and true. Time will heal. They will come to see it differently. They are a robust people who will build a new and better life for themselves in Africa. And when the scars of history have healed, Africa will remember their courage and their great talent, and take them to its heart.

It is hard to think like that now, but it will happen. In times to come, after many decades, when black and Afrikaner sit side by side, these long centuries will be forgotten. They will be a dream without reality or interest. Only in the minds of old men and scholars will they survive. Only there will the faint traces of the long-drawn-out struggle whose climax we are witnessing live on.

As for the immediate future, the prospects are both good and bad. South Africa is a most richly endowed country. It has a vast territory, and a population which is not yet too large. It has been lavishly provided with mineral and agricultural resources. It has a substantially literate people, which includes some of the most resourceful and innovative minds in all Africa. The capacity of both black and white for kindness and good is great. They have, too, that supreme human quality of being able to rise above the past and look to new futures. South Africa may yet provide a nobler example to all the world. But will circumstances conspire for, or against, them? No one can say.

In the meantime, as we stand on the brink of this epoch-making period of South African history, the people of South Africa, and all those who wish them well, can only share the eloquent hope of the hymn of black liberation. That hymn, soon to be sung as the anthem of the new South Africa, says simply *Nkosi Sikelel' iAfrika*. God Bless Africa.

BIBLIOGRAPHY

BOOKS

If a book has been published outside Britain, the place of origin is given, as well as the publisher and year of publication.

Adam, Herbert and Giliomee, Herman. *Ethnic Power Mobilized: Can South Africa Change?*, Yale University Press, 1979

Benson, Mary. *Nelson Mandela*, Penguin Books, 1986

——*South Africa: The Struggle for a Birthright*, IDAF, 1985

Biko, Steve (Edited by Arnold Millard). *Black Consciousness in South Africa*, Vintage, New York, 1979

——*Testimony of Steve Biko*, Maurice Temple Smith, 1979

——*I Write What I Like* (Edited by Aelred Stubbs). Heinemann Education, 1978

Breytenbach, Breyten. *True Confessions of an Albino Terrorist*, Faber, 1984

The Cambridge History of Africa (8 volumes), Cambridge University Press, 1977 onwards

The Commonwealth Group of Eminent Persons. *Mission to South Africa: The Commonwealth Report*, Penguin Books, 1986

Crapanzano, Vincent. *Waiting: The Whites of South Africa*, Granada, 1985

Davenport, T.R.H. *South Africa: A Modern History*, Macmillan, Johannesburg, 2nd edition, 1978

De Klerk, W.A. *The Puritans in Africa: A History of Afrikanerdom*, Rex Collings, 1975, Penguin Books, 1976

Desmond, Cosmas. *The Discarded People*, Penguin Books, 1971

Elphick, Richard. *Kraal and Castle: Khoikhoi and the founding of white South Africa*, Yale University Press, 1977

Elphick, Richard and Giliomee, Hermann (Editors). *The Shaping of South African Society, 1652 – 1820*, Longman, Cape Town, 1979

Farwell, Byron. *The Great Boer War*, Allen Lane, 1976

Frankel, Philip H. *Pretoria's Praetorians: Civil-Military Relations in South Africa*, Cambridge University Press, 1984

Giliomee, Hermann and Schlemmer, Lawrence (Editors). *Up Against the Fences*, David Philip, Cape Town, 1985

Grant, Kenneth W. *The Militarization of South African Politics*, I.B. Tauris & Co, 1986

Guy, Jeff. *The Destruction of the Zulu Kingdom*, Longman, 1979

Hanlon, Joseph. *Apartheid's Second Front: South Africa's War Against Its Neighbours*, Penguin Books, 1986

Harrison, Nancy. *Winnie Mandela: Mother of a Nation*, Gollancz, 1985

Hepple, Alex. *Verwoerd*, Penguin Books, 1967

Huddleston, Trevor. *Naught for Your Comfort*, Collins, 1956

Ingham, Kenneth. *Jan Christian Smuts*, Weidenfeld and Nicolson, 1986

Innes, Duncan. *Anglo American and the Rise of Modern South Africa*, Heinemann Educational Books, 1984

Inskeep, R.R. *The Peopling of Southern Africa*, David Philip, Cape Town, 1978

Joseph, Helen. *Side by Side*, Zed Books, 1986

Kane-Berman, John. *Soweto: Black Revolt, White Reaction*, Ravan, Johannesburg, 1978

Leach, Graham. *South Africa*, Routledge & Kegan Paul, 1986

Lee, Emanoel. *To The Bitter End: A Photographic History of the Boer War*, Viking, 1985

Lehmann, Joseph. *The First Boer War*, Buchan and Enright, 1985

Lelyveld, Joseph. *More Your Shadow*, Michael Joseph, 1985

Lewin, Hugh. *Bandiet: Seven years in a South African prison*, Heinemann, 1981

Lipton, Merle. *Capitalism and Apartheid*, Temple Smith/Gower, 1985

Lodge, Tom, *Black Politics in South Africa Since 1945*, Longman, 1983

Luthuli, Albert. *Let my people go*, Collins, 1962; Fount Paperbacks, 1982

Magubane, Bernard Makhosezwe. *The Political Economy of Race and Class in South Africa*, Monthly Review Press, 1979

Mandela, Nelson (Edited by Ruth First). *No Easy Walk to Freedom*, London, 1965

Mandela, Nelson. *The Struggle is My Life*, IDAF, 1978

Mandela, Winnie (Edited by Anne Benjamin). *Part of My Soul*, Penguin Books, 1985

Marks, Shula. *The Ambiguities of Dependence in South Africa*, Ravan, Johannesburg, 1986

Marks, Shula and Atmore, Anthony (Editors). *Economy and society in pre-industrial South Africa*, Longman, 1980

Marks, Shula and Rathbone, Richard. *Industrialisation and Social Change in South Africa*, Longman, 1982

Morris, Donald R. *The Washing of the Spears*, Jonathan Cape, 1966

Motlhabi, Mokgethi. *Black Resistance to Apartheid*, Skotaville Publishers, Johannesburg, 1984

Nolutshungu, Sam C. *Changing South Africa: Political Considerations*, Manchester University Press, 1982

Pakenham, Thomas. *The Boer War*, Weidenfeld and Nicolson, 1979

Paton, Alan. *Ah, but your land is beautiful*, David Philip, Cape Town, 1981
——*Cry, the beloved country*, Jonathan Cape, 1958
——*Hofmeyr*, Oxford University Press, Cape Town, 1964
Phillipson, D.W. *African Archaeology*, Cambridge University Press, 1985
Plaatje, Sol T. (Edited by John L. Comaroff). *The Boer War Diary of Sol T. Plaatje*, Macmillan, 1973
Ransford, Oliver. *The Great Trek*, John Murray, 1972
Slabbert, F. Van Zyl. *The Last White Parliament*, Sidgwick & Jackson, 1985
South African Research Service (Edited and compiled). *South African Review II*, Ravan, Johannesburg, 1984
Wheatcroft, Geoffrey. *The Randlords: The Men who made South Africa*, Weidenfeld and Nicolson, 1985
Wilson, Monica and Thompson, Leonard (Editors). *The Oxford History of South Africa* (Volume 1), Oxford University Press, 1969 (Volume 2), Oxford University Press, 1971
Woods, Donald. *Biko*, Paddington Press, 1978

ESSAYS OR BOOKLETS

Buzan, Barry and Nazareth, H.O. 'South Africa versus Azania: the implications of who rules,' *International Affairs*, Volume 62, no 1, Winter 85-6
Gutteridge, William. *South Africa: Strategy for Survival?* Conflict Studies no. 131, The Institute for the Study of Conflict, London, 1981
——*South Africa: Evolution or Revolution?* Conflict Studies no. 171, The Institute for the Study of Conflict, London, 1984
Macshane, Denis; Plaut, Martin; Ward, David. *POWER! Black workers, their unions and the struggle for freedom in South Africa*, Spokesman, Nottingham, 1984
Maggs, Tim. 'Iron Age, south of the Zambezi', *Southern African Prehistory and Palaeoenvironments*, edited by Richard Klein. A.A. Balkema, Rotterdam and Boston, 1982
Marks, Shula. 'Khoisan resistance to the Dutch in the seventeenth and eighteenth centuries.' *Journal of African History*, xiii, 1, 1972.
'The Myth of the Empty Land,' *History Today*, London, January 1980.
South Africa – in the 1980s – State of Emergency. CIIR, London, 3rd Edition, 1986

INDEX

Note: The index does not include references to the maps or illustrations, which are listed at the front of the book. Names of organizations are not inverted. South African Acts of Parliament are entered under laws.

217